The Encyclopaedia of
Classic Saturday
Night Telly

The Encyclopaedia of
Classic Saturday Night Telly

Jack Kibble-White
and Steve Williams

First published in Great Britain in 2007 by
Allison & Busby Limited
13 Charlotte Mews
London W1T 4EJ
www.allisonandbusby.com

10 9 8 7 6 5 4 3 2 1

ISBN 0 7490 8031 0
978-0-7490-8031-0

Typeset in 11/16 pt Futura Light by
Terry Shannon

Printed and bound in Cornwall by MPG.

JACK KIBBLE-WHITE is the author of *The A-Z of Cool Computer Games*, which is also available from Allison & Busby, and is co-author of *TV Cream: The Ultimate Guide to '70s and '80s Pop Culture*. Jack writes about popular culture for publications and websites such as *ScriptWriter Magazine, bbc.co.uk, Off the Telly* and *TV Cream*, and has acted as programme consultant to Channel Four. He makes the occasional appearance on radio and television, usually to talk about old telly.

STEVE WILLIAMS is co-author of *TV Cream: The Ultimate Guide to '70s and '80s Pop Culture*. He is a regular contributor to *Radio Times* and writes on a weekly basis for *TV Cream*, where he has been compiling the site's listings guide for the past four years. He is a regular contributor to the TV criticism site *Off the Telly*, writing articles on all aspects of contemporary television, and has used his research skills to provide information for a number of organisations, including BBC1 and LWT.

Jack Kibble-White
dedicates this book to Sweetpea.

Steve Williams
dedicates this book to Mum, Dad and Julie.

ACKNOWLEDGEMENTS

We would like to thank Chris Diamond, Chris Hughes, Ian Jones and Graham Kibble-White for their help and expert assistance. Thanks also to Mike Kibble-White and Kathy Speirs for their proofreading expertise.

Thanks also to the magnificent website *offthetelly.co.uk*, which provided a home for a very early version of this project and to Jeremy Beadle who generously provided us with a foreword plus many words of encouragement while we were writing this book.

We would also like to express our gratitude to the following roll call of superb people who all contributed in some way: Louis Barfe, Lionel Blair, David Bodycombe, Andrew Collins, Martin Cunning, Paul Daniels, Alistair McGown, Lee McMurray, David Oliphant, Justin Scoggie and Graeme Wall.

And finally a special thanks from Jack goes to Rose whose love and support helped him every step of the way.

FOREWORD

Jack Kibble-White and Steve Williams are an untapped national treasure. Their knowledge and understanding of television is exceeded only by their enthusiasm for the subject.

I have long admired their perceptive analysis of programmes. Their overview is always based on meticulous and often first-hand research. I well remember reading their detailed examination of *Game for a Laugh*. I marvelled at the insight. At last here were writers who understood the essence of the show; the problems and the decisions made to overcome them. Their forthright and honest opinions resulting from clear thinking and deep intelligence were genuinely welcomed. Their appreciation of the creative personality balanced with sound knowledge of the technical issues make them mentors to be respected.

I cannot think of anybody better armed to present a record of Saturday Night Television than Jack and Steve. Reading this you will learn the history of a special brand of entertainment but the lessons are universal.

If you harbour ambition to be a part of the increasingly complex world of television I suggest this book is a must-read.

On the other hand if you are simply a fan of television this book will heighten your viewing pleasure by giving you fascinating behind-the-scenes secrets.

I do hope producers out there will realise Jack and Steve can help make their programmes brighter and more rewarding by employing them – or simply buy this book and learn.

Jeremy Beadle
13 August 2006

INTRODUCTION

'Saturday night is the happiest night of the week,' sang Mike and Bernie Winters. The comic duo's delight was plain to hear, and you could imagine that up and down the land families were cheering them on while metaphorically breaking out the bunting as they too celebrated the arrival of the best evening of the week. Of course, those families had done the same thing seven days previously, and would do the same again seven days hence; because the brothers were right – on Friday evening we are still recovering from the working week, and on Sunday the spectre of Monday morning looms large. Indisputably then, Saturday night is the happiest night of the week.

In its own way Saturday night telly has contributed to this welcome state of gaiety – be it Noel Edmonds facing down a rugby tackle from a clearly overexcited Mr Blobby, or Brucie cavorting with a contestant before imploring the audience 'didn't they do well?' Shows such as *Baywatch*, *The Price Is Right* and *Strictly Come Dancing* are big, bold and totally escapist in exactly the same way that programmes like *EastEnders* aren't (at the time of writing, Saturday is still the only night of the week not to take advantage of the easy ratings winner of a regular soap episode).

But why is Saturday night television so notable? The writers of this book doubt they will be putting together a follow-up looking at, say, Tuesday night's output; mainly because no one really remembers which shows were regularly transmitted on that day of the week. But think of *The Generation Game* or *Russ Abbot's Madhouse* and you inevitably think also of Saturday nights. Unarguably the one trait shared by all of the most successful Saturday night telly shows is that their greatness is inextricably tied up in their 'Saturdayness'.

A large part of Saturday night television's enduring popularity can be traced back to the Fifties. The then newly launched ITV relied heavily on variety acts and quiz shows to tease viewers away from the already established BBC. Initially this meant screening major variety shows on a Sunday evening (the only night of the week that entertainers weren't already booked up to work in the theatre), but as television's popularity grew, stars became ever more willing to turn down stage work in favour of an opportunity to ply their wares in front of the growing television audience.

ITV Series such as *Saturday Showtime* and *The 64,000 Question* were devastatingly popular and an under-siege BBC recognised that it looked a bit old and stuffy in comparison. It needed to hit back with similar high-quality entertainment shows of its own. The major battleground for this conflict was Saturday nights, the place where exciting new light entertainment programmes were attracting the largest audiences.

By the turn of the decade, the glamour and glitz of variety was retaining its massive popularity, but the programmes themselves were changing. Before it has been enough just to record the on-stage acts of various performers, but now entertainers such as Arthur Haynes and Morecambe and Wise were producing material specifically tailored for the small screen.

While the Sixties gave us such Saturday night success stories as *Juke Box Jury* and (for a while) *Dee Time*, it was the Seventies that presented us with the era today remembered as the high water mark of Saturday night television. Shows such as *The Generation Game* and *Look – Mike Yarwood!* were enjoyed by the entire family, providing shared talking points for the schoolyard or shop floor on Monday morning. With half the entire population of the United Kingdom tuning in to watch such programmes, any rising entertainer worth his or her salt now realised that the pinnacle of their career was to be awarded a show of their own on Saturday nights. As a result, there grew within the television industry an increasing fixation on the all-important Saturday night telly line-up.

By the mid-Seventies, the BBC had not only recovered its position against ITV, but was now dominating. A finely balanced schedule of drama with *The Duchess of Duke Street*, chat presided over by the crazily sideburned Parkinson, early evening escapism in the form of *Doctor Who* and of course the aforementioned and all-conquering *Generation Game*, ensured that most viewers simply never bothered to switch over to see what ITV were doing.

Into the Eighties and the well-loved entertainers of the previous ten years gradually gave way to a new breed of Saturday night star. American dramas such as *CHiPs* and *The A-Team* offered viewers explosions and spectacle galore, while the likes of Noel Edmonds and Jeremy Beadle proved that entertainers with no discernible talent other than an ability to communicate could make it on television's biggest night of the week. Yet with television remote controls and home VCRs becoming ever more commonplace, our Saturday night entertainers had to work even harder to gain our attention. Unsurprisingly, this era signalled the end of the entertainer as an easy-going, well-loved figure.

Saturday night telly of the Eighties can be best summed up in one word – 'brash'. Shows such as *Game for a Laugh*, *Blind Date* and *The Price Is Right* were noisy, raucous, and above all not the cosy kind of television the long-term Saturday night viewer had grown accustomed too. Even the BBC, once a paragon of sobriety, got into the habit of yelling at the viewer, with series such as *The Noel Edmonds Saturday Roadshow* willing to dispense gunge liberally around the studio set.

The big Saturday night acts of the Eighties, your Cilla Blacks and Cannon and Balls did still engender warm feeling from their fans, but they also managed to irritate at least as many viewers as they amused. This contrasted with the previous decade when you couldn't find a member of the British public with a bad word to say about Morecambe and Wise or Mike Yarwood.

This state of affairs remained in place for much of the Nineties, with Noel, Cilla and Beadle continuing to dominate the Saturday night schedules, arguably in some cases a bit after their peak. However, with the proliferation of television channels plus the increase of other affordable leisure activities, television audience numbers as a whole were now on the decline, and viewers tended not to turn on their sets until later on in the evening.

With its emphasis on large-scale family entertainment, Saturday night telly was hit particularly hard and by the start of the twenty-first century it had fallen from being the most-watched night of the week to the least-watched. By the time Cilla finally decided she'd had enough of peeking round that partition, *Blind Date* (which had once commanded up to 17 million viewers) was being watched by fewer than 4 million.

Programme makers fought hard to entice viewers back with series such as *Pop Idol* mining our new-found fascination in watching bizarre, talentless individuals undergoing ritual humiliation for our entertainment. Meanwhile the BBC explicitly tried to recreate Saturday night's sense of nationally shared moments by hosting an occasional series of interactive quiz shows under the banner *Test the Nation*. Yet the press bemoaned the state of our Saturday night telly and Channel 4 even broadcast a one-off two-hour documentary under the self-explanatory title *Who Killed Saturday Night TV?*

In recent years there has been a definite up-turn. Variety, for so long an unfashionable term, is back in favour with programmes such as *Strictly Come Dancing* and *When Will I Be Famous?* allowing non-singing variety acts a chance to appear on our screens once again. Family drama, in the shape of *Doctor Who*, *Primeval* and *Robin Hood* has also re-emerged, and at the time of writing our Saturday night telly is more entertaining and popular than its been for a decade or so. It's as if Saturday night television has finally remembered that, whatever else it might be, it should always be in some way a celebration that at last the best night of the week has come round again.

This book then, is a celebration of all those celebrations. It's a (mainly) warm-hearted sift through British Saturday night television's back pages, remembering its most notable programmes, best-loved stars, and – in some cases – most God-awful television moments. You'll see that *The Generation Game*, *Blind Date* and *Noel's House Party* all feature, as well they should, but we haven't just gone for the big hitters. Some of the less well celebrated, although not necessarily less loved, Saturday night shows get a mention too; as well as a few of the spectacular flops that have stunk out our telly screens. And all eras are catered for, with the variety days of the Fifties happily rubbing shoulders alongside the pop star wannabes of *The X Factor*.

It's worth pointing out that in trying to pull together a list of shows to write about, we've had to make some determinations as to what actually constitutes a Saturday night television programme. Our rule of thumb has been (with a couple of honourable exceptions) to include only series where the majority of episodes have been screened on the night in question. Regrettably, this has meant no room for *Blankety Blank*, *The Professionals*, *You've Been Framed!*, *Dee Time*, *Family Fortunes*, *Roland Rat: The Series*, *The Adventures of Robin Hood*, *The Avengers*, *The Muppet Show* and countless other programmes that all possessed the right aesthetic, but had the misfortune of being scheduled on other nights more often than on Saturday nights.

The entries that have made it through are laid out in that handy A–Z format so beloved of these sorts of books, so feel free to skip around and check that your favourite shows have made it in there (yes *Copy Cats* is in – result!). You should also notice that those programme names that appear in bold within one entry have entries all of their own somewhere else in the book, meaning that the so-inclined reader can at last trace the Noel Edmonds trilogy of Saturday night shows, or take a nostalgic wander through those great American action series of the Eighties.

Of course you can just read it cover-to-cover; we don't mind what you do to be honest – as 'Our Graham' used to say on *Blind Date* with that slight hint of laughter in his voice 'the choice is yours'.

3-2-1

Yorkshire Television for ITV

29 July 1978 to 24 December 1988 (154 episodes)

'It's a quiz, it's a game, it's fortune and fame!' So went the opening to one of ITV's most durable, and most baffling, Saturday night series.

3-2-1 was a shameless attempt to create a rival to **The Generation Game**. It was based on a Spanish show (somewhat inevitably, *Uno Dos Tres*) with the name referring to the fact the series was a quiz show, a game show and an entertainment spectacular all rolled into one. All of this from the unlikely setting of Kirkstall Road, Leeds.

Fast-talking Ted Rogers oversaw proceedings. Three

married couples took part in the opening quiz and, inexplicably, the winners were eliminated, coming back the following week to build up their stash of cash. The other couples went forward to watch a series of comic sketches, songs and novelty acts, all based on that week's theme, after which they would be presented with a cryptic clue. Each clue related to a specific prize, and the contestants' job was to avoid the rubbish and find the Mini Mayfair or trip to Benidorm.

Famously, the clues were utterly impenetrable ('Bernie'll tell you, 'ere it's gone, but now you'll know the big trip's on'), making great play of anagrams and sound-a-like words. Whether any contestants were actually able to understand them or simply picked a prize at random is a moot point ('Well, ERE goes from Bernie, which leaves three letters, BNI, but now you'll know the big trip's on, and this would have tripped you up in a big way, yes, you've done it, you've rejected Dusty Bin!').

Originally Ted was assisted by a company of comedians, Chris Emmett, Duggie Brown and Debbie Arnold, who would interrupt proceedings. In addition there was also The Gentle Secs; a collective of six hostesses, each from a different country (apparently to give the show an 'international' flavour). Ted also had a 'chauffeur' who would come on and do bits of business, as well as, of course, Dusty Bin, the show's mascot who served as the ultimate booby prize for those contestants who failed to decipher those cryptic clues. Such reckless over-manning was testament to the money thrown at the series. So flush with cash were the early shows that Ted even strolled around the audience offering pound notes for correct answers to trivia questions.

3-2-1 was an instant hit, with the series becoming a staple of the weekend schedules. No doubt the huge amount of gimmicks Yorkshire TV stuffed into the show helped – Ted's three-finger salute, Dusty Bin's exploits, the video games the contestants had to play, even the flying YTV chevron in the opening titles – all had massive child appeal and helped to cement it as a family favourite.

As it continued throughout the Eighties, the show was changed slightly – thankfully ensuring the loser of the first round was now eliminated. The cast changed throughout, with troupes such as Lipstick and The Brian Rogers Connection replacing The Gentle Secs. A big-name singer or comedian would top the bill each week, dependent on that week's theme. Given that the themes were supposed to add a bit of variety to proceedings, it was funny how often they seemed to be Music Hall (where Ted could do his Danny Kaye impression), Fairy Tales or Cruise Ships.

Ratings eventually began to decline in the mid-Eighties. The final series abandoned the idea of themed shows altogether and instead simply developed a straightforward formula of quiz, songs and comedians (including early appearances from the likes of Phil Cornwell). The show came to an end in 1988, apparently considered too tacky for the modern ITV.

Sadly, post-3-2-1 Ted Rogers' career stalled, as he failed to land a replacement series and experienced some well-publicised financial difficulties. In recent years, however, 3-2-1 has become a staple in the schedules of Challenge TV, so much so that shortly before his death in 2001 Ted recorded new links for evenings of repeats. No matter how many times they were repeated, however, those cryptic clues remained completely unfathomable.

The 64,000 Question

ATV Network Production for ITV

19 May 1956 to 18 January 1958 (80 episodes)

Bringing high tension to the masses well over forty years before **Who Wants to be a Millionaire**, *The 64,000 Question* was one of a suite of game shows, including *Double Your Money* and *Take Your Pick*, to arrive on British screens during the hot flush of ITV's first year of transmission. The show was based on the hit American series of (almost) the same name, *The $64,000 Question*. However, whereas the US series was able to award a then unprecedented actual $64,000 to the winner, the UK version found itself restricted by regulations governing TV prize money to a jackpot of just £1,600 (64,000 sixpences), rising to £3,200 come the end of 1956 (64,000 shillings).

Nonetheless, this was still a sizeable amount, and one that allowed *The 64,000 Question* to crank up the tension. In fact, quizmaster Jerry Desmonde and 'custodian of the questions' ex-Detective Superintendent Robert Fabian (whose real-life policing adventures formed the basis for the successful series *Fabian of the Yard*) could often be found posing for publicity photos while kneeling in front of a large safe containing the questions.

The quiz itself was pretty straightforward. Contestants would have to answer questions of increasing value on a chosen specialist subject. The 100 and 500 teasers would be easy enough, however the questions came in two parts for the 1000 and 2000 teasers, and continued to increase in complexity until the 64,000 question itself required seven correct answers. The path to the top prize was therefore arduous, requiring the contestant to appear on a total of six consecutive editions. Stringing out encounters in this way was incredibly popular, and viewers would become so hooked by the performance of a contestant on the 8000 question that they simply had to tune in the following week to find out what happened next.

The show spawned a spin-off series, *The 64,000 Challenge*, featuring members of the public going head-to-head against previous *64,000 Question* contestants. Seven episodes were broadcast from 15 June to 31 August 1957, each presided over by Robin Bailey and, as with the parent programme, the producers were keen to point out that the accuracy of the answers could be vouched for by *Encyclopaedia Britannica* (a statement which further enhanced both programmes' intentional air of gravitas).

The 64,000 Question was regularly amongst the top five most watched programmes. However it was brought to an end in 1958. It made a brief return to our screens in 1990 under the full title of *The $64,000 Question*, but even then the top prize was still only £6,400.

All Creatures Great and Small

BBC1

8 January 1978 to 24 December 1990 (90 episodes)

All Creatures Great and Small oozed charm in a non-contrived sort of a way; the tinkling theme tune was the musical equivalent of a hillside stream, and the title sequence itself the epitome of pastoral tranquillity and bonhomie. More importantly, the series' characters, both regular and incidental were almost to a man utterly endearing. From the flamboyant Siegfried Farnon (Robert Hardy), to the innocently roguish Tristan Farnon (Peter Davison), not forgetting the litany of 'yokels' and amusingly pompous upper crusts, this was a world that you wanted to live in. Of course, James Herriot (Christopher Timothy) himself was a model of charm and patience, while his wife Helen (originally played by Carol Drinkwater) was the perfect example of an old-fashioned, supportive wife.

For three series, *All Creatures Great and Small* worked through the original Herriot novels with James and company cementing the image that they spent most of their time sticking their arms up cow's backsides and tending to dogs owned by ridiculously upper-crust ladies. But by the time the Second World War was rearing its head in the show, the source material was drying up and, in contrast to previous series' conclusions, the supposedly final run that commenced in 1979 ended with the rather gloomy prospect of James and Siegfried preparing to 'join up' and go into battle.

This downbeat note was a strange way to draw the programme to a close and unsurprisingly the public appetite for more remained undimmed over the intervening years. Although Christmas specials were served up in 1983 and 1985, it seemed inevitable that a full-blooded return to Darrowby would follow. And so it was that, some eight years after the original run had finished, *All Creatures Great and Small* returned to Saturday nights. At first glance the formula looked to be much the same. However, having grown unhappy with the development of her character, Carol Drinkwater elected not to reprise her role. In her place Lynda Bellingham, who is a perfectly fine actress, lent Helen a slight, but unwelcome element of brittleness. Peter Davison also pared down his involvement in the new run, so in came John McGlynn as the proto-ecologist Calum Buchanan.

All in all though, the storylines remained pretty much the same (although one episode featuring the demonstration of an artificial vagina provoked questions from viewers regarding *All Creatures Great and Small*'s suitability as family viewing), and the series continued to cast its spell on the telly-watching populace. By the time it drew to what one must assume to be its ultimate conclusion in 1990, the action had moved on to the early Sixties. Perhaps sensing that the charm of *All Creatures*...could not survive the turbulence of the Swinging Years, the programme was allowed once again to come to an end. This time round the audience recognised that it was right to let go of James, Siegfried and the rest and let them pass into the afterlife of an utterly warm and pleasant television memory. Two years later the mantle was picked up by ITV's inferior *Heartbeat* and rural dramas found themselves slipping off Saturdays and over to Sunday nights.

An Audience With...

LWT for ITV

26 December 1980 to ongoing
(44 episodes as of 9 December 2006)

There are few things more glamorous on television than an ITV light entertainment show. Compared to the often half-hearted efforts on the BBC, programmes recorded in LWT's cavernous Studio One, with its enormous audience, have always managed to impress through sheer scale if nothing else. Probably the most exciting of all was *An Audience With...* – not only were the people on stage famous, but so were those watching!

Although never a regular series, *An Audience With...* is one of the longest-running strands on British TV, starting way back on Boxing Day 1980 when Dame Edna Everage took to the stage in front of 'her' peers. The concept was established from day one; the star delivers a stand-up act or wheels out some anecdotes, while the celebrity audience, relentlessly placed in shot, cues in the routines with some carefully scripted questions.

Offering over an hour of the star, it's unsurprising that *An Audience With...* has served as the best example of the work of numerous performers, with Billy Connolly, Victoria Wood and Bob Monkhouse all recording shows that stand as perhaps the definitive record of their act. However, it initially only appeared on a very occasional basis, with just one episode between 1988 and 1994.

Since then, the series has turned up with increasing frequency, which, although welcome, has somewhat diluted its prestige. Where once we had Dudley Moore, Mel Brooks, Joan Rivers, Jackie Mason and Peter Ustinov we now have to endure the likes of Brian Conley, Joe Pasquale and even the cast of *Coronation Street*. The show's format has changed down the years too; originally it was a spotlight for comedians and entertainers, but these days it's more often a platform for musicians, such as Cliff Richard and Donny Osmond, to run through their back catalogue, often conveniently at the same time a Greatest Hits album is being released. At least in 2006 Take That and Lionel Richie made things a little more exciting by broadcasting their episodes live.

An Audience With... remains a regular part of the Saturday night schedules, although the audience cutaways seem to have become more frequent in recent years, as if the number of celebrities that can be lured into the studio is of more importance than the identity of the star actually doing the business up on the stage. Sadly, this means we'll probably never again get to enjoy the rather halting attempts at identifying audience members that Kenneth Williams so memorably essayed on his *An Audience With...* – 'Er, Matthew? It is Matthew, isn't it? ***Game for a Laugh***?'

Ant and Dec's Saturday Night Takeaway

Granada Television for ITV1

8 June 2002 to ongoing
(46 episodes as of 21 October 2006)

What if you could win everything shown in the TV ad breaks? This vaguely interesting concept formed the rather weak backbone to Ant and Dec's second attempt at establishing a successful Saturday night entertainment series. Since the rise of the Tyneside twosome in the Nineties, it seemed inevitable that sooner or later they would bag a primetime Saturday night slot. But the failure *Slap Bang with Ant and Dec* demonstrated that without a proper hook even they – the anointed future of light entertainment – were going to struggle.

Saturday Night Takeaway wisely built the entire show round an end game in which a member of the audience got

an opportunity to not 'just watch the ads – win them'. Each week a contestant was plucked from the audience and asked a series of general knowledge questions. However, given the brevity of the quiz, it was difficult to care much whether 'Sheila from Dagenham' actually went home with the star prize or not. Perhaps recognising that the 'Win the Ads' game wasn't actually that good, its role in the show was greatly diminished after the first series.

However, pretty much everything else about *Takeaway* was great. The first episode set the tone with an excellent ruse in which the duo appeared live on a cinema screen and informed a stunned audience that one of their party had a £3000 prize waiting for them at home that had to be collected before the end of the show. This stunt was not in itself new (**Noel's House Party** and 'NTV' had hacked into a cinema screen a few years earlier), but it established *Takeaway* as an 'anything can happen' sort of a show – ideal for Saturday night viewing.

That same edition also featured the introduction of what was obviously designed to be a major element. 'Banged up with Beadle' saw the one-time Saturday night prankster locked up in a fort in the Solent for the duration of the series. Each week he would be joined by a member of the public, and between them they would have to master a new skill that, if performed successfully live on the Saturday night show, would earn the member of the public £5000, plus a privilege for Beadle to make his incarceration more bearable. 'Banged up with Beadle' even spawned its own spin-off show in 2002 – *Ant and Dec's Banged Up with Beadle.*

Probably much against the programme's wishes Beadle actually got on very well with his fellow inmates, meaning that hoped-for arguments rarely ever surfaced. Ironically, the only disagreement of any significance occurred during the first week when Beadle threatened to walk out after being told he had failed a yoga task. It took the intervention of an executive producer to resolve the situation, ensuring that at the end of the show, the lucky member of the public was awarded their prize money after all.

For the second series we lost Beadle plus other items such as 'Make Ant Laugh' that had felt like a hangover from *Slap Bang* anyway. In their place came celebrity hidden-camera shenanigans with 'Ant and Dec Undercover' and 'What's Next?' – five minutes of unscripted and unprepared nonsense as our two hosts were invited to take part in a Wild West shoot-out or try and slam-dunk a few hoops with a team of crack basketball players. Whatever the situation, Ant and Dec's unfailing ability to improvise amusing banter never deserted them.

Perhaps the most memorable addition though was 'Little Ant and Dec'. The diminutive duo's *raison d'être* was to conduct slightly cheeky interviews with various celebrities ranging from Kylie Minogue to Tony Blair. Over the years *Takeaway* has become a bigger and more ambitious spectacle. For example, the 2006 series saw Ant and Dec abseil down the side of the London Studios, and take a variety of vehicles out for a hair-raising spin on a race course. Meanwhile, celebrities were inveigled into ordinary people's lives in the clever and original hidden-camera strand 'Stars In Their Lives'.

But however ingenious or impressive these various items might be, it's really the boys' bonhomie, comic timing and, above all, genuine affection for each other that really keeps viewers tuning in, and you have to figure that as long as Ant and Dec remain the best of friends there will always be an appreciative and loyal audience waiting to lap up their latest antics.

Aspel and Company
LWT for ITV

9 June 1984 to 20 June 1993 (118 episodes)

Parkinson had his Yorkshire grit. Wogan specialised in homespun blarney. Harty essayed camp bemusement. Michael Aspel, on the other hand, appeared not to have a unique take on the role of chat show host. However he did have bags of affability and easy charm, and as *Parkinson* was to the Seventies, so *Aspel and Company* became a familiar part of an Eighties Saturday night.

When he took on the show, Aspel had already proven himself adept at most things on TV – indeed, he managed to pull off a rather bizarre shift from reading the news to presenting kids show *Crackerjack*. Later stints asking questions to people who couldn't speak English on *Miss World* and keeping the peace between Una Stubbs and Lionel Blair on *Give Us a Clue* established him as a safe pair of hands. Yet the chat show had its roots in the wireless, as during his lengthy stint on London's Capital Radio, Aspel notched up several hundred interviews with famous people. This was enough of an apprenticeship to allow him to translate his talent for chat to television.

Starting off with a guest list of Richard Clayderman, Tracey Ullman and Paul McCartney, Aspel proved himself to be the perfect host of a relaxed talking shop. His gentle manner meant that guests opened up, yet our man possessed the rigour and quick wit to ensure interviews kept on the rails. Some moaned he didn't ask tough questions, but this was

Saturday night and not the place for an interrogation. Aspel didn't even mind what and how much his guests plugged just so long as they were entertaining in the process.

Aspel also seemed entirely without embarrassment and throughout the run was happy to answer any questions his guests might have on how old he was (he'd just passed his fifty-first birthday when the first series began), when he lost his virginity and even, thanks to Jackie Collins, what he called his penis (his 'dickie', fact fans).

Everything seemed to run like clockwork, except for one notable occasion. Oliver Reed's memorable appearance, where he emerged with an overflowing pint glass and proceeded to sing an unintelligible version of 'The Wild One', has gone down in the annals of history (compare and contrast with his appearances on *Saturday Night at the Mill* and *Sin on Saturday*). However Aspel remained unflappable throughout, and seemed content to simply let Ollie get on with it and let the edit suite sort it out.

Sadly, *Aspel and Company* ended on a low note. In 1993, the series was moved from Saturday to Sunday, and was also broadcast live, which Aspel was rather uneasy about. Then there followed the notorious appearance by Arnold Schwarzenegger, Sylvester Stallone and Bruce Willis – a real coup, but one that came at a heavy price. Aspel had to agree to discuss nothing but the trio's newly opened Planet Hollywood restaurant, even going as far as to read out the menu on air. This rather shameless selling-out inevitably spelt the end for the series. Still, as the most likeable man on telly, he didn't moan once and still had the likes of *This Is Your Life* and later *Antiques Roadshow* to keep him busy.

The A-Team

Carnell Productions/Universal [shown on ITV]

22 July 1983 to 17 October 1987 (95 episodes)

'Crash, bang, wallop, it's *The A-Team.*' So proclaimed *TV Times* back in July 1983 as it announced the arrival of one of the Eighties most iconic television series. Starting with a 105-minute opening episode, *The A-Team* began in the UK on Fridays before being moved to Saturday early evenings in 1984. Deliberately created to get the viewers' blood pumping, *The A-Team* was high-octane stuff, featuring the weekly adventures of a former Vietnam combat squad on the run from the law and forced to live as soldiers of fortune.

The line-up consisted of four pleasingly delineated and distinctive characters: Dwight Schultz as Murdock (the crazy one), Dirk Benedict as Templeton Peck – better known as Face (the smooth con-man who regularly became embroiled in some yawn inducing skirt chasing), George Peppard as Colonel John 'Hannibal' Smith (the cigar-chomping leader of the pack) and Mr T as B.A. Baracus. Of the quartet, it was Mr T who made the biggest impact. His temperament,

© Photos International/ Rex Features

liking for bling and massive physical frame set him apart from pretty much every other action hero on telly. His surly behaviour also struck a chord with the younger audience, who could relate to his simplistic outlook on life (although it's probably not unfair to point out that there was something of the child in all of the four characters).

Not that characterisation was *The A-Team*'s defining attribute. While BBC dramas of the time (such as **The Tripods**) featured characters embarking on noble quests and learning important lessons about themselves, *The A-Team* relied on blowing up lots of stuff, and sending jeeps hurtling through the air at every given opportunity. The series' massive success (in the UK in 1984 it attracted more than 16 million viewers) was predicated on a tightly defined formula that was much loved by viewers, and later much dissected by observational comedians.

The ingredients for any given episode included an attractive woman for Face to chat up, the trading of insults between Murdock and BA, Face donning some form of disguise to infiltrate that week's gang of baddies, aerophobic BA having to get into a plane, and of course the set piece finale in which the team would find themselves hauled up in some kind of enclosed space, only to uncover a stray oxy-acetylene welding torch, a massive vehicle and enough scrap metal to armour-plate a bus. The triumphant final reel would then see the team in their improvised battle vehicle wreaking havoc and flipping jeeps galore, while a nation of teenage boys looked on and cheered in front of their television sets.

Formulaic it might have been, but *The A-Team* managed to

display a level of invention that kept things highly entertaining. One week the team might be called upon to defend a group of shopkeepers from a protection racket, and (literally) the next they would be pressed into service to transport a harvest of melons to a local market.

All was going swimmingly until 1987 when, provoked in part by Michael Ryan's horrific killing spree in Hungerford, the Independent Broadcasting Authority decided to clamp down on what it saw as gratuitous violence on ITV. *The A-Team* was an obvious target and sometimes as much as nine minutes were cut from a 48-minute episode, leaving the plot in a disjointed state that was very difficult to follow. Obviously, this was an unsatisfactory situation, but before ITV could take any decisive action, word came through that the Americans had decided to axe the series anyway.

Barrymore
LWT for ITV

21 December 1991 to 28 June 1997 (67 episodes)

'Here we go — late coach party.' And so would start another sequence of unscripted Barrymore-fuelled mayhem. Can there ever have been another entertainment series that spent so much time with the cameras trained on the studio audience, and can there ever have been another entertainer who could make such mileage out of donking old men over the head with the end of a microphone?

Building an entire show around Michael Barrymore's bantering with Joe Public was an obvious idea, and after a one-off Christmas special (written by comedians Stewart Lee and Richard Herring), the *Barrymore* series proper

featured the eponymous host welcoming talented or just eccentric members of the public onto his rather basic set (consisting of two large sofas set at an obtuse angle positioned in front of what appeared to be the partitions from ***Blind Date***). Barrymore would carry out a pretty straightforward interview, all the while chipping in with loads of comic asides to the audience ('They're not all locked up, are they?'), before finally allowing his guest to perform their act (which he would invariably attempt to upstage).

The first show was notable for a bizarre opening as our host spotted BBC Sport executive Brian Barwick in the audience and made great play of throwing him out of ITV premises ('You're BBC, you shouldn't be here'), while inviting the entire audience to hum along to the tune of *Match of the Day*. But the rest of the series was full of equally strange and memorable moments. During the filming for one edition, Barrymore initiated his usual shtick of aggravating a member of the audience, only to be shooed away as the embarrassed recipient of his attention confessed she was on a date with her secret lover and didn't want to be seen on telly by her husband. Other in-the-crowd antics involved our man attempting to walk along the partitions that separated sections of the audience, and physically grovelling on one poor lady before dragging her, a step at a time, down towards the studio floor.

But those who joined him on the sofas weren't safe either. Ernie, an 81-year-old Jewish comedian was well into his act ('I have sex nearly every night...nearly on a Monday, nearly on a Tuesday...') when a heckler informed him, quite correctly as it turned out, that his flies were undone. Amidst the peals of laughter Barrymore was unable to resist dropping in a circumcision gag and then went on to make great play of pulling Ernie's zip up for him.

A regular insert to the show was 'My Kind of People', where the *Barrymore* road show would set up in a shopping centre and invite members of the public to sing songs, tell jokes or perform magic. Of course they would have to endure Barrymore arsing about behind them before, if they were good (or bad) enough, getting an invite to appear on the main show. This open-house policy resulted in some of the most weird and wonderful entertainment acts in Britain getting national airtime. Yodellers, roller-skating gymnasts, female OAP bikers and human gnomes were all put to the service of fuelling Barrymore's limitless potential for mucking around.

The show enjoyed three series of massive success, blighted only by the odd big production number during which Mike would attempt to sell himself as a serious singer (the most memorable of these was perhaps a maudlin reading of the Barry Manilow hit 'Never Met A Man I Didn't Like' including changed lyrics to reflect Barrymore's pedigree as a 'Bermondsey Boy'). Yet due to his prodigious talent, such excesses seemed excusable.

As Barrymore began to earn the epithet 'troubled entertainer', his show shifted its focus away from members of the public and on to fellow celebrities (with the likes of Spike Milligan, Hinge and Bracket, Paul Young and Frank Bruno all making an appearance). Perhaps this was simply to distinguish the programme from *Michael Barrymore's My Kind of People* – a spin-off from the similarly titled item in *Barrymore*, or maybe Mike simply felt more comfortable in the company of his fellow pros. Although *Barrymore* wound up in 1997, its memory lived on in *Michael Barrymore's My Kind of Music* – a pretty rubbish musical quiz show that never really allowed its host to stretch his now long-forgotten comedic muscles.

The Basil Brush Show
BBC1

14 June 1968 to 27 December 1980 (154 episodes)

For years, Saturday nights on BBC1 would start with a programme aimed at the younger members of the audience, normally involving a puppet of some kind. Cast adrift from the usual weekday and Saturday morning children's programmes, these shows were normally made by the light entertainment department. As such they would include all the usual trappings of a standard variety programme – including a pop band or two, who in exchange for plugging their latest single would have to participate in a hugely demeaning sketch with the star of the show (involving said star getting their names wrong or making jokes about their hair). The master of this art was undoubtedly the esteemed Basil Brush.

Created by Peter Firmin and voiced by Ivan Owen, the upper-class fox first made his debut as one of *The Three Scampis* (broadcast as part of ITV's long-running pre-school series *Small Time*), but soon cast off his partners to become a solo star in his own right, helped by regular appearances alongside David Nixon. Eventually Basil was given his own BBC show, and a fixture of the Saturday teatime schedules was born.

The eponymous series was never-changing, with Basil perennially pissing off his long-suffering human sidekicks, Mr Rodney (Bewes), Mr Derek (Fowlds), Mr Roy (North), Mr Howard (Williams) and Mr Billy (Boyle). Contrived gags and daft puns were the order of the day, most obviously in the familiar closing sequence when the 'Mister' would attempt to tell a story (such as 'Basil the Buccaneer') during which Basil would act up something chronic.

For those who worked with Basil, the association could stick – Derek Fowlds went on to enjoy a long and distinguished acting career, most obviously in *Yes Minister*, but a generation would forever know him as 'Mr Derek'.

Throughout the run, numerous big-name pop stars would appear, mainly because *The Basil Brush Show* was one of the few places outside of *Top of the Pops* to showcase contemporary pop music. In fact over the years pretty much the whole gamut of pop music was represented on the show with acts such as Leapy Lee, Gilbert O'Sullivan, The New Seekers, Pilot, Brotherhood Of Man and Wings all making an appearance. However it must be noted that the George Martin who wrote almost all of Basil's scripts was a former stand-up comedian and not the Beatles producer.

When the show finally came to an end in the early Eighties, Basil conceded the slot to a number of other juvenile series, including *The Keith Harris Show*, *The Krankies Elektronik Komik* and *Roland Rat: The Series*. Meanwhile, Basil ligged around a number of ITV kids' programmes, such as *Basil Brush's Joke Machine*, until he went into semi-retirement in the late Eighties.

That wasn't quite the end though, as in the twenty-first century, Basil was 'relaunched' with a new voice (Ivan Owen having since died), a new body and a new setting. The irrepressible fox had now became the star of a sitcom shown as part of Children's BBC.

Baywatch

The Baywatch Company/Tower 12/Tower 18
[shown on ITV]

6 January 1990 to 19 July 1997 (122 episodes)

As well as being (according to its star David Hasselhoff) 'the most popular television series in the world', *Baywatch* holds the distinction alongside **The New Adventures of Superman** of being the last American drama show to make a significant impact on Saturday nights. Like many of the previous US hits, *Baywatch* found success by defining and then sticking firmly to a winning formula. In this case an exotic location, soft rock soundtrack, easy to follow morality tales and scantily clad beauties.

Although lead actor, David Hasselhoff, was persistently heard complaining about the lack of 'emotional stories' ('I don't want to come out of this in five or six years and have people say, well he talked to a car and then he ran down the beach'), viewers were turning on in their millions to enjoy some brainless entertainment and as many slow-mo shots of buff lifeguards running into the sea as the producer's could contrive. In fact, such was the show's popularity in the UK that when, due to poor ratings Stateside, NBC decided to cancel it after the first series, ITV organised a consortium of contented buyers to pre-finance another run.

Of course without ITV's help *Baywatch* would never have secured the services of its most iconic cast member. Pamela Anderson first appeared as C.J. Parker in the third series, and with her arrival *Baywatch* perfected its winning formula. As if to prove the point, by its fourth year it became established as the fastest-produced drama on television (churning out twenty-two episodes in only five months). However, the production line couldn't last for ever and British viewers got tired of Hasselhoff, Anderson and the others' heavy moralising; even the gratuitous slow-motion shots accompanied by histrionic soft rock incidental music were beginning to pall.

By the end of 1997 (just two years after ITV had seen fit to bill repeats of the show as *Golden Baywatch*), the channel jettisoned the series altogether, allowing Sky One to pick up the rights. Today the show never seems to be off our screens thanks to some digital satellite channel or other airing repeats. In fact, as you are reading this there is probably some British channel somewhere right now showing the same bevy of lifeguards hurling themselves headlong into the same surf for the umpteenth time today.

Beadle's About

LWT for ITV

22 November 1986 to 31 October 1996 (94 episodes)

Although it may surprise his detractors, *Beadle's About* is generally regarded as the 'Rolls-Royce' of hidden-camera shows, and many of the programme's most successful stunts are now considered classics of the genre. The show diverged from standard hidden-camera series such as **Candid Camera** by concentrating on stings set up for pre-selected targets. While this made the stunts all the more difficult to stage (each one was tailor-made for a specific person, so there was no opportunity to remount it and try it again with someone else if it went wrong), it also allowed for the introduction of a little bit of natural justice, as long-suffering wives could get one back on their irritating 'look-at-me-I'm-a-bit-wacky' husbands.

Of course, certain set-ups live longer in the memory than others and particular highlights include the overweight Golightly family trashing a bed shop in Orpington, a bogus Queen Mother stealing items from an antiques shop, a husband and wife visiting a military museum only for the husband to start up one of the tanks and trash the exhibits, and the various and many workplace stunts involving employees (usually on their first day at a new job) being asked to shred and then reassemble documents or other equally ridiculous tasks.

Although the camera work and (particularly) the sound on *Beadle's About* were first rate, odd shots obviously taken after the stunt had happened did crop up and a sequence featuring actress Annette Badland as a foreign princess was notable for the inclusion of a number of close-ups and reaction shots that clearly weren't caught at the time the prank was being played.

Of all the *Beadle's About* stunts, there is one that is commonly agreed to tower above all others. Apparently its genesis came not from Beadle, but from the man who gave us such great children's telly programmes as *Jigsaw* and *Eureka*, Clive Doig. After much logistical planning (that resulted in the ruse becoming one of the most expensive hidden-camera stunts ever filmed in Britain) the game was on.

The target selected was an unsuspecting farmer's wife on her way home from an appearance in a local pantomime. While she had been out, Beadle and co. had embedded a fake meteorite in her garden. Her initial reaction was priceless, and with very little persuasion from the 'authorities' gathered at the scene (really Beadle's stooges), she willingly serenaded the steaming lump of rock (she was fed a line to the effect that meteors were attracted by creativity). In so doing she caused an 'alien' to appear from within the debris. Here was the pivotal moment of the entire, elaborate scam. Fabulously undeterred, the target enquired whether the extra-terrestrial would like a cup of tea. At this point the audience at home wet themselves, as did Beadle and the poor woman's friends (all watching the action unfold on monitors from the comfort of a forty-seat coach situated in a nearby field). As Beadle himself concedes, he couldn't have scripted a better outcome.

Surprisingly, although 1996 was the year of *Beadle's About*'s most acclaimed stunt, that same year the powers-that-be deemed the series had come to the end of its natural life and the show was cancelled. This was a particularly sad moment for petty agitators who realised that the by now famed 'I thought it was Beadle' defence would no longer wash in a court of law.

Big Break

BBC1

30 April 1991 to 13 May 2000 (215 episodes)

The BBC's attempts at game shows in the Eighties and Nineties were not, perhaps, the greatest programmes to come out of Television Centre. There was a feeling that the corporation only commissioned them for the sake of it, and with the licence fee preventing them from giving away huge prizes, they couldn't help but look slightly ragged next to the more glamorous, expensive ITV opposition. And a bad BBC game show could generate critical ire like nothing else on television.

Not for nothing then, did Jim Davidson introduce the first episode of *Big Break* by announcing, 'This is my first show for the BBC and, if it doesn't work out, we're both snookered!'

Big Break's most obvious influence was the long-running ITV series *Bullseye*. On that show contestants had to exhibit a general knowledge and some skill at darts to win big prizes, while guest professional players would turn up to throw a few arrows and add a bit of credibility to proceedings. On *Big Break*, each week, three members of the public would be teamed up with professional snooker players, and the punters would have to answer questions to win time for their team-mates to pot balls on the in-studio table. If they could do this successfully, prizes would be on offer – but not very big ones, obviously, as this was the BBC. Davidson asked the questions, and bantered with the show's 'referee', John Virgo, whose presence clearly helped attract big names – virtually every famous player appeared at least once during the run.

With a loudmouth comedian in charge, a show based around a pub game, and a raucous stompalong theme sung by Captain Sensible, *Big Break* was clearly not particularly cerebral viewing. However, it was incredibly popular. The first episode pulled in 16.5 million viewers, and it became a staple on Saturday evenings for the entire Nineties.

While always able to attract big audiences, *Big Break* couldn't help but become something of an anachronism – this was very much a quiz show of the old school. Later in the run the programme devolved into a kind of half-hour comedy routine between Davidson and Virgo, with the actual game taking second place. Worse still, at times it appeared to be on for ever, umpteen episodes being recorded in one go and then flung out for months and years on end. If BBC1 was particularly stuck, you would sometimes have to sit through two or three shows a week.

In *Big Break's* favour, the programme's contestant policy deserves some credit, as the show specifically appealed for disabled and ethnic minorities to appear. Yet by 2000, it was hard to work out what such a tacky series was still doing on the BBC, especially when even ITV had dropped the majority of its cheap and cheerful quiz shows. Eventually the huge stockpile of episodes ran out, and the Beeb didn't seem particularly enthusiastic about making anymore. Still, at least Jim could concentrate on **The Generation Game** instead. Oh dear.

The Billy Cotton Band Show

BBC

29 March 1956 to 20 July 1968 (168 episodes)

For those of a certain age, a hollered 'wakey wakey!' and a frantic rendition of 'Somebody Stole My Girl' is the epitome of television variety. Billy Cotton had been at the helm of his big band since the Twenties, and had landed his own radio show in 1949. As with much else in the early days of television, it was simply ported straight over to the new medium, and stayed popular for twelve years.

The concept of *The Billy Cotton Band Show* was almost an anachronism when it began, with the musicians harking back to an older era of dance bands. This faithful troupe provided the backing for guests from the world of comedy and music, with many of the big names from both fields appearing (Russ Conway, Frankie Vaughan, Spike Milligan).

There was also room for some up-and-coming names, including a very young Ted Rogers (who on one edition sang 'Mambo Italiano'). Meanwhile Kathie Kay and Alan Breeze were Cotton's regular sidekicks, helping to bring a familiar mixture of comedy and up-tempo musical numbers to the masses (in the process perfecting a formula that would be used in countless BBC Saturday night shows throughout the next two decades). The show specialised in songs such as 'Don't Dilly Dally On the Way', but an edition in June 1967 acknowledged the growing importance of contemporary music by finding space to include a rendition of Procol Harum's 'A Whiter Shade of Pale'.

Cotton was well into his fifties by the time the series started, and as it continued, he was obviously getting too old to join in with the hoofing and slapstick, and spent much of the programme standing slightly off-stage clutching his sides. By this point, the series had become something of a family affair, with his son Bill Junior taking over the producer's reigns. Indeed it served as a useful training ground for BBC producers, with Johnnie Stewart (creator of *Top of the Pops*) and Michael Hurll (*The Late Late Breakfast Show* and much else) also taking a turn.

For much of its run *The Billy Cotton Band Show* shared Saturday evenings with the equally prestigious *The Black and White Minstrel Show*, with each series airing on alternative Saturdays. Yet while the title to the Minstrels show never changed (except for the odd one-off occasion to recognise Christmas or other holidays), the *Band Show* went under a number of different names during its twelve-year tenure. A few early episodes were billed as *Wakey, Wakey!*, while later on the names *The Wakey Wakey Circus* and *The Wakey Wakey Tavern* cropped up on a few occasions. From 1965 onwards the show was permanently rebranded as *Billy Cotton's Music Hall*. Yet to most viewers it remained simply *The Billy Cotton Band Show*.

The series finally came to an end in 1968, when Cotton retired before dying of a heart attack in 1969. A giant show in its day, it has been wheeled out every now and then to represent Sixties TV, as part of the BBC's fiftieth anniversary programming in 1986, and during a Sixties season on BBC4 in 2004. Bill Junior, meanwhile, went on to commission every light entertainment show on the BBC for the next decade or so.

The Black and White Minstrel Show

BBC

14 June 1958 to 21 July 1978 (174 episodes)

First appearing on our screens under the fantastic name *The 1957 Television Minstrels*, this series has latterly gained notoriety for its use of white performers with 'blacked-up' faces. However, *The Black and White Minstrel Show* was actually a staple of Saturday nights for over twenty years and for a while was the flagship programme of BBC light entertainment. The Minstrels were involved in the grand opening of BBC Television Centre in 1961, with their backing dancers The Television Toppers prancing around the concrete doughnut, and were also one of the first variety shows to be broadcast in colour.

The group were already a going concern before they made it to television, touring the nation's theatres under the auspices of their creator George Mitchell. The seeds of their television debut were actually sewn some nine years before they hit our screens. In 1948 producer George Inns watched the BBC's rather static one-off television special *The Kentucky Minstrels* and vowed that he would one day produce something of a similar nature, albeit on a far larger and more spectacular canvas. When it arrived on our screens in 1957, *The Black and White Minstrel Show* was dubbed 'the fastest show on television'. Pace, movement and a constant stream of different camera shots, marked the series out as something new and different.

Each episode consisted of various medleys of popular songs crooned by the monochrome men, specialising in the sort of standards that your grandparents could sing along to, often harking back to the Deep South (ironically for most of the vocalists, the 'Deep South' referred to Wales, with the likes of Dai Francis and Les Want donning the black make-up). An awful lot of high-kicking up and down superfluous staircases seemed to be the order of the day, and when the Minstrels weren't regaling us with the likes of 'Old Man River' they would offer us a selection of songs from around the world (although usually from South America or Italy) performed in front of a suitably themed set. Over the course of one 45-minute episode up to fifty songs could be featured, with seven or eight included in each medley.

The Black and White Minstrel Show was immediately and hugely popular. Having produced just seven editions within the space of its first year, from September 1959 onwards the series was broadcast on a fortnightly basis (not that uncommon in those days, but pretty rare in the world of television scheduling today). In 1961 *The Black and White Minstrel Show* attracted over 15 million viewers and won both the Golden Rose and Silver Rose awards at the inaugural Rose d'Or Festival in Montreux. The series was also credited with being one of the first BBC shows to win back audiences who had previously been wooed over to ITV by that channel's intensive diet of variety spectaculars.

As well as the crooning, each episode of *The Black and White Minstrel Show* featured the odd comic interlude. The first chap to assume the role of the Minstrel's funny man was

Kenneth Connor, closely followed by Stan Stennett. The likes of Leslie Crowther would later build their reputation delivering gags on the series, while Keith Harris (with a proto-Orville) made his TV debut on the show.

Harris' spots were pretty typical of the kind of comic turns that *The Black and White Minstrel Show* featured. One routine, involving a crudely constructed puppet of boxer Muhammad Ali, included the terrible and somewhat suspect pun 'your mother warned you to stay away from dark alleys'. Similarly dubious, an effervescent Don Maclean started one of his comedy sets with the proclamation 'a clean face at last!' (before launching into an excruciating impression of a 'Chinaman'). Famously, later in the run, a young Lenny Henry found himself working as comic relief, something that seems a bizarre choice today, but at the time Henry was grateful for the exposure.

Linking between the big music numbers and comedy spots was George Mitchell himself. By no means a born showman, his understated delivery of such uncharismatic lines as ' for our finale tonight we've chosen some music by George Gershwin which we hope you'll all enjoy', suited the style of presentation when the series began, but by its latter years, looked somewhat creaky.

For much of its run, the rather dubious nature of the series was either never remarked upon, or simply laughed off; 'blacking up' had been a staple of light entertainment for decades. However, some of the Minstrels recalled they'd often pop out the stage door for a cigarette between takes while still in full make-up, much to the surprise of the black labourers working on a nearby building site.

It's remarkable to think that *The Black and White Minstrel Show* retained its popularity throughout almost the entire Seventies (it was one of the Top Ten most watched programmes of the week as late as 1976). However the concept, as well as the politics, was becoming ever more outdated. Variety shows were falling out of favour on television, and *The Black and White Minstrel Show* was no more immune than any other series. By 1978 the show was no longer viable.

Since then, *The Black and White Minstrel Show*'s only appearances have been as part of serious documentaries on race relations. The show has never been screened as simply a piece of archive television or as a piece of entertainment. When it was left out of a season of programmes to celebrate BBC Television's fiftieth anniversary in 1986, Bill Cotton was hauled onto the television show about television, *Open Air*, to answer criticism that by not screening what had clearly been a well-loved and popular series at the time, the BBC had bowed to political pressure.

Of course, it's probably fair enough that *The Black and White Minstrel Show* is not shown anymore, but the fact remains it had little, if any, malice in its construction, and was simply an old-fashioned variety show of the type that happens to have become, with the passing of time, as dated as its morals.

Blind Date

LWT for ITV

30 November 1985 to 24 May 2003 (356 episodes)

If there is one programme synonymous with British Saturday night television over the last twenty years it has to be *Blind Date*. This light-hearted dating show actually began in America as *The Dating Game*, a highly controversial series that featured such unambiguous exchanges as one chap answering the question 'What would I like most about you?' with the rather too on-the-nose response: 'My cock'.

The British version was an altogether tamer programme, with contestants briefed to shake hands when they first met, and the couples who actually got to go on a date being closely chaperoned to ensure they went their separate ways at nightfall. This is not to say though that the programme couldn't occasionally be saucy; presenter Cilla Black peering her head around the famous partition that separated the 'picker' from the 'pickees' and expressing mock shock at a risqué comment from a contestant wearing a pair of personality socks, became a regular Saturday night occurrence.

Whether the show appealed to you or not really depended on what you made of those contestants. It could be said that it was *Blind Date* that pioneered the concept of members of the public coming on the telly to try and be 'funny' in their own right. Revolutionary as this was, it also meant that loads of people with no specific skills, save perhaps a strong belief in their own entertainment value (and an inherent ability to be bloody irritating), saw the show as a perfect springboard to a long-dreamt-of career in television presenting.

Of all the 'eccentrics' that perched upon one those famous stools, perhaps the most memorable was also one of the first. Paul Nolan (who appeared from behind the partitions in 1987) milked his fifteen minutes of fame for all it was worth, launching into a number of highly exaggerated impersonations of celebrities such as Bruce Forsyth and Norman Wisdom; all of which tickled Cilla greatly, while prompting many viewers at home to launch into a tirade about 'prats who think they're funny'. Although his appearance led to neither a long-term romance, nor, come to think of it, a long-term television career (Paul was last spotted running an entertainment business in Newcastle), it did secure *Blind Date* the kind of press coverage that became instrumental in sustaining the show's fortunes.

In this regard, *Blind Date* broke further ground and established a rapport with the tabloids that would later be copied by reality television series such as *I'm a Celebrity...Get Me out of Here* and *Big Brother*. While most of the press coverage focused on those contestants who turned out to be cheating love rats, the marriages of Alex Tatham and Sue Middleton and 'golden oldies' David Fensom and Lillian Morris were both big news.

For thirteen years, *Blind Date* changed very little; the only real development being the adoption of filmed inserts as opposed to photographic montages to represent the Blinders' date, and the resultant increase in footage of females pushing wacky males into swimming pools, lakes or other similarly wet locations (and of course if the date had taken place somewhere dry then the male would have to suffer an ice cream in the face instead). But by 1998 audiences for terrestrial television were on the decline thanks to the increasing take-up of satellite and cable television. *Blind Date* was no more immune than any other programme, and average ratings were 4 million down on the series' heyday. By way of retaliation the show was afforded an increased budget, new scriptwriters and new producers, and discussions began in earnest regarding a radical revamp. Initially it was decided that contestants would be picked 'randomly' from the studio audience, but this was discarded in preference to the tried and tested format and *Blind Date* teetered on as before.

1998 also saw the first concerted rumours that Cilla Black would be heading for pastures new. It emerged that Zoë Ball, Kirsty Young or (unthinkably) GMTV's Eamonn Holmes were all being lined up to replace the great lady. Change, however, finally arrived in 2002 with the addition of a 'ditch or date' element and a new spin-off show called *Blind Date Kiss & Tell*.

Now, pickers had to reject one of the pickees at the end of the question and answer session, and choose one of the two remaining contestants to accompany them on their date. But that was not the end of it. At this point, the picker's loved ones were encouraged to give their opinion as to whether the chosen contestant should be 'ditched' in favour of the final contestant who still remained out of the picker's view. The studio audience, too, expressed their opinion by vigorously shouting 'ditch' or 'date' as the picker was asked to either re-affirm their choice or expel the second pickee in favour of the final contestant. If it sounds complicated and awkward, that's because it was.

However, viewers roundly rejected the new look and, perhaps sensing that *Blind Date* was in terminal decline, Cilla announced on the special one-off live 4 January 2003 edition that she intended to quit at the end of the show's eighteenth series. Apparently, no one in the production team had been made aware of her intentions and, caught in a tailspin, the programme makers elected to 'ditch' *Blind Date* itself later that year.

Will *Blind Date* ever return? Absolutely – although it won't be Cilla cajoling the picker into selecting contestant 1, 2 or 3. Whomever her ultimate successor might be it is highly unlikely that they will be able to carve as successful a niche in popular culture as the first lady of Saturday night television. After all, there are very few people as skilled as Cilla at walking that fine line between encouragement and reprimand, and even less who can provide such easy fodder for rubbish impressionists.

Bob Monkhouse on the Spot
BBC1

22 July 1995 to 27 July 1996 (12 episodes)

The history of Bob Monkhouse's television career is in a way the history of television comedy itself. From his first appearance on the medium in the late Forties, to almost immediately before his death in 2003, Monkhouse was never out of work.

By the Nineties, most people knew him as a game show host. For Monkhouse, this was no problem as he was certainly adept at them – **Bob's Full House**, *Family Fortunes* and *The Golden Shot*, among many others, were all huge successes. However, the odd sharp one-liner aside, he didn't get many chances to remind viewers of his comedic pedigree. Anyone who saw Bob's stand-up act was well aware of his mastery of the one-liner, and it seemed a waste of a major comedy talent to see him simply trading quips with Garry Bushell on **Celebrity Squares**.

Undoubtedly the turning point in the public's perception of Monkhouse came when he guested on an episode of *Have I Got News for You* in 1993. Rather than simply stringing tired old gags together, he came out with a stream of funny, sharp and topical quips. At a stroke Bob was reinvented as a contemporary and relevant comedy star for the Nineties. This led to his first all-comedy TV series for years.

Bob Monkhouse on the Spot was a straightforward stand-up show with one man and his microphone entertaining a studio audience. Much of the material was based on the week's news and was testament to Bob's ability to move with the times (although few comedians were as adept at recycling old jokes). It also served as a great way for Bob to continually stretch himself, with each episode ending on a startling set-piece where he improvised his way from one subject to the other.

All in all, it was an impressive performance that showed an old-school entertainer prepared to take on the dangerous comedy challenge of improvisation. In recent years it had seemed that improvised comedy was the preserve of alternative comedy performers such as John Sessions and Paul Merton, and so to see an established entertainer put his reputation on the line like this made for thrilling television. A welcome injection of topicality also helped give the show a certain edge, as did Bob's willingness to take on risqué subjects. All in all, *On the Spot* was a real highlight in the great man's long career.

Bob claimed the series generated 'the best reviews of my life', but this wasn't enough to ensure *On the Spot* lasted for more than two series. However, it did enough to ensure that Bob proved as popular with the younger generation as he'd been among their parents, and even their parents before that.

Bob Says Opportunity Knocks

BBC1

21 March 1987 to 2 June 1990 (48 episodes)

'Star – That's what they call you / How long you've waited to get where you are'. Just as the original **New Faces'** boom-crash intro had established that talent show's star-making aspirations, Kiki Dee's imaginatively titled 'Star' ensured that viewers new to the programme, immediately understood what the return of the longest-running and most successful talent show on British television signified. For over twenty years, *Opportunity Knocks* had been a monolithic presence on ITV but its arrival, after a nine-year hiatus, on the BBC marked the show's first foray onto Saturday nights (surely its natural home) since 27 July 1968.

While the original run had been defined by presenter Hughie Green's almost mafioso aspirations to create a light entertainment firmament of which he was the Godfather, the BBC slipped the impeccable Bob Monkhouse into the role of impresario and chief cheerleader. As with the Green years, *Bob Says Opportunity Knocks* offered up no stunt critics, and instead provided unstinting support for the featured acts, as well as an opportunity for the performers to show something of their real lives in a brief film featuring them going about their day-to-day business (an idea adopted by pretty much every subsequent talent show).

BobKnocks (the Monkhouse-endorsed abbreviation of the show's title) also introduced a crucial innovation to Saturday night television – phone voting. Here for the first time the public were able to circumvent the rather tedious and long-winded process of filling out a postcard, by simply dialling the telephone number that corresponded to their favourite act. As a result, whereas the original series had only ever been able to attract around 16,000 postcard votes, *BobKnocks* registered half a million telephone calls.

In truth a lot of the acts that appeared were pretty forgettable. The first series finale (broadcast live from the London Palladium) managed to pack ten separate acts into its tight 45-minute running order, all of whom (with the honourable exception of *Coronation Street* actress Debra Stephenson) retreated back into obscurity once the series was over. Even the eventual winners, Rosser and Davies failed to kick on from this promising start, and with an early Nineties musical project in collaboration with Rick Wakeman excepted, little more was heard from this gently comic musical duo who had pledged to be 'friends to the end'.

Other acts that lived long in the memory, but not in career terms, included first-series entrants the Balfour Chorus – a kind of underpowered G4, who delivered an accomplished if rather subdued version of the Queen classic 'Bohemian Rhapsody' (strangely an enduringly popular track with talent show contestants). Later series foisted onto the world Darren Day who sustains a career in showbiz to this day. Series two and three winners Jane Harrison and Brenda Cochrane were also able to carve a sustainable niche in the entertainment industry, but in the main *BobKnocks* was conspicuous for failing to produce as many success stories as its earlier incarnation.

After the third series, Bob decided that (as he put it) opportunity was now knocking elsewhere, and for the reincarnated *Opportunity Knocks'* fourth run, one-time contestant and now successful comedian Les Dawson was drafted in as host. But with **Stars in Their Eyes** coming into view over on ITV and the decline in interest in novelty acts, *Opportunity Knocks* was rested once again at the end of 1990.

Bobby Davro on the Box
TVS for ITV

19 May 1985 to 19 April 1986 (7 episodes)

Bobby Davro is the epitome of the prawn cocktail crisps-type of impersonator (which means that although his impressions are nothing like the person he's trying to be, you somehow know who it is just the same). He first came to prominence in 1984, thanks to an appearance on the middle-of-the-road Jimmy Tarbuck-helmed variety series *Live from Her Majesty's*. Sharing the bill with Cleo Laine, Bernie Winters and Brian Conley, he stole the show with a send-up of Freddie Starr plus some pot shots at pop stars of the day. This blistering performance led to immediate offers of work and by the beginning of 1986 Davro had his own show on telly plus a regular part on the Saturday evening comedy series **Copy Cats**.

Bobby Davro on the Box was just one of six different series that the comic made for ITV between 1986 and 1991 and in truth they were all pretty much the same. Understanding that his selling point was his youth, Davro shied away from taking off politicians and focused instead on contemporary targets such as George Michael, Bob Geldof and Jonathan Ross (in fact Davro reckons he was the first person ever to 'do Wossy'). However, of all his impersonations, perhaps the most accomplished was his Max Headroom. 'I hope people won't think we cheated and used Max Headroom voice tracks, because we didn't. The make-up and wardrobe people did a fantastic job and I'm very pleased,' proclaimed the comic back in 1986.

Yet for all its attempts at breaking new ground, *Bobby Davro on the Box* was pretty conservative stuff. Sketches such as Davro and comedy partner Jessica Martin performing 'Total Relapse of The Throat' (a spoof of the Bonnie Tyler hit 'Total Eclipse of the Heart') was hardly the work of a great subversive. Nonetheless, the programme's title sequence (with Davro endlessly changing channels on a television which seems to broadcast nothing but Bobby Davro mid-impression) was still less dated than other shows around, and the brevity of his sketches gave *On the Box* a welcome sense of pace.

For a time, the audience loved it, and him, and by 1987 that title sequence seemed to be becoming a reality, with Bob turning up on every light entertainment show going. However, the clock was already ticking and with alternative comedians invading telly via the influential **Saturday Live**, Davro couldn't help but look a bit corny and weak in comparison. It didn't help his cause that he had a tendency to keep trotting out the same impersonations long after they'd lost their currency (most obviously typified by sending up the cast of pre-schooler's favourite *Rainbow* long after the programme had been cancelled).

It seemed that audiences grew tired of Davro rather quickly, and after an ill-advised switch to the BBC to present **Public Enemy Number One**, his television career hit the doldrums. His last major show, *Bobby Davro: Rock with Laughter* provoked London's *Evening Standard* critic Victor Lewis-Smith to describe it as an 'insult to the audience', before proclaiming, 'I can't see this, or anything remotely like it, getting back on air. Ever.' Given that Bobby's most memorable appearance since has been as a contestant on reality television series *The Games* (where his high points consisted of a belly flop into a swimming pool and screeching 'Daddy's a winner' after he just about managed not to be completely crap at curling) it looks as if Lewis-Smith was spot on.

Bob's Full House

BBC1

1 September 1984 to 27 January 1990 (115 episodes)

Bob's Full House was nothing less than the ultimate distillation
of those 'Middle England with a soupçon of bonkers' studio-
based game shows that the BBC excelled at during the
Eighties. All present and correct were a *'Blankety Blank* gone
posh' set (complete with superfluous rotating central column),
perfectly pitched prizes (a 'state-of-the-art' vertical music centre
and a matching set of his and her bathrobes, to mention but
two), brilliant 'wrong answer' sound effects, and loads of
great catchphrases, of which the best was undoubtedly 'in
bingo lingo it's clickety-clicks, it's time to take your pick of the
six'.

On screen, *Bob's Full House* looked effortless, but the show
actually took a year to develop with the game going through
an unprecedented thirty-seven revisions (there were even plans
at one time to broadcast live with viewers at home able to
play along using a bingo card included in the pages of *Radio
Times*). The version that eventually ended up on our screens
was, in fact, dead simple. The contestants were each
equipped with a bingo card, and over three rounds had to try
and light the corners, the middle line and the whole card
respectively by correctly answering as many questions as
possible. The first two rounds were relatively sedate and low-
key, with host Bob Monkhouse bantering away in fine style,
including exerting his comedic superiority over the inevitable

moustachioed contestant 'from Accounts' who had aspirations of being a bit barmy ('Nurse – he's out of bed again!'). But by the final round the tension became palpable, helped in no small part by Monkhouse dropping the off-the-cuff witticisms in favour of overemphasised and much mimicked scoring updates ('Jo NEEEEDS three for a full house, David NEEEEDS two...'). Brilliantly, contestants who got a question wrong were frozen out from answering the next one, in a move that Bob referred to as being 'wallied'.

The victor of the main game would go on to face 'The Monkhouse Mastercard'; an over-elaborate rotating numerical structure that resembled an airport departures board. Here they would have just one minute to try and answer fifteen questions and reveal the letters of a mystery holiday destination hidden under each of the numbers ('Your first letter is "M" – let's hope it's not Manchester!'). But what made the end game so compelling was its stop-start nature. After each correct answer, Bob would pause the countdown to allow the contestant to pick a number, and would then offer a few heightened words on the state of play before allowing the game to recommence. This meant that although the round was only meant to take sixty seconds, it could actually last anything up to three times as long, depending upon how much effort Bob invested into playing with our nerve endings.

Undeniably, of all the many elements that ensured *Bob's Full House*'s success, the most important was the host himself. Each show would open with Bob chatting to the contestants, excavating their utterances for any signs of a quick one-liner or impromptu observation ('Jo, if your nose is running and your feet are smelling, then it means you're upside down'). Yet Bob knew how, and when, to switch from gregarious host with a funny line for almost everything ('many of the prizes have hours of use left in them'), to serious quizmaster, and his imperceptible verbal acceleration as the quiz headed towards the final straight meant that each edition was guaranteed a thrilling conclusion.

Boys and Girls

UMTV for C4

1 March 2003 to 17 May 2003 (12 episodes)

If **The Price Is Right** epitomised crass Saturday night television in the Eighties, then there is no doubt that its spiritual heir in the twenty-first century was C4's appallingly noisy *Boys and Girls*. Billed as a 'battle of the sexes' and coming from the makers of the superlative **Don't Forget Your Toothbrush**, it sounded brilliant, but what we actually got was a rather sorry mixture of **Red Alert** and C4's infamous late night youth series *The Word*.

As was the case with the aforementioned *Red Alert*, the studio audience played a central role. They were split into two groups based on whether they were a boy or a girl (hence the name of the programme) and were rather noisily invited to take part in a succession of mostly witless games. However the meat of the show revolved around three contestants picked from each team battling it out to earn the right to choose a member of the opposite sex to join them for a frantic seven days spending C4's money. Over the course of the week the couple would live together and get challenged to buy various consumer items, before returning to the show the following Saturday hoping to leave still clutching their purchases.

Initially host Vernon Kay proclaimed that the couple's fate would be determined by a viewer phone vote, however this was sidelined in favour of a studio game in which the twosome had to answer a series of 'true or false' questions. The reason for the change was never made clear, but it is hard to resist the thought that the programme makers had tuned in to the fact that all the contestants were utterly obnoxious and that the TV audience would never allow any of them to retain their prizes.

Boys and Girls owed much of its existence to the fact that Chris Evans was the supposed genius shoring up the whole operation. He did make the occasional on-screen appearance (principally to chaperone the winning couple off the set on the back of a golf buggy), but in the main his presence could be felt through the supposed 'water cooler' moments that peppered the show. Of these, perhaps the most heinous was 'Parents on Parade'. This thankfully short-lived item featured a member of the studio audience's mum and dad walking onto set with no clothes on. Ten years earlier such a stunt might have held some genuine shock value, but not only had *The Word* already comprehensively covered this ground, but C4's own Friday night game show *Something for the Weekend* had tried and failed to make bums and willies a popular feature of weekend television viewing only four years earlier.

One item that did make it through the show's twelve-week run was 'Babe or Minger'. This lowbrow concept took the game show *Your Face or Mine* and turned it into a straightforward shoutfest during which members of the audience would rank each other based on physical attractiveness.

C4 invested a lot into the show. Quite apart from the

reputed £500,000 budget for each episode, it enjoyed not one, but two spin-off series: *Boys and Girls Friday* and *Boys and Girls Do It with Dougie*. However, the investment was not rewarded, with the first edition attracting only 1.1 million viewers and later episodes failing to improve much on that. By the end of the run it was clear that it wasn't going to be coming back for a second series. Sadly, this was one programme that definitely deserved the label 'minger'.

The Brian Conley Show
LWT for ITV

22 February 1992 to 22 July 1995 (24 episodes)

The tragic dichotomy at the heart of Brian Conley is that, although undoubtedly a highly polished and talented performer, he is also King of the Slappable Face People. His one-liners may be great ('I was with this band on a cruise ship and we were sailing round Bermuda, when the bloke playing the triangle disappeared'), and his verbal delivery accomplished (his spoonerism-heavy version of *Cinderella*, in which the prince is mistakenly described as a 'fart smeller' instead of a 'smart fella' is easily comparable to the best of Ronnie Barker), but he is a performer who it is hard to warm to. It doesn't help that his singing voice sounds like a cross between a cruise liner crooner and a voice over for a massive furniture sale advert, but in his defence it does make for a good Al Jolson (Conley's most celebrated impression).

Arguably the last all-round entertainer to have his own signature entertainment series, Conley's career in television blossomed when appearing as a warm-up man on the first edition of the game show *Catchphrase*. A load of technical problems meant that the young entertainer was extensively called upon to keep the audience amused and he caught the eye of a number of television big-wigs.

The Brian Conley Show was sort of like a stage show on television. Each edition would begin with a song, and then Conley would walk around the stage, changing costume en route, and launching into a number of sketch scenarios. He developed a strong relationship with his theatre audience and, although it whiffed a bit of Bruce Forsyth, to see Conley berating the front row ('Shut it!') or, better yet, getting down amongst them for some close-quarter insults (such as asking one member of the audience to close their legs while pretending to polish another's bald head) was to watch a performer at the top of his game.

Although a number of sketches featured one-off characters, Conley developed a suite of regular comedic roles such as Dangerous Brian – a stuntman dressed in an all-in-one silver jumpsuit who would indulge in a number of supposed high-risk ventures, all for the sake of big-budget, carefully choreographed physical comedy; and Septic Peg – a rather too on-the-nose parody of *The National Lottery*'s fortune-teller, Mystic Meg. Although not the most inspired comic creation in the world, Septic Peg did give vent for Conley's notable predilection for verbal comedy, culminating in the sketch that opened the one-off special *Brian Conley – Alive and Dangerous*. Here the would-be soothsayer was united with her real-life inspiration. The two traded lines such as Meg proclaiming, 'I am serious about the paranormal,' with Peg responding, 'and I'm seriously abnormal' and the audience rocked with laughter.

Without a doubt, Conley's most popular character was surly children's TV presenter, Nick Frisbee. Based half on Philip Schofield and half on Jim Davidson, Frisbee would sit in his would-be 'broom cupboard' and read off a string of silly jokes ('How come Postman Pat can afford a personalised number plate?'), while all the time being upstaged by a glove puppet called Larry the Loafer. Frisbee's catchphrase, 'it's a puppet' (which Conley would bellow every time the audience voiced their sympathy for the much abused Larry), was actually an ad-lib that only became much repeated once the production team caught on to how funny it was (well, it was certainly far more amusing than Frisbee's intended catchphrase: 'Hi, chilblains'). Incidentally, although the part of Larry the Loafer would later be played by Ray Tizzard, it was originally future *Popstars* judge 'Nasty' Nigel Lythgoe with his hand up the puppet's posterior.

Although never the most original or modern of programmes, *The Brian Conley Show* worked very hard at producing a slick, reasonably ambitious, Saturday night family comedy show. In fact, to broaden its appeal even further, a game show element in the guise of 'Conley's Car Boot Quiz' was introduced in the third series. By the time the curtain fell in 1995, Conley had become a big star, and ITV's second-highest-paid entertainer (just behind Cilla Black). But while admittedly very talented and now highly paid, there was never any danger of Conley becoming as well loved as the **Blind Date** star – well, not until he wiped the big, smug grin off his face anyway.

Bruce Forsyth's Big Night
LWT for ITV

7 October 1978 to 4 April 1980 (13 episodes)

'You get criticised if you're trying something new, you get criticised if you do the same old thing.' So bemoaned a rueful Bruce Forsyth on the set of this ill-fated entertainment extravaganza. In fact, on this particular edition of *Bruce Forsyth's Big Night*, the eponymous host spent ten minutes of precious airtime bitching about press coverage of the show: 'with all that pre-press it made people think when the show started, glitter was going to come out of the set and, you know, it was going to be so sensational. It's like everything else; when people say "you must see that", when you go and see it for yourself you're a bit disappointed.'

Beneath the veneer of bitterness you had to concede that Brucie had a point. Since leaving the BBC in 1977, the

public and press alike had wondered where 'the most important man in television' (according to the *Guardian*) would turn up next. When news filtered through that he would be hosting an entertainment extravaganza on ITV you couldn't help but be curious. The fact that the series was going to cost a reputed £1000 a minute to make, would run for between ninety minutes and two hours, and would be shown up against Bruce's old series, **The Generation Game**, sent the press haywire.

Yet for all the hype and excitement, *Bruce Forsyth's Big Night* had a fatal flaw; it never really had a proper hook. Instead, the show was made up from loads of different sections of variable quality. 'Sofa Soccer' featured a television viewer delivering 'left a bit...right a bit...' instructions to a cameraman in an attempt to fire a football into a goal. Meanwhile Steve Jones presided over members of the public trying to get celebs to correctly guess certain words in a kind of 'You Say, We Pay' style in a section labelled 'The Pyramid Game'. The UK Disco Dancing Championships provided a degree of spectacle, plus ghastly and inventive dancing in equal measure, while mini editions of ancient radio sitcom 'The Glums' and 'The Worker' kept the comedy quotient up.

But above all, *Bruce Forsyth's Big Night* was about the host himself. Vast swathes of the show were given over to Bruce answering the audience's unscripted questions, or getting a member of the public to run through a comedy sketch with him ('it's not "nice", it's "neee-ce"'). And of course, there was plenty of time allotted to allow our host to demonstrate his excellent microphone technique while crooning some old show tune or other. This need to show off even extended to his interchanges with the various guest artistes. Acts of the calibre of Sammy Davis Jnr would have to put up with Bruce's hilarious impressions of them ('I'd just like to say sincerely…"sincerely"') before being expected to participate in a duet with the ever-present host.

What made all of this worse was the fact that each item would go on for what felt like an eternity (often up to ten minutes). This, in retrospect, was the series' fatal flaw. Whereas later shows such as **Noel's House Party** recognised the virtue of keeping each element short and sweet, *Bruce Forsyth's Big Night* lost loads of viewers who simply couldn't be bothered to sit through ten minutes of turgid disco dancing on the remote chance that they might be rewarded with a bit of Cannon and Ball afterwards. It didn't help matters when after only the second show, the programme's director, Paul Smith, walked out on the production complaining that the running order was being changed so much that his task had come to resemble directing a news bulletin.

Unfortunately performers of the calibre of Rod Hull & Emu, Bette Midler, Elton John, Liza Goddard and Colin Baker weren't enough to paper over the cracks, and with a retrospective New Year's Eve highlights special on 31 December 1978, *Bruce Forsyth's Big Night* was over. Or rather, it was almost over. Bizarrely on Good Friday 1980, the show returned for a one-off special, but even then, the combined might of Kenny Lynch, Derek Griffiths, Joan Collins and Jimmy Tarbuck could not alter public indifference.

Buck Rogers in the 25th Century

A Glen A. Larson Production in association with
Universal Television [shown on ITV]

30 August 1980 to 25 September 1982 (33 episodes)

'The year is 1987,' explains the world's most serious voice, 'and NASA launches the last of America's deep space probes. In a freak mishap Ranger 3 and its pilot, Captain William "Buck" Rogers, are blown out of their trajectory into an orbit which freezes his life support systems and returns Buck Rogers to Earth 500 years later.' It's at this point that the funkily fussy bass guitar riff kicks in and somewhat ruins the sense of solemnity of what has, so far, been an utterly gripping title sequence. Still, as a way of luring science-fiction fans away from *Doctor Who* (which was showing on the other side), this promise of effects-heavy, deep-space action was difficult to resist.

Adventures were of the swashbuckling variety, with our eponymous hero wisecracking his way through various battles against the evil Princess Ardala (played with a careful adherence to her stereotype by Pamela Hensley), with his cohorts Colonel Wilma Deering (Erin Gray sporting too much lip gloss and tight-fitting jumpsuits) and Dr Huer (played by Tim O'Connor, who is not a Scouse comedian) in tow.

Much humour was made at the expense of the culture clash between Buck's homespun American ideals and his colleagues' supposedly more enlightened twenty-fifth century ways. But among the pristine brigade of future dwellers Buck was able to find a soulmate, albeit in the form of a smart alec robot called Twiki (voiced by Mel Blanc of Daffy Duck fame). Twiki's main function was to complement the action with an occasional show-stealing rendition of his catchphrase 'Bidi bidi bidi'. In one episode, 'Cruise Ship to the Stars', Twiki actually discovered a female version of himself. Naturally she opined 'Boodi boodi boodi'.

Despite its ambition of scale, *Buck Rogers in the 25th Century* was produced on a meagre budget, meaning that effects shots were recycled with alarming frequency. In particular the same sequence of a starfighter blasting off into space could be relied upon to turn up at least twice an episode. Rather more alarmingly, child actor Gary Coleman turned up twice during the course of the first US season. His role as a 'cosmic whizz-kid' probably best typified the series' lack of dramatic aspirations. Yet to its target audience this mattered not one jot. Indeed, the series was sufficiently colourful in design and content that for those of the right age it appeared to be a very rich concoction indeed, and *Buck Rogers in the 25th Century* was, for a brief spell, massively popular with the kids, even finding his way into the pages of juvenile publications such as *TV Tops* and – proving that Buck definitely had a way with the ladies – girls' comic *Jackie*.

Bugs

Carnival Films for BBC1

1 April 1995 to 28 August 1999 (40 episodes)

There are few major drama series that have withstood the test of time quite as poorly. Self-consciously designed to ape the adventure series of the Sixties and Seventies, *Bugs* was so busy trying to walk the line between *The Avengers* and *The Professionals* it never managed to leave its own footprint in the sands of telly history.

By 1995 there had been an absence of any major British escapist drama on Saturday nights for the best part of a decade. When *Bugs* came along it seemed to have been genetically developed to fill the gap. Its premise (three techno troubleshooters taking on the forces of evil) was well in keeping with telly's strong lineage of action and adventure series, however its casting (Craig McLachlan and Jesse Birdsall – two ex-soap stars – and Jaye Griffiths from *The Bill*) was an obvious nod to the current power base within television drama.

Save for the occasional sight of Ed (played by McLachlan until series four when he was replaced by Steven Houghton) scaling the side of office blocks, *Bugs* offered little in the way of truly stand-out action scenes or dramatic spectacle. Instead, each week the viewer was served up a perfectly competent slice of hokum, which somehow managed to avoid being in anyway quirky or distinctive.

Loads of episodes seemed to end up with one of the three

operatives having to defuse a high-tech bomb, while the other two barked instructions into an earpiece, and this feeling of sameness wasn't helped by the show's rather limited design palette (lots of blue lighting or torch lights seemed to be the order of the day). Indeed the casual viewer was often left wondering if they'd tuned in to a repeat of the previous week's adventure.

In later series a conscious attempt was made to try and humanise the lead characters, principally by invoking that classic soap opera trick of a love triangle between two of the leads and one other peripheral character. A proper recurring baddy was added to the mix in series two, but there was an overriding sense that even with these changes, somehow the whole was less than the sum of the parts.

Bugs did manage to make it to four series (albeit with the last three episodes slung out at the height of summer when audiences were at their lowest). However, after its demise there was still some small spark left in the adventure series genre and the revived **Randall and Hopkirk (Deceased)** kept things ticking along into the twenty-first century. By then of course, the triumphant return of **Doctor Who** demonstrated exactly how this sort of telly should be done.

Candid Camera
ABC/LWT for ITV

10 September 1960 to 28 December 1974 (146 episodes)

'Just like the lady – the Mona Lisa – smile, you're on *Candid Camera*.' The granddaddy of all hidden-camera shows started out on American radio back in 1947 where it was broadcast under the title *Candid Microphone*. But it didn't make its UK debut until 1960, when the Brits' introduction to 'the TV series that turned the public into megastars' came courtesy of Bob Monkhouse. Undoubtedly one of Britain's most promising comedians of the time, Monkhouse presided over *Candid Camera* with an enthusiasm that is slightly grating in retrospect but was actually just the ticket back in the day. However, even his zeal was tested during an early stunt in Blackpool when he attempted to sell £5 notes for £4 10s. The comic was convinced that he wouldn't get any takers, but ended the day £50 down.

Of the many stunts undertaken down the years, the one that seems to attract most attention also happens to be one of the earliest: the car with no engine. Much hilarity ensued when the driver (played with utter conviction by Jonathan Routh) asked a garage mechanic to take a look at it, claiming he couldn't get it to start. 'How did you get here?' enquired the mechanic with no small measure of disbelief. 'We drove from Basingstoke,' Routh replied.

Other memorable moments included replacing the pins in a Harrow bowling alley with ones that shattered upon contact with a bowling bowl, the cutlery that moved thanks to a magnetic counter, and the birdman of Basingstoke (Routh again) who with as much charm and sincerity as he could muster tried to persuade visitors to a local park that he could actually fly ('I had a nasty crash this morning. I was coming in from Croydon and the wind changed and I ended up in those trees over there').

Unlike later hidden-camera series, *Candid Camera* worked on the assumption that members of the general public were, by and large, decent folk. This supposition was never more tested than during a carefully choreographed stunt in which Routh and another stooge sat either side of a target in a café and kept asking the poor fellow to pass them various condiments and cutlery. Such a premise was simple but devastatingly effective, and in a way this summed up the appeal of *Candid Camera*.

But perhaps the best stunt of all was the one in which Routh posed as a registrar and persuaded a member of the public to act as a witness to a (fake) wedding. Routh then became confused as to who was marrying whom and proceeded to try and marry the witness to the bride. As was typical with *Candid Camera*, the same stunt would be carried out on a number of different victims. On one occasion Routh actually succeeds in having a witness complete the vows and even place a ring on the bride's finger, even though the poor chap mumbles that he 'doesn't quite follow this'. Having completed the ceremony, the victim protests that he is already married, to which Routh replies simply, 'Mister Babcock, this is bigamy.' Priceless.

The original UK run wound up in 1965, but was revived some nine years later presented by series producer Peter Dulay. With the exception of an infamous goldfish-eating incident (during which Dulay went into a pet shop and plucked slivers of carrot out of fish tanks before swallowing them whole claiming they were actual fish), the stunts just weren't as memorable as those in the original run; probably because the incomparable Jonathan Routh was by now no longer involved.

Cannon and Ball

LWT/Yorkshire Television for ITV

28 July 1979 to 25 August 1990 (71 episodes)

For a comedy act built on the slimmest material, Cannon and Ball are to be applauded for notching up a creditable seventy-one shows during their eleven-year reign on Saturday night television. Theirs is a traditional act consisting of a 'pull up the cuffs'-style straight man in the form of Tommy Cannon, and an overly aggressive 'naughty boy' in the shape of Bobby Ball.

Alarmingly, when you boil it down, all of their routines can be described by reference to a mere handful of slogans, mannerisms and sketch ideas. First of all there are Bobby's catchphrases: 'I thank you, I thank you and once again I thank you', 'You little liar', 'You'll do for me' and, most famously, 'Rock on, Tommy'. Then there are the various physical and vocal mannerisms such as Bobby threatening to poke someone in the eye, yelling 'Shut it, lady' to someone in the crowd and contriving to pull a neck muscle to punctuate a particularly voluble diatribe. Finally there are the sketches themselves.

These usually feature either Tommy taking part in a pursuit or activity that in some way excludes Bobby; or Tommy being continually interrupted by Bobby while attempting to complete a performance that, crucially, has aspirations towards high culture. This particular routine turned up so many times that by the end of the Eighties most of the audience could probably improvise their own version.

The duo started out as a straight musical act appearing under a number of different names (including 'The Shirelle Brothers', 'The Harper Brothers' and, best of all, 'Bobby and Stevie Rhythm') but over time they added comedy to their performance. Although the gags were pretty crummy (Bobby used to wave his camera around on a piece of string and yell 'look at that, it's a movie camera'), there was something about the two, and in particular the way Bobby could get the crowd's sympathy when Tommy attempted to shun him, that saw them grow in popularity.

It is almost impossible now to appreciate just how successful Cannon and Ball were in the Eighties, but their series attracted massive audiences, and their live shows sold out across the land. Yet they weren't without their critics, and Bobby's on-screen aggression was considered by some as something that may well have worked well in the working men's clubs but was a bit too strong for the small screen.

Much like their act, their television series stuck to a rigid formula (or rather it did for its first six series): there would be the opening stand-up routine and then a performance by a top pop act (such as Grace Kennedy). After this would come a series of sketches performed in front of minimal set dressing, then another musical act, before a final stand-up routine in which Tommy would explain to Bobby what he was going to be doing for the rest of the weekend and, more importantly, how it wouldn't involve Bobby. Cue public sympathy and the duo leaving the stage their own separate ways, before reuniting once again to show us that they really were pals. After that there would just be time for the twosome's signature tune, 'Together, We'll Be OK' ('laugh me a laugh, grin me a grin...'), and that would be the end of the show.

Unsurprisingly a number of jokes and routines resurfaced throughout their television tenure with an early skit in which the duo played invisible snooker turning up again later on as a game of invisible poker. Meanwhile, Bobby was still using the line 'I'm a sex object – I want sex and they object' when the boys appeared on *I'm a Celebrity...Get Me out of Here* in 2005. By 1986 no one could dispute that a change was long overdue. *Cannon and Ball* metamorphosed into a sitcom in which the two played themselves living in a London flat, but this didn't really catch on. There was even talk that their employers, LWT, were simply trying to wind down the lad's highly lucrative contract (supposedly, one of the clauses meant that even though they were living together at the time, two separate limousines were required to transport them to rehearsals).

Having turned down an offer to go to the BBC, Cannon and Ball recorded their final Saturday night series *Cannon and Ball's Casino*. This was a rather flawed variety game show in which our two hosts led contestants through a series of general knowledge questions and silly charades in attempt to win a star prize. But beyond the fact that the studio audience sat around tables and drank champagne, the whole casino concept was totally superfluous, and the game show element never really worked. Today the twosome refer to the show as a 'monkey on their backs'.

After just one series, the duo was shifted off Saturday nights altogether and had one final crack at television with *The Plaza Patrol*. But by then, the writing was well and truly on the wall. Sadly, television comedy had moved on, and where once Bobby's outbursts had seemed outrageous and exciting, by the Nineties there was no one remotely interested in still 'rocking on'.

Carrott's Lib

BBC1

2 October 1982 to 30 December 1983 (17 episodes)

It's easy to suggest that before the arrival of 'alternative comedy' in the late Seventies, television humour was confined to frilly-shirted men dispensing mother-in-law jokes. Yet there was another approach, with a wave of comedians graduating from the folk scene of the Seventies.

Rather than simply rattle through a set of identikit jokes that could be delivered by any comedian, the 'folkies' told stories from their own lives, ensuring their routines were distinctly personal. Most of them also had a musical background, and almost all wrote their own material. Perhaps the leading name was Billy Connolly, but a Birmingham comedian called Jasper Carrott had garnered a big reputation, especially on his home patch of the Midlands. Before too long Carrott had released a string of successful albums ·– as well as, unforgettably, the single 'Funky Moped'.

He then made the move into television, with *An Audience with Jasper Carrott* for LWT. This was a straightforward stand-up show, notable for the fact that it was presented as Carrott entertaining the audience with the cameras looking in, as opposed to the star directly addressing the camera as had been the style of the time. Carrott's tales of Midlands life struck a chord, and numerous other ITV specials followed.

In 1982, he was lured over to the BBC, but there was a slight problem – Carrott claimed he'd used up three years' worth of touring material in one six-part series and couldn't rely on anecdotes for much longer. Therefore, *Carrott's Lib* was based more on topical comedy, with much of the material derived from the week's news. For this Carrott was assisted by a team of writers skilled in satire, including future *Have I Got News for You* panellist Ian Hislop.

Better yet, *Carrott's Lib* was broadcast live and, rather than opening titles, each edition started with a huge audience laugh and Carrott announcing, 'That's the best joke I know'. With the electric energy of a live show, plus a platform from which to poke fun at the politics of the day, *Carrott's Lib* meant a return for Saturday night satire for probably the first time since the great flowering pioneered by *That Was the Week That Was*. Sadly like that earlier show, the pressure in having to come up with brand new gags each week meant only two series were ever broadcast.

Casualty

BBC1

6 September 1986 to ongoing
(582 episodes as of 19 May 2007)

The average Holby City A&E patient is either someone whose predicament is the ironic consequence of an earlier decision they made, or else it's a poor sap whose condition in some way reflects, or inadvertently comments on, whatever personal problem is currently affecting the doctor or nurse treating them.

Casualty almost never made it to our screens at all. Apparently the BBC had originally toyed with the idea of making a picturesque hospital drama starring Hannah Gordon. In its early years especially, *Casualty* was about as

far away from that gentle kind of programming as it was possible to get. The series started out being all about 'issues' and in its first year alone touched on alcoholism, drug abuse, AIDS and football violence. However, the show's major concern was the decline of the National Health Service. This theme was predominantly and rather ploddingly explored through the character of Ewart Plimmer (Bernard Gallagher), the manager of the hospital nightshift. A principled man, Plimmer was shown to be forever at loggerheads with the upper tiers of management. This was all worthy stuff, but a little bit dull and also somewhat dated. It was probably not a big shock then when an announcement was made on 12 September 1987 that the second series was to be *Casualty*'s last.

However with the introduction of Elizabeth Straker (Maureen O'Brien) as *Casualty*'s first out-and-out villain, audiences grew to more than 10 million and rather then cancelling the show, *Casualty* was moved to Fridays where it tackled even weightier issues. By the time it was back on Saturdays a few years later, though, the programme had shed its campaigning spirit in favour of focusing on viewer-grabbing storylines. Although some hardcore fans bemoaned this change, on the plus side we no longer had to put up with Kuba Trzcinski (Christopher Rozycki), the irritating 'comedy' porter that had dogged the corridors of *Casualty* for its first three years. And it wasn't as if the show had completely lost its ability to create controversy. An episode in the seventh series, 'Boiling Point', was considered to be so sensitive that it was hastily rescheduled to the later time of 9.30 p.m. and preceded by the announcement that 'this episode features riot scenes of some power and impact'.

Another change, implemented from 1989 onwards, saw the series' location come in for a subtle overhaul. Whereas in the early years Holby was simply Bristol under another name, now all such connections to that metropolis were severed and Holby became a generic British city. One of the stranger consequences of this was that long-standing character Duffy (Catherine Shipton) mysteriously shed her West Country accent.

By the mid-Nineties *Casualty* had become all about the lives of its regular characters. For those interested in the plight of the patient this was a disappointment, but most viewers welcomed the show's move into soap opera. Less popular, however, was an attempt at technical innovation. The first few episodes of the ninth series were broadcast with a post-production filmic effect that was supposed to make the series look grittier and more 'American'. But viewers hated the change and bombarded the BBC until the decision was reversed, and *Casualty* returned to its familiar and homely 'video look'.

As the show marched on through the Nineties it stuck close to its winning formula. The occasional big set piece in which all hell broke loose became a pretty much annual occurrence with riots, sieges and plane crashes all turning Holby into possibly the UK's number one trouble spot.

The Christmas 2005 special edition of the occasional crossover series *Casualty @ Holby City*, saw a confluence of catastrophes as a number of *Casualty* regulars found themselves trapped under a crumbling bridge in the company of some highly toxic material. Of course, a major disaster wasn't quite enough, and doubtless viewers were unsurprised to see mainstay Charlie Fairhead (played with ever increasing wisdom and ennui by Derek Thompson) trying to save lives, while all the while having to contend with the knowledge that his young son had just run away from home.

March 2007 brought another memorable episode as famed screenwriter Richard Curtis co-penned a story featuring not only Angus Deayton playing himself, but the return after an absence of eighteen years of actress Brenda Fricker (a mainstay from the first few series as the kindly nurse Megan). The episode was designed to highlight the issues surrounding the treatment of mental health and so unsurprisingly threw up a number of complex moral dilemmas for the resident cast to grapple with. It seems that surgery can never be simple in *Casualty*.

C.A.T.S. Eyes

TVS for ITV

12 April 1985 to 6 June 1987 (30 episodes)

Given the popularity of American series such as **The A-Team** and **Starsky and Hutch**, it's no surprise that British television tried to muscle in on the act. *C.A.T.S. Eyes* was rather like a UK version of *Charlie's Angels*, except that whereas the Angels found themselves solving crimes on cruise ships and casinos, the agents of the Covert Activities Thames Section division spent much of their time pounding Chatham, Rochester and other parts of Kent (although they did make it to Amsterdam for one episode).

C.A.T.S Eyes actually came from the demise of *The Gentle Touch*. Yet while that earlier show majored on grim, urban crime (the finale of the penultimate series saw Detective Inspector Maggie Forbes caught up in a grenade explosion), *C.A.T.S Eyes* took the Forbes character (played by Jill Gascoigne) and transplanted her into an altogether sillier and less realistic world. The first, feature-length edition, 'Goodbye Jenny Wren' introduced the series' premise; Maggie was drafted in to C.A.T.S Eyes (the newly established Home Office covert security operation masquerading under the guise of the 'Eyes Enquiry Agency') to replace a previous agent who had been killed in the line of duty. Unsurprisingly, her arrival created tension with the two remaining original members, particularly with computer boffin and all-round tomboy Fred Smith (Leslie Ash). But by the close of the first story Maggie had proven herself, and had become fully integrated into the group.

The third member of the original line-up, Pru Standfast (Rosalyn Landor) was the head of the trio, but was best remembered for her exceptionally haughty manner and school-matronly charms. In fact Landor left *C.A.T.S Eyes* at the end of the first series, with the press blaming her departure on friction between the three leads. Her character was replaced by Tessa Robinson (Tracy-Louise Ward), who, while similarly well spoken, was altogether less uptight than Pru. The final member of the team was Home Office official Nigel Beaumont (Don Warrington). He contributed little to each week's adventures save from providing the initial briefing in a manner very reminiscent of the eponymous figure in *Charlie's Angels* (albeit Warrington did actually make appearances on screen).

The team's adventures admittedly lacked much of a cerebral dimension, but were a welcome change of speed from most British dramas of the time and featured set-ups every bit as imaginative as anything you would find in **The A-Team**. One edition, 'Frightmare', even dipped a tentative toe into the murky waters of fantasy, as Fred's sanity was pushed to its very limit while she attempted to guard a valuable jewel. The show was savaged by the press for its 'thin plots, unimaginative scripts and dodgy politics' and today it is probably better remembered for its deficiencies rather than its dramatic attributes.

Celebrity Squares

ATV/Grundy/Central for ITV

20 July 1975 to 26 August 1996 (186 episodes)

Come 1974, ITV's Sunday afternoon game show *The Golden Shot* (which was produced by the Midlands company ATV) was floundering. After Bob Monkhouse had been 'let go', partly thanks to mutterings that he'd accepted bribes to get prizes featured, the show had stumbled along with Norman Vaughan and Charlie Williams. Although both were fine comedians in their own right, they were each completely unable to cope with the complicated mechanics of the series. Only one man seemed to have the quick wit to cope with the sort of problems you got on a live show featuring crossbows, so eventually ATV swallowed their pride and invited

Monkhouse back. He agreed, on the condition they bought the rights to the American format *Hollywood Squares* and let him host it.

Sure enough, when *The Golden Shot* ended in 1975, *Celebrity Squares* moved into exactly the same slot, before shifting to Saturday nights the following year. The new show was rather more glamorous than the dowdy *Shot*, in part thanks to the dazzling showmanship of host Bob Monkhouse, but mainly due to the presence of the nine celebrities who inhabited the programme's oversized noughts and crosses board.

Each week, Bob would ask the celebrities a general knowledge question, and contestants would then have to decide whether the answer given was correct. If they got it right, their 'square' would turn into either an X or an O and on the game would continue until one of the contestants managed to secure a line on the board, thus winning the game.

So far, so simple, but Bob ensured that it was a fast-moving and funny show by having, inevitably, a one-liner on hand for every question and every celebrity. Added humour came from Kenny Everett providing the voice-overs (Everett was bored witless in between announcements and spent most of the show playing Scrabble with his agent). He was later replaced by Lance Percival. However *Celebrity Squares* retained its popularity right up until it was finally dropped in 1979.

Over a decade later, Bob was ensconced at the Beeb, before Central (as ATV had become in 1982) decided to lure him back over to the commercial channel, and Bob suggested that *Celebrity Squares* could be ripe for a revival.

The new series proved to be as successful as ever; Bob had the talent and experience to helm this sort of quiz in his sleep. However it was all fairly unexceptional and ended again after just a few years, when Bob moved back to the BBC. Since then, it has occasionally been rumoured that the show would return, with Channel Five once apparently intending to launch a new version for 'the *Heat* generation'. Perhaps fortunately, this has so far failed to make it to the screen.

Copy Cats

LWT for ITV

30 November 1985 to 5 December 1987 (20 episodes)

Copy Cats was Saturday night television at its most anaemic. It actually started out as a Sunday night sketch series called *Go for It* featuring the dubious collective talents of Les Dennis, Dustin Gee, Bobby Davro, Johnny More, Aiden J. Harvey, Allan Stewart and Ann Byrne. But while Les Dennis and Dustin Gee managed to jump ship for the BBC, the rest of the cast (Byrne excepted) wound up duplicating pretty much the same show, but on Saturday nights instead.

Although all of the Copy Cats were equal in status, for the two years he was in it, Bobby Davro was a little more equal than most. Davro himself reckons this was because he was willing to take risks, but given how middle-of-the-road his material was it's difficult to work out quite what he's referring to. Not that it was only Davro who failed to innovate – the targets for impressions were, by and large, pretty uninspired with anyone who was easy to do finding themselves shoe-horned into a *Copy Cats* sketch. Particularly notable for their frequency though were Cilla Black, Joan Rivers and Frank Carson.

Many of the sketches featured impressions not of other celebrities but of other fictional comedy characters (such as Kevin Turvey and Jimmy McJimmy). 'Of course, I'm actually doing an impression of someone doing an impression,' remarked Allan Stewart. 'It isn't more difficult – just a little bit weird'. Weird was one way to describe it, but others felt it was a form of plagiarism. More to the point, while Jimmy McJimmy was still then part of the current Russ Abbot canon of characters, Rik Mayall had abandoned Kevin Turvey back in 1982, making *Copy Cats'* appropriation of somebody else's comic creation not only artistically dubious, but in this instance, totally behind the times.

All three series attracted sizeable audiences though, and in 1987 there was even a theatrical tour. But If *Copy Cats* is remembered for anything today then it's surely for its closing title sequence in which the performers would group together on bar stools and sing a few bars of a song before pausing to let rip with a quick gag or impression. Apparently this was the 'Cats'' favourite part of the show, and each week they would good-naturedly duel it out to come up with the best impression or joke. Unfortunately most weeks nobody won.

Crime Traveller

Carnival Films for BBC1

1 March 1997 to 19 April 1997 (8 episodes)

Crime Traveller was the ultimate distillation of that favourite listings magazine phrase 'enjoyable hokum'. The series starred Michael French (then incredibly popular having just played the part of David Wicks in *EastEnders*) as Detective Jeff Slade and Chloe Annett as police scientist Holly Turner, but also featured popular actress Sue Johnston in a supporting role as Slade's suspicious boss Grisham. The show's premise was really no sillier than most sci-fi shows: each week Holly and Slade (for some reason he was rarely ever referred to as 'Jeff') would use the time machine situated in Holly's flat to nip back a few hours or days to solve a seemingly unfathomable crime (cue rather understated time travel special effect that consisted only of clocks running backwards, lights shining up a wall, and a computer screen showing lots of geometrical squares that transmute into a kind of tunnel to presumably connote reverse chronological travel).

There was a clearly stated set of rules regarding time travel that meant the characters couldn't travel to the future ('it doesn't exist'), nor indeed change the past. More crucially though, they had to make sure they didn't meet their past selves (as so doing would cause a 'temporal schism') and, above all, guarantee they were back in front of the time machine at the exact moment they began their expedition into the past. This particular rule became a lynchpin for the series, providing pretty much every episode with at least one race against the clock as Slade and Holly desperately attempted to avoid the grisly fate of becoming stuck in a 'loop of infinity'.

It wasn't only the rules governing time travel that were strict, there was an unerring rigidity to the programme's formula that worked both for and against the show. On the debit side, the regular supporting cast remained inflexible and unchanging in their outlook from episode to episode. Grisham was forever infuriated by Slade's maverick tendencies and superfluous police officer Morris (Paul Trussell) stuck close to his role as resident comic meathead. This just left Nicky (Richard Dempsey) as the posh-but-nice copper, seemingly played by a twelve-year-old boy with a James Harries haircut, and Danny (Bob Goody) the kindly but confused caretaker; both of whom never strayed far from their wafer-thin characterisations. And it wasn't just the characters that remained forever in stasis. Slade's wardrobe consisted only of a camel-coloured jacket, sky-blue shirt and dark blue slacks.

The flipside to this rigidity, though, was the enjoyment that could be had from watching the scenes in the early part of the episode and attempting to work out how they would be revisited later on. This led to some attentive viewing as you tried to work out whether the car following Slade actually contained Slade from the future.

While never as bad as the critics suggested, *Crime Traveller* was flawed. The viewer was expected to understand the sometimes quite convoluted repercussions of time travel, but other elements of the plot were so obviously signposted, it was as if the programme makers thought we were thick.

Worse still, the series never really deviated away from the formula defined in the first episode. The only time it did try something different ('The Revenge of the Chronology Protection Hypothesis' begins with Holly already having travelled back in time, but attempting to disguise the fact from Slade), *Crime Traveller* managed to transcend its otherwise rather limited aspirations and turn in a story that worked very well on its own merits.

It probably wouldn't have hurt the show either if it hadn't chosen to end each episode on the sort of upbeat note already much lampooned by comedy series such as *Police Squad* over ten years earlier. Still the sub-*Tales of the Unexpected* theme tune that followed was undeniably ace, even if the starscape that accompanied each week's closing credits was completely irrelevant.

Dempsey and Makepeace
LWT for ITV

11 January 1985 to 1 November 1986 (29 episodes)

Perhaps ITV's most transparent attempt at a US-style action series ever, *Dempsey and Makepeace* was billed as a direct replacement for *The Professionals*. Like that earlier series it featured two crime-busting operatives, this time members of Scotland Yard's SI10 section. But whereas the contrast between Bodie and Doyle had been largely aesthetic (one had straight hair, the other curly), here the two really were poles apart.

The accepted rules of telly necessitated that the female of the duo, Detective Sergeant Harriet Makepeace (Glynis Barber) got the upper hand over the wise-talking Yank Lieutenant James Dempsey (Michael Brandon) and a lot of comic interplay was harvested from Dempsey's continuing ability to underestimate his partner. For example, on their first meeting the American 'tec entirely failed to spot his soon-to-be colleague posing undercover as a waitress. The scene concluded with Dempsey commenting, 'Having done a light perusal I would say your man is not here', only to be served with the rejoinder 'you just spoke to him'. Clearly the American cop would have to get used to having egg served directly onto his face on a regular basis.

Critics hated the show, but the audience were less appalled; the shorthand characterisation and 'slow burning fuse of attraction' (which is how the publicity material described the relationship between the two main characters) appealed enormously. It didn't harm things when reports began to surface of a real attraction growing between Barber and Brandon (although there were also newspaper stories doing the rounds that painted Barber as rather temperamental, with a habit of running off the set in floods of tears).

For twenty-nine episodes Dempsey and Makepeace kept their fictionalised streets of London clean of crime. Invariably they would do whatever it took (including Dempsey going undercover as a bare-knuckle fighter in one episode) to bring the bad guys to account, and, by and large, the public loved it. After three series Barber chose to try and further her career in Hollywood. Brandon, meanwhile, was distraught that things had come to an end. However, he and Barber married in 1989, and ever since there has been the occasional talk of some kind of *Dempsey and Makepeace* revival – usually coming from the lips of the two leads though and, somewhat tellingly, nobody else.

The Des O'Connor Show
ATV for ITV

29 May 1963 to 28 December 1973 (79 episodes)

Imagine being continually parodied and sent up on prime-time television for two decades. It would ruin your career, wouldn't it? Not so for Des O'Connor, who realised that every time he turned up to be insulted by Eric Morecambe, he confirmed himself as a man without a shred of ego.

No surprise, really, as throughout his lengthy career Des has prided himself on being down to earth. Indeed, right at the start he specifically decided not to adopt a stage name to point out that he was a normal bloke who happened to sing and tell jokes. This relentless ordinariness seems to have had genuine appeal, given in 2003 he claimed to be the first man to have had his own peak-time TV show every year for forty years.

A sizeable percentage of this period was spent on Saturday nights via umpteen series for ATV in the Sixties and Seventies. With Jack Douglas as his regular sidekick, Des welcomed most of the major names in showbiz for unchallenging songs and comedy sketches. If it wasn't exactly producing hugely memorable moments of telly, Des's charm meant it was entertaining enough. There were some notable aspects, however, most obviously when Des was the first person on British telly to work with The Muppets.

At ATV, Des was a stablemate of Morecambe and Wise, of whom he was a great fan. The feeling was mutual, but on screen Eric continually joked about the quality, or otherwise, of his musical talents. Des didn't mind a bit, and regularly appeared to receive another ribbing. It all kept him in the public eye and confirmed his status as a genuinely nice bloke.

ATV boss Lew Grade attempted to sell *The Des O'Connor Show* to the USA, and in 1970 and 1971 two entire series were made with American writers, American producers and American guests. Exactly what British viewers made of this transatlantic mix is uncertain, but the shows were successful enough in the States. In the end, however, Des decided that becoming a star in America was far too tough and concentrated on his home market.

However it did have a lasting effect on his career. To promote the series, Des found himself appearing on dozens of chat shows, and enjoyed the experience – he had a natural charm that perfectly suited such programmes. Des's agent was so impressed he suggested he host a chat show of his own. Des hot-footed it to the BBC where *Des O'Connor Tonight* became a huge success, and overshadowed his previous light entertainment work.

The Dick Emery Show
BBC1/2

13 July 1963 to 7 February 1981 (162 episodes)

A huge star in the Seventies, Dick Emery is perhaps one of the last big names from that decade yet to enjoy a renaissance. Somehow he seems destined never to be mentioned in the same breath as the likes of comedy giants Morecambe and Wise and The Two Ronnies.

Perhaps it's because his work was always fairly raucous and exaggerated. It involved extensive dragging up and silly costumes, and didn't seem to have much in the way of any subtext. Journalist David Quantick once expressed surprise that the BBC allowed Emery to portray a skinhead character whose comedic trait was constantly shaking piss down his trouser leg. Clearly, Emery was one of the last big television comedians to be influenced by music hall and his act conveyed all the vulgarity that came with that association.

Although it started off as a fairly straightforward sketch series, with scripts recycled from American telly from the likes of Mel Brooks, *The Dick Emery Show* soon found its own niche, with Emery's own comedic characters coming to the fore. Memorable creations such as the toothy vicar and Mandy (of 'ooh, you are awful' fame) mainly appeared in film sequences where a hapless interviewer would meet them on the street and ask them innuendo-laden questions that would forever be misunderstood, with hilarious consequences. Of course, this meant you always knew more or less what was going to happen, but that wasn't the point – it was all about the anticipation of how you were going to get to the punchline.

© Rex Features

Inevitably, given the larger-than-life characters and catchphrase repetition, Emery's comedy had a particular appeal for children, and for a while he became the face of Airfix, with the *Dick Emery's Airfix Club* advertorial syndicated in numerous comics. Sadly there was no 'Hello, honky tonks' business here, simply his picture above the latest news on the Messerschmitt BF109.

Emery's unchallenging bawdiness seemed the perfect fit for Saturday nights, with a shift to weeknights for one series in 1976 proving unsuccessful. There were some changes made during the marathon run, with the occasional special show – such as the edition in 1981 filmed entirely on location in Majorca. Eventually the series ran out of steam, and so the comic decided to give up sketch shows in 1982 and move into new areas. The result was *Emery Presents*, two series of spoof detective shows which although still played for laughs allowed for (slightly) more subtle characterisation. Unfortunately, he died shortly after the second series.

Dick Turpin

A Gatetarn, Seacastle production, in association with
LWT for ITV

6 January 1979 to 6 March 1982 (31 episodes)

Undoubtedly one of the best title sequences of all time, and just perfect for those long winter evenings, *Dick Turpin* opened up with a series of beautifully shot silhouettes of men cavorting around on horses in front of gallows and trees. All the while, a wonderfully strident, galloping theme tune confirmed your suspicions: this was going to be a slice of perfect Saturday night nonsense.

The show was pretty similar to the historical adventure series that ITV had excelled at down the years; our eponymous hero (Richard O'Sullivan) returned from 'fighting for England' to discover that the local sheriff, John Glutton (Christopher Benjamin) had taken his family farm. 'I am going to ruin Glutton and everyone around him,' vows Turpin in the opening episode. 'I shall wear them down, like water on a stone.' So was set in motion a series of escapades in which Turpin and his young sidekick Swiftnick (Michael Deeks) would present themselves as a perennial thorn in the side of Glutton and his horrible henchman Captain Nathan Spiker (David Daker).

An enjoyable set piece action scene routinely turned up about two-thirds of the way through each episode and O'Sullivan (who looked like he was only just about in the right physical shape to take on such stunt work) always rose to the challenge. Be it slugging it out with a podgy bloke who purported to be the local thug, or engaging in one of those sword fights that seemed to span several rooms, there was little in the way of tension, but plenty of spectacle and over-the-top sound effects to enjoy during these welcome up tempo moments.

After twenty-six episodes, a feature film in the guise of *Dick Turpin's Greatest Adventure* was produced. The original cast were joined by some additional American guest artistes in a transparent attempt to appeal to the US market and although the film received a theatrical release it was serialised by ITV over the course of 1981.

It's fair to say that *Dick Turpin* was infused with a kind of carefree attitude; the same basic storylines were regularly recycled and the dialogue was made up from a strange mixture of modern vernacular with the odd antiquated phrase thrown in for good measure ('get off your prancer' was the favoured instruction when attempting to persuade a would-be highway robbery victim to dismount). But none of this really mattered. Thanks to some top-rate cinematography, and wonderfully realised locations, the series looked fantastic, and with O'Sullivan and his supporting cast turning in such likeable performances, the lack of historical realism and surfeit of formulaic plots didn't detract from the enjoyment one bit.

Dixon of Dock Green
BBC1

1 April 1961 to 1 May 1976 (442 episodes)

Saturday night television needs something of a sparkle about it. It's the only night of the week yet to be colonised by soap operas, presumably as ordinary workaday television seems out of place. The exception, however, was *Dixon of Dock Green*, which spent twenty years on a Saturday night with its own brand of down-to-earth drama.

In the Forties, actor Jack Warner was best known for his liberal use of the catchphrase 'Mind my bike!' in radio comedies of the day. However, Warner's portrayal of PC George Dixon in the 1949 crime film *The Blue Lamp* marked the beginning of a major career change. Although Dixon was killed off fairly early in the picture, there was something about Warner's interpretation of the heroic and scrupulously fair copper that stuck in the public's mind, and so in 1955, the BBC decided to resurrect the character for his own series.

Dixon of Dock Green quickly became a staple of Saturday night viewing, and was probably cherished as much for its never-changing format as for its stories and excitement. Each episode began with a whistling Dixon strolling into shot, before addressing the camera directly with his latest tale of police drama. The emphasis was on stories of domestic life in which George and his colleagues invariably proved themselves to be stoic, caring, dignified and reliable (although a now infamous episode in which Dixon recommends the occasional slap to keep the 'good lady' in line undermines this slightly).

Hugely popular in its early years, it's probably fair to say that *Dixon* was pretty anachronistic almost as soon as it began. Six years into its run though, it began to draw unfavourable comparisons with its BBC stablemate *Z Cars*, a rather more modern take on policing featuring speeding cars, extensive violence and shouting coppers. Jack Warner, however, remained unconcerned, citing the programme's popularity with the real-life police force, who doubtless appreciated the programme for portraying one of their own as a fundamentally decent individual.

Series creator Ted Willis was also initially bullish, saying that although the programme's concentration on the cosy side of police life may not have provided the full picture, it was no less accurate than other series that emphasised the darker aspects.

While the critics might have harped, *Dixon of Dock Green* remained hugely popular, pulling in its highest audiences in 1971. By this point, the ageing Warner had been 'promoted' to desk sergeant and spent most episodes looking on in a fatherly manner while his younger colleagues, most notably Peter Firth's DC Andy Crawford, got stuck into the action. The scripts were sharpened up slightly and covered slightly more sensational topics, but everything still always worked out happily ever after.

By 1976, Jack Warner was eighty, and if the series had looked somewhat outdated opposite *Z Cars*, now it was being compared to *The Sweeney*. Imagining Dixon working alongside Regan and Carter took some doing, and *Dixon of Dock Green* seemed to be rapidly transforming into a period piece. Indeed, perhaps the most famous moment from the later years was not any searing piece of drama, but a notorious out-take when an actor was unable to deliver the words 'Dock Green nick' without turning it into something rather less suitable for family audiences.

It's hard to work out exactly how the series managed to continue for so long, but obviously few at the BBC wanted to kill off a programme – and a character – that had become so loved and welcomed by the audience, and furthermore finding long-term Saturday night hits was an incredibly difficult business. Dixon's retirement finally brought down the curtain on the series. Right up to his death in 1981, however, Jack Warner remained hugely proud of his role as the honest, straightforward copper who had brought comfort to millions.

Doctor Who

BBC1

23 November 1963 to ongoing
(723 episodes as of 30 June 2007)

So is *Doctor Who* the epitome of cringe-making television, or the best sci-fi programme ever made? Well, it's still with us some forty or so years after it first began, and although the series has had its fair share of bottom-clenchingly embarrassing moments (think the seventh Doctor, Sylvester McCoy, facing up to a giant Bertie Bassett monster), it rather obviously has done more things right than wrong.

Although many would claim that it was the arrival of the

© Rex Features

Daleks (in only *Doctor Who*'s second story) that put the series on the map, much of the credit for the show's longevity must be attributed to the fact that the original premise (that of a man travelling through space and time in a ship that is bigger on the inside than out) was not only brilliant, but brilliantly, and economically, conveyed in the first ever episode 'The Unearthly Child'. It also helped that early aspirations towards making the programme educational were dropped in favour of placing the Doctor (originally played by William Hartnell who is best remembered for his bad moods, bad teeth and creepy Kaftan hat) and his travelling companions in positions of ever increasing jeopardy.

A plethora of robotic, organic and, in some cases, even vegetable monsters began to dominate the programme, edging out real-life historical figures. From 14 January 1967 onwards, every single *Doctor Who* story (with the exception of the two-part 'Black Orchid' transmitted in March 1982) would feature an evil alien villain, some monsters or both.

In 1966, the series faced the first of its many brushes with termination when it became clear that the ageing Hartnell would have to leave. There was the possibility of re-casting and carrying on as if nothing had happened, but the production team came up with the bold idea of allowing the Doctor to renew himself in the guise of a new body. This crucial concept (which would later become known as 'regeneration') not only allowed the show to live on past the shelf life of its lead actor, but established the central character of the Doctor as unearthly in origin (over the years we would come to learn that he was a Time Lord and came from the planet Gallifrey).

By 2005, ten actors had taken on the role of the Doctor on television, all of whom had been memorable in their own way, but it is perhaps Tom Baker that remains the most popular Doctor of them all. This is in part because he was brilliant at it, and also because he played it for the longest time (seven years), but you have to concede that he was also lucky enough to take on the role when BBC's Saturday night line-up was at its strongest.

While the aforementioned Daleks might remain *Doctor Who*'s most famous adversary, the Time Lord has faced a litany of memorable baddies; and tussles with Cybermen, Ice Warriors, Sea Devils and even humanoid foes such as The Master have created enduring images that have burnt into the minds of a generation. In fact *Doctor Who*'s ability to create memorable images is one of its most distinctive attributes and in particular the show's end-of-episode cliffhangers have always been hard to beat.

In the Eighties *Doctor Who* was moved from its traditional home on Saturday nights and put up against *Coronation Street*. By then the quality of the programme had taken a dip and the show found itself unable to compete against the big-budget American television series that were now popular on British telly. When *Doctor Who* was finally cancelled in 1989, it had long since become something of a national joke.

During its long spell in television exile there were a number of attempts made by independent production companies to bring the good Doctor back to our screens. Terry Nation and Gerry Davis (creator and co-creator of the Daleks and the Cybermen respectively) tried to persuade the BBC to let them produce a new series. So too did the programme's first ever producer Verity Lambert. A short-lived American-funded revival did surface in 1996, but it failed to attract the necessary audience in the US and so never got beyond a one-off TV movie.

When it finally came, *Doctor Who's* eventual return (in 2005) was nothing short of a triumph. In the course of only thirteen episodes the programme regained its place at the top table of Saturday night television. It probably helped that the new series looked amazing, and featured a much respected actor in the lead role (although Christopher Eccleston's ability to play the lighter moments always seemed a little suspect). But best of all this new series had great stories; and never more so than when the Doctor became embroiled in a lush wartime adventure with a creepy gas-masked kid. This was definitely *Dr Who's* finest ever script and saw school kids the land over scaring the bejesus out of their parents by quizzically intoning, 'Are you my mummy?'

Doctor Who's massive wave of popularity was further bolstered by the arrival of David Tennant in the lead role at the end of the 2005 run. Somehow Tennant, a self-confessed *Doctor Who* fan, seemed far more comfortable in the part than Eccleston had ever been, and the new man brought a superb emotional range to the Doctor that had hitherto remained unseen.

Billie Piper's impeccable performance as Rose also gave *Doctor Who* something it had never had before: a companion who had a proper home to return to when she grew tired of time travelling. This was a major departure from days of yore when, with very few exceptions, the companions' personal histories were completely ignored as soon as they stepped foot into the TARDIS. Not only were Rose's family members referred to, but her mum, dad and boyfriend actually featured in the occasional adventure. The result of all this was that when Rose and the Doctor finally parted company in 2006, it made for some of the most emotionally charged popular drama shown that year.

Inevitably *Doctor Who*'s renewed success attracted some competition, but the series remained well ahead of its 'me-too' rivals (including ITV's *Primeval* and the BBC's own revived version of *Robin Hood*) both in terms of critical opinion and number of viewers. *Doctor Who* also established itself as an important part of BBC1's Christmas Day line-up (the original run was shown on Christmas Day only once), becoming a firm Yuletide tradition after only two years.

Most remarkable of all, by 2007 the show was able to boast an incredible four ongoing spin-off series, a situation unprecedented for a British television drama. For those who had remained loyal to the Doctor during his sixteen-year exile from our screens, the eventual pay-off had certainly proven to be well worth the wait.

Dog Eat Dog

BBC1

14 April 2001 to 2 November 2002 (30 episodes)

Friends Like These had been a success for the BBC – a strong programme, cheaply made, that could run and run. *Dog Eat Dog* was another variation on the theme. This time six contestants battled it out for supremacy over five studio challenges involving physical and mental agility. The twist here was that prior to entering the studio, the contestants had been sent on an outdoor pursuits weekend to allow them to work out their fellow competitors' strengths and weaknesses.

As the studio challenges unfolded, the contestants each had to nominate the person who they felt to be least equipped to carry out a specific skill-based task. The one with the most nominations would have to take on the challenge, knowing that if they failed elimination from the show awaited.

Capably hosted by Ulrika Jonsson, the element of nastiness and backstabbing had clearly been purloined from the Beeb's biggest recent hit, the daytime smash *The Weakest Link*. The success of the association rubbed off as the second series found *Dog Eat Dog* beating **The Premiership** on ITV. However it would be fair to say that even the production team would hardly consider the show one of the all-time greats of Saturday nights.

The series was certainly competent enough, but occasionally the forced backstabbing came across as achingly contrived, while the games proved either dull or, in the case of the first series final elimination game Stealth, completely incomprehensible. Here the remaining two contestants would race each other to cross a walkway made up of a grid of squares. Supposedly, if a contestant attempted to cross too quickly then an alarm would be set off and they would be forced to retreat a square. That was the theory anyway, but in practice it all looked decidedly random, and it proved impossible to predict who would make it to the end first.

The final round continued this slightly anticlimactic theme, with the last remaining contestant having to select the losing contestants that they felt most likely to get a particular general knowledge question wrong. If the losers collectively got three out of the five questions correct they would split the prize money between them, but if they failed all the money would go to the 'Top Dog' (the name awarded to the victorious contestant).

This scenario would usually be accompanied by scenes of gritted-teeth jollity as the losers had to show themselves to be 'good sports' and heartily congratulate their vanquisher. However, occasionally the show would bear witness to the odd bad loser who very obviously felt disinclined to join in the festivities. In such circumstances Ulrika would sashay in front of them to bring proceedings to a close, but it still left viewers with a sour taste in the mouth that felt a little inappropriate for what was just meant to be a teatime game show.

As such, despite enjoying three series within twelve months, when the trend for 'nasty' shows waned, *Dog Eat Dog* quietly came to an end.

Don't Forget Your Toothbrush

Ginger Television for Channel Four

12 February 1994 to 25 February 1995 (25 episodes)

Channel Four's Saturday night schedule has almost always been devoted to serious drama or documentary. They weren't in the business of going up against the likes of **Blind Date**, but instead provided an alternative to the other channels. This didn't always mean that light entertainment was completely out of the question – **Saturday Live** had mixed **Game for a Laugh**-esque production with innovative new comedians. Now it was time for the game show to undergo a similar makeover.

Don't Forget Your Toothbrush was the concept of Chris Evans, who in 1992 burst out of seemingly nowhere (in reality, London radio and short-lived satellite network BSB) to become host of *The Big Breakfast*. His quick wit and boundless enthusiasm were the main reasons Channel Four moved from a distant third to a clear first in the breakfast market. Eager to hold on to a rising star, Channel Four gave him the chance to move to primetime.

The first attempts at producing *Don't Forget Your Toothbrush*, however, were less than successful, with the press gleefully reporting that the pilot episode had been a complete disaster. The concept behind the series – members of the audience compete to win a holiday and, as the name suggests, leave right after the show – was sound enough, but it was proving tough to make it work on screen. An unlikely saviour was found, though, in the shape of William G Stewart. At the time he was best known as the no-nonsense, straight-laced frontman of the afternoon quiz *Fifteen to One*, but he had many years' experience behind the camera, most notably presiding over the demented **The Price Is Right**.

A second pilot was shot, and everything suddenly came together. In a way, *Toothbrush* used many of the same techniques as **Noel's House Party** (a series Evans confessed to being a huge fan of, and had even appeared in via an NTV 'hit' in 1993). Each week there would be in-studio games with unsuspecting members of the studio audience, who would find the contents of their bedrooms being brought on stage, or their prized possessions being dangled over the River Thames, ready to be released if they failed a task. A musical guest would sing a few songs each week, accompanied by a band led by Jools Holland, who also acted as Evans' sidekick. The guest artiste would then be invited to participate in a weekly quiz against one of their biggest fans to see who knew the most about them. Meanwhile the audience were encouraged to sing and cheer along, and become part of the fun.

The whole show led up to the main game, played in the final ten minutes, where members of the audience were plucked at random and took part in 'Light Your Lemon'. Two destinations would be offered – one somewhere like Barbados, the other somewhere like Blackpool. The contestants would have to answer questions, and if they got five right they'd be off on the exotic holiday right there and then. If they got five wrong first, though, they'd be off to the dowdy seaside resort, and there'd be a viewer on the telephone who'd try and get the star prize instead (memorably, one week the home viewer had been watching the other side when he was phoned). This often made for exciting television, but in the penultimate episode of the first series the stakes were significantly raised, when the competing couple weren't just playing for a holiday for themselves, but for the whole studio audience. As promised, the two-hundred-strong crowd went on to enjoy a week in EuroDisney – one of the biggest prizes ever given away on British television.

Initial critical reaction was mixed, but after a few weeks, everyone was talking about *Don't Forget Your Toothbrush*. It didn't even make it into Channel Four's own top ten until the middle of the run, and the 3 million or so watching was nothing compared to the nearer 13 million watching *Blind Date*. Of those 13 million, most probably couldn't remember what had happened the minute the show had finished. *Toothbrush* viewers remembered the time a member of the audience was offered a random choice of three cars to win, and ended up going home with Evans's own Ferrari. They also remembered the regular segment when the show cut to a camera shot of a street and invited the residents to flash their lights on and off to be chosen to win cash prizes. The sight of whole towns joining in said much about the power of the show.

Don't Forget Your Toothbrush went on to win BAFTAs and the prestigious Golden Rose of Montreux, and the concept was sold to dozens of broadcasters around the world, making

Evans a massive amount of money. But despite its impact, the series was incredibly short-lived, ending after just over a year. Evans claimed that the person who fronted *Toothbrush* was a different person to him in 'real life' and he simply didn't want to do that sort of thing anymore. The programme clearly also consumed ideas at a tremendous rate, and it's likely that if it had gone on for much longer it would become rather less inventive.

Oddly, the BBC then bought the *Toothbrush* format, and went as far as piloting their own version with MTV presenter Ray Cokes, but this never made it onto the screen. It's hard to see how it would have succeeded without the man who dominated the show, but the fact the Beeb were willing to go ahead with a new version anyway proves how successful it was deemed to be. For many, it remains Evans's best TV work.

The Duchess of Duke Street
BBC1

4 September 1976 to 24 December 1977 (31 episodes)

What Saturday night television programme today would dare try and get away with dialogue such as: 'Widowers are prone to exotic fashions and you are perfectly right to treat them with the utmost circumspection'? But such lines were commonplace in *The Duchess of Duke* Street, a series that attracted up to 14.6 million viewers as part of the BBC's formidable mid-Seventies Saturday night schedule. Period drama was a real winner some thirty years ago with series such as *Edward VII*, *Upstairs, Downstairs* and *The Forsyte Saga* establishing a healthy appetite for the bedazzling world of the turn-of-the-twentieth-century social climbers and step scrubbers.

The Duchess of Duke Street followed the rising fortunes, but troubled life, of Louisa Trotter (Gemma Jones), an ordinary working-class girl with a talent for cooking who, thanks to a liaison with royalty, found herself moving up the ranks of servitude until she became owner of the opulent Bentinck Hotel. From here Louisa could observe the trappings and indiscretions of the wealthy and significant, and on regular occasions would chip in with a slice of homespun wisdom which, although well meaning, usually came across as rather irksome (such as declaring all women who have left their husbands to be 'trouble'.)

As was the way, Louisa surrounded herself with a cast of

likeable, if at times eccentric characters. Her trusty head-waiter Merriman (John Welsh) was a cantankerous old fellow, while the porter, Starr (John Cater), was more concerned about his dog than actually shifting any luggage. As agreeable as these regular faces were, any decent period drama requires the odd rogue or bounder, and it was something of a hallmark of the series that smooth-talking scoundrels could be uncovered by goading them into making an angry outburst, from which they would then attempt to reverse back into their gentlemanly persona before Louisa fixed them with a withering gaze ('I'd drop the whole bleedin' thing if I was you').

True, the odd scene might begin with an actor conspicuously stationary on their mark halfway down the stairs, waiting for their cue to begin, but in the main *The Duchess of Duke Street* was a well-put-together series, drawing upon the BBC's obvious strength in portraying period detail. Whether today's viewer would share Louisa's code of conduct is debatable, but her abilities to see off the likes of a swarthy Robert Hardy (an actor typical of the stock that featured in the programme) are still to be admired.

The Dukes of Hazzard

Lou Step/Piggy Productions/Warner Bros [shown on BBC1]

3 March 1979 to 30 December 1986 (147 episodes)

The *Dukes of Hazzard* was one of those programmes that found a winning formula, and then stuck close to it. Each week an adventure in which the 'modern-day Robin Hood' Duke boys took on some injustice or other was spun out in a pleasingly yarnish manner involving loads of car chases as the cousins careered round the countryside in their beloved 1969 Dodge Charger, the General Lee. Invariably, there would be run-ins with the law, but strangely in Hazzard County none of the cops ever thought of simply strolling up to the boys' house and waiting for them to get back from their latest foray into needless wheel spinning. Instead the likes of Cletus or Enos (the law enforcement agents always had stupid names) would try in vain to chase the boys down and, for their troubles, would inevitably end up piling their cop car into a tree.

It's probably fair to say that nothing was taken particularly seriously on *The Dukes of Hazzard*. The narration (a rare device for such shows) was delivered in a laconic and slightly bemused style by country and western star Waylon Jennings (he provided the catchy theme tune too), that ensured any potentially dramatic moments were suitably diffused ('friends, now the cheese is going to get more bite'). Similarly, the numerous car chases were accompanied by ferocious banjo picking that gave these sequences a freewheeling spirit totally devoid of tension. Probably just about the only serious elements in the series were the Duke boys themselves. Crucially one needed to be blond and the other dark-haired, but beyond that there was very little to distinguish them: Bo Duke, the blond-haired one (played by John Schneider) was perhaps a touch more impetuous than his elder cousin Luke (Tom Wopat), but both of them played each week's adventure with a pretty straight face.

By no means could the same be said for *The Dukes of Hazzard's* most memorable double act – Boss Hogg (Sorrell Booke) and Rosco P (which stood for Pervis) Coltrane (James Best). In any given episode, we would alight upon Boss Hogg dressed in his customary Southern gentlemen attire of an all-white suit, with a napkin forced down his shirt, munching on some chicken wings or bon bons and berating Rosco for some act of stupidity or other ('Rosco, you'd better sneeze as your brain is getting dusty!'). The put-upon P Coltrane would in turn punctuate every response with his idiot laugh and a propensity to refer to anyone and everyone as his 'little bitty buddy'.

Other regular characters included Uncle Jesse (Denver Pyle), the oddly underused Cooter Davenport (Ben Jones), Flash (Rosco's trusty pooch) and, perhaps most memorably, Daisy Duke (Catherine Bach) who, according to Jenning's narration in the first ever episode, 'drives like Richard Petty, shoots like Annie Oakley, and knows the words to all of Dolly Parton's songs'. Bach became much talked about thanks to her proclivity for wearing a tiny pair of shorts (which she apparently made herself) that showed off a set of pins that were reputedly insured for $20 million.

Broadcast just after the football results, *The Dukes of Hazzard* was a big hit, especially with younger viewers. However disaster struck during the fifth series when a pay dispute meant that John Schneider and Tom Wopat left the show. A couple of stand-in cousins, Coy (Byron Cherry) and Vance (Christopher Mayer) turned up behind the wheel of the General Lee for eighteen episodes, and rather ungraciously earned the off-screen nickname 'The Scabs of Hazzard'. Happily the dispute was soon resolved and Schneider and Wopat returned to their rightful place – careering up and down the many obstacle-strewn dust tracks of Hazzard County.

But the hiatus of the 'proper' Duke boys seemed to put *The Dukes of Hazzard* into a downwards spiral, and after just two more series, the show was cancelled. A couple of TV movies followed ('The Reunion' in 1997 and 'Hazzard in Hollywood' in 2000), before the original cast were finally rested for the 2005 big-screen version featuring Seann William Scott and Johnny Knoxville. Inevitably, it failed to recreate the myriad charms of the television series, most heinously neglecting to accompany the closing credits with a sequence that purported to portray the Duke boys attempting to flee a police car, but in actuality just showed the General Lee driving round and round the same tree.

Fame Academy

Initial Productions for BBC1

4 October 2002 to ongoing
(50 episodes as of 16 March 2007)

By rights *Fame Academy* shouldn't really be featured in this book at all (in that it spent more time on other nights of the week than on Saturdays), but it sums up twenty-first-century Saturday night telly far too neatly to be ignored.

The success of **Popstars** and **Pop Idol** had shown how effective the melding of reality and talent shows could be, but the BBC had shied away from playing any part in the genre, lest they be accused of dumbing down. However a series that had proven a hit on Spanish television looked like it could be something a little different – a more thoughtful, 'BBC' take on the concept.

To avoid a clash with *Popstars: The Rivals*, BBC1 scheduled *Fame Academy* on Friday nights. The idea was that instead of simply being a straightforward sing-off, *Fame Academy* would actually follow the hopefuls as they lived together and underwent rigorous training to hone their talents in songwriting, dancing, musicianship and so on. There'd still be evictions, of course, but the hope was that this hot-housing process would help uncover long-lasting musical talents rather than flash-in-the-pans. The live shows were based in the cavernous Shepperton Studios, with an enormous audience and a giant stage.

Sadly, early episodes were shambolic, with judge and

legendary music radio bigwig Richard Park claiming after the first show that he would have given it 'five out of a hundred' for musical aptitude. Throughout the run there was a definite improvement – thanks, clearly, to the training that the wannabes underwent in their spell at the academy – and by the end of the series the show had actually garnered a loyal audience. Contestant Lemar even went on to win a Brit award. However it hadn't been a huge hit, and though a second series appeared in 2003, major changes were afoot.

The most obvious came in the scheduling. The BBC announced that, for some reason, there were no other slots available and so the new series would have to go out on Saturday nights. Coincidentally, of course, *Pop Idol* 2 was just about to start in exactly the same slot on ITV, with the two going head to head every week. Generally *Fame Academy* would start ten minutes or so before *Pop Idol*, but you could never watch both.

This seemed a rather stupid idea, but it could have been argued that the two series were very different and thus appealed to different audiences...until you actually saw the new *Fame Academy,* that is. One of the major criticisms of the first series was that it had been confusing, with the 'teachers' nominating three pupils for eviction each week, whilst the rest of the students were simply allowed to perform their latest routines, free from the stress of imminent expulsion. For the second series, the show was dramatically simplified – everyone was now up for eviction every week.

The over-the-top setting of the first series was also dropped, with the action relocating to the piddly performance space of the academy itself. This meant that whereas before, the contestants had been able to dance and make a bit of a spectacle, now all they could do was stand there and sing. Just like on *Pop Idol*.

This slavish copying of the rival series even went as far as the viewer telephone numbers, which ludicrously were just one digit different to those used on *Pop Idol*. With the show getting rid of virtually all its unique selling points there hardly seemed to be a reason for it to exist, given *Pop Idol* was doing the same thing at the same time on the other side. This was unfortunate as there was a great deal more variety in the type of music and contestant that took part in *Fame Academy* – most notably the winner, Alex Parks, a sensitive singer-songwriter with an acoustic guitar.

That said, there was one other notable aspect of *Fame Academy*. Cat Deeley and Patrick Kielty were hosts for both series, and Kielty's job was to get an opinion from the judges after each performance. Richard Park took up the time-honoured role of the plain-speaking judge we were all supposed to boo, and he certainly approached the job with gusto, once brilliantly telling one of his fellow judges that to say a wannabe was 'better than Madonna' was 'dangerous rubbish'.

Somewhere along the line, however, Park and Kielty fell out massively, with Kielty taking all Park's comments as a personal affront and Park simply getting more miserable with each show. It was said the two were given dressing rooms miles apart and avoided each other in the corridors, and the absolute hatred between the two was grimly fascinating to watch. Some of the arguments – including Park bellowing 'Oi!' when Kielty tried to cut him off – looked as if they were about to lead to flying fists. This wasn't put on for the cameras; they clearly hated each other's guts.

Although the second series was the last proper run of *Fame Academy*, the show has made a semi-regular return every few years with celebrities taking the plunge for Comic Relief. Kielty and Park can't even put aside their differences for charity though, with Park being censured by the BBC for being caught on camera giving Kielty the wanker sign on one such edition. One of the contestants, Nick Knowles, went even further by squaring up to Park backstage after the show. Take it outside, will you?

Families at War

Channel X for BBC1

29 August 1998 to 29 May 1999 (9 episodes)

The script seemed already written. As **Noel's House Party** was breathing its last, a new series was to begin on Saturday nights that would take light entertainment in a completely new direction. The old guard had been pushed out and the next generation were now in charge. At least, that was the plan.

Vic Reeves and Bob Mortimer were familiar faces on BBC2, and their recent take on the comedy panel game, *Shooting Stars*, had achieved some remarkable viewing figures, while also broadening Vic and Bob's appeal to those who were unmoved by the capers of The Man With The Stick and Judge Nutmeg. Therefore thought was given to launching the pair on BBC1, and after revitalising the panel game, overhauling the Saturday night game show seemed the obvious next step.

However *Families at War* was not envisaged as a vehicle for the duo. Reeves and Mortimer simply came up with the idea and intended to bequeath it to a different host, while they stayed firmly in the background. Hence it was originally pitched as a show starring Shane Richie and Ulrika Jonsson, but the BBC more or less said that if it was a Reeves and Mortimer series, it would have to have Reeves and Mortimer in it. In the event, Vic and Bob did present, with *Watchdog* host Alice Beer joining them to act as 'umpire'.

Families at War was a fairly simple show. Reeves and

Mortimer would lead two teams of three family members, each of whom would play a game based on one of their talents. They would go head to head with judges choosing their favourites, and whichever family got the most votes would go into the final in the hope of claiming big prizes.

So far, so ordinary, but there were plenty of touches that showed signs of the creators' influence. For example, each contestant would introduce themselves via a specially written song, along the lines of 'I'm Carol, a beautician/Waxing an ape is my ambition'. Meanwhile, the show's jury was made up of such august bodies as twelve jockeys from Gillingham and twelve shoe salesmen from Surrey.

Most obviously devised by Vic and Bob were the games that the contestants had to play. One contestant reckoned that his special skill was milking cows, so he was engaged to squirt milk from a fake cow's udders in order to repel zombies. Another participant held records in power jogging, a sport that involved running while carrying heavy weights, and so was required to jog on a treadmill while giving a piggy-back to Leo Sayer, who sang throughout.

This level of innovation and wit was hugely unusual for Saturday nights, but after eight years of *Noel's House Party* the bright new hopes managed to last just eight weeks. Indeed, with an average audience of just 3.4 million viewers, *Families at War* was one of the least successful BBC1 shows of the decade. One obvious reason for this was the ludicrous scheduling of the show alongside **Big Break**, the epitome of outdated light entertainment.

It also proved that while Vic and Bob had a loyal

audience, most of them would be nowhere near a television at six o'clock on Saturdays. It's fair to say that the BBC got it wrong, and had it been fronted by someone else it may have proven more popular. Remarkably, here's a programme that might have been improved had Shane Richie been involved.

Still, for providing us with the unforgettable sight of Leo Sayer slipping off a treadmill and being eaten alive by a crash mat, *Families at War* will never be forgotten by those who saw it. Whomever they were.

Friends Like These

BBC1

6 November 1999 to 1 March 2003 (51 episodes)

Friends Like These was a pretty straightforward kind of a show: each week, five twentysomething male friends took on five twentysomething female friends at a number of individual challenges ranging from 3-D puzzles to identifying different types of food and drink and even mundane tasks such as threading a series of needles. The winners went through to the final, where each of the five had to answer a question about one of the others. Cruelly, if they got it wrong, it would be their friend who would miss out on the star prize holiday. A further twist, however, was that the members of the team who had been successful could gamble their tickets to win back a place for their loser mates. This meant that either everybody or nobody would end up going, and so ending the episode on a pleasingly cruel moral dilemma.

Equally as important as the format were the show's presenters. Ant McPartlin and Declan Donnelly were then best known as hosts of *SMTV Live*. They were perhaps unique in that they combined youthfulness (they were both in their mid-twenties) with several years' experience in television, having started as child actors on *Byker Grove* a decade earlier. This meant they had a pleasing 'old school' professionalism about them and a desire to transcend the ghetto of youth programming.

As well as appearing young and fresh both in front of and

behind the camera, *Friends Like These* also appealed to the BBC as it was extremely cost-effective. All the challenges took place in the one medium-sized studio, which, with clever set-dressing and imagination, never looked too cheap or repetitive. The signs were that it was going to be a long-runner, and this looked even more likely when the show managed to continue after the hosts' departure to ITV. Coming in the opposite direction was Ian Wright, the former Arsenal footballer whose personality made him an obvious TV talent. Wright's first series enjoyed a notable success when it beat the ITV opposition in the ratings – **Slap Bang**, hosted by, er, Ant and Dec.

Despite this, *Friends Like These* was never a huge ratings winner and it came to a natural end a few years down the line. What it had proved, though, was that Saturday night telly could appeal to young people without having to try too hard.

Game for a Laugh

LWT for ITV

26 September 1981 to 23 November 1985 (58 episodes)

Game for a Laugh was the show that shifted the balance of power on Saturday nights away from the BBC, and in so doing brought about the demise of none other than **The Generation Game**. It also established the careers of two of ITV's most important Saturday night presenters, Matthew Kelly and Jeremy Beadle. All this despite a senior ITV executive of the time insisting you couldn't make light entertainment stars out of men with beards.

Game for a Laugh was originally going to be called *The People Show*. However, the eventual title came about from a misreading of some notes scrawled down by the show's producer (who had been listening to disc jockey Ray Moore's late night radio show the previous evening, and illegibly

© London Weekend Television/ Rex Features

jotted down the phrase 'good for a laugh').

Even with a title in place *Game for a Laugh* was a difficult programme to describe; a typical episode might include members of the public trying to identify a celebrity simply by touching his or her head, a filmed insert depicting rock and roll star Joe Brown returning to his first job as a steam locomotive fireman, a report on the annual raft race from Loch Tay to Aberfeldy, and, as a climax to the show, an elaborate practical joke such as placing a lady's entire home furnishings in an auction (which she is then made to bid for). Pretty much nothing was off limits and apparently, members of the studio audience were actually warned that if they were invited by Beadle to take part in a game they were duty bound to accept the offer.

Although the balance of the four presenters Sarah Kennedy (the school-matronly one), Henry Kelly (the sensible one), Matthew Kelly (the slightly camp one) and Jeremy Beadle (the naughty imp who, apropos nothing, would occasionally produce a pair of scissors and snip a bit off Henry's tie) seems, in retrospect, to be perfect, the truth is that the programme's presenting line-up could very well have been different: Terry Wogan, Cilla Black and Selina Scott were all invited to take part and Bruce Forsyth later bemoaned the fact that he wanted to present the show but was never approached.

Although each show was recorded twice – once on a Wednesday and once on a Thursday – there was a conscious attempt to make each episode of *Game for a Laugh* feel live and so presenters corpsing, or items going wrong usually made the final cut. The show also featured as much as twice the number of camera shots as other programmes of equivalent length so that it felt fast-paced and energetic.

The hidden-camera stunts that closed each edition were undoubtedly a high point. The very first featured a traffic cop setting up his unsuspecting wife by bringing the arm of a giant digger crashing down into the roof of their car (in truth it wasn't their car at all but a specially rigged duplicate, with all the strengthening of the bodywork removed so that it would crush in a pleasingly dramatic fashion). Later stunts would see a man's home turned into a grotto, and one unsuspecting husband's night out became altogether more memorable when his wife made a surprise appearance on-stage as a dancer.

This made for entertaining telly, but *Game for a Laugh* had a critical weakness; it was a voracious consumer of new ideas. Items such as fooling a member of the audience into believing that a pair of twins was actually only one person could only be attempted once before we got wise to what was going on. Similarly, there were only so many whimsical reverse car drivers, Liberace impressionists and diminutive versions of pop acts that could be featured on the show. Later episodes included items that simply weren't as cleverly thought out as those from the early years. In particular a game in which a member of the audience was invited to stick stars on the parts of a muscleman's body beginning with the letter 'b', provoked hysterical laughter from the studio, but failed to entertain the viewer at home who had seen far more inventive things on earlier editions.

At the end of the third series Matthew, Sarah and Henry all decided that enough was enough and left. Beadle was joined by regional news reporter Lee Peck, breakfast telly cook Rustie Lee and magician Martin Daniels (comedian Duncan Norvelle was briefly considered as a camp replacement for Matthew Kelly). Poor old Rustie Lee seemed to find the programme rather overwhelming and while her raucous laughter had been endearing on breakfast television, it became annoying on *Game for a Laugh*. It wasn't much of a surprise when she was replaced by Debbie Rix for the fifth series.

But after fifty-eight episodes of nudists, stunt Tiger Moth aeroplanes, members of the audience who had just featured in the previous filmed item standing up to give us a wave, countless appearances by the Roly Polys, silly games in which husbands got to kiss Miss United Kingdoms while their wives remained utterly oblivious, vegetables talking to children, gnome farms, haggis hurling and Beadle proclaiming 'this week what we are looking for is…', *Game for a Laugh* came to an end on 23 November 1985. The show's legacy though survives in the form of pretty much every subsequent Saturday night entertainment series. From rubbish souvenir trophies that in some way feature the programme's logo, to presenters hurtling down a flight of stairs at the top of the show, the ghost of *Game for a Laugh* is everywhere. You could say that to this day it remains watching us, watching you, watching us, watching you.

The Generation Game

BBC1

2 October 1971 to 31 December 2005 (412 episodes)

For many, *The Generation Game* is the epitome of Saturday night. It helps that the concept can be encapsulated in two sentences: Here's an expert doing something. Now you try it.

The concept was famously devised by a Dutch housewife, and her show, *Een Van De Aacht* (*One from Eight*) topped the ratings in the Netherlands. The BBC bought the rights, and fiddled with it so all that remained from the original was the conveyer belt at the end.

Bruce Forsyth was host, thanks to his superb stint at the helm of the 'Beat the Clock' strand on *Sunday Night at the London Palladium* a decade previously. Bruce was certainly in his element in charge of proceedings, able to send up and parody the hapless contestants ('I'll just make a note of that…') while ensuring there was obvious affection.

Where *The Generation Game* really worked was that everyone seemed to be having a wonderful time. The final conveyer-belt game was supposed to be a test of memory, but Bruce practically read out the entire list of prizes. Nobody cared; it was all just good clean fun.

Bruce was with the show for seven series, but come 1977 he was getting a little tired. Having to learn the rules for five different games a week was starting to take its toll. Eventually he defected to ITV and the disastrous **Bruce Forsyth's Big Night**. So what of *The Generation Game*? The series remained sturdy, so it was decided to continue it with a new presenter.

In came camp comedian Larry Grayson. Larry's hapless approach was the antithesis of Brucie's domineering and slick personality. It soon became obvious, however, that while Larry was an accomplished comedian, he had some trouble coping with the complexities of the games. This problem was solved by giving his 'assistant' a much greater role. With Bruce, Anthea Redfern's role was basically to bring contestants on and off. In Larry's version, however, it would be up to Isla St Clair to introduce and explain the games, while Larry simply stood back and added a pertinent comment ('Seems like a nice boy!') where appropriate.

In fact, Larry's stint at the helm of the *Gen Game* was even more successful than Bruce's, topping 20 million viewers on regular occasions. However the audience tailed off during Grayson's fourth series in 1981, due to the appearance of **Game for a Laugh** on ITV. Larry and Isla decided to call it a day and the series ended after over a decade.

Fast-forward to 1990, and the BBC asked Brucie if he'd like to return to *The Generation Game*. Bruce dug out some tapes and was surprised by how funny it remained. So come September he was back in charge. It proved to be a huge success, bringing in a new audience who hadn't even been born when the first incarnation was going out.

The Generation Game had established itself as a hit all over again, but after five series, Bruce again found it becoming a strain. In his final year, he was absent for one show due to illness and Jim Davidson filled in. It was no surprise, then, when Bruce decided to return to ITV and less gruelling shows such as **The Price Is Right** and *Play Your Cards Right*. So who'd take over the hot seat next?

Perhaps this would be the carrot to convince Michael Barrymore to finally leave ITV? Might Dale Winton be given the opportunity to do the show that had always been his ambition? Or would it be Jim Davidson, who already had experience of the series?

Surely Davidson's reputation as something of a rogue with a shady past meant he was hardly suitable as the host of the number one family show? Seemingly not, as come 1995, Davidson was now in charge full time, joined by weathergirl Sally Meen. Davidson was something of an acquired taste, and clearly struggled in his first series, unable to bond with the contestants to any great extent or develop much of a relationship with Meen.

Still, the show continued for several more years, and eventually he gained his confidence. Sadly, this was to be his failing. Somewhere along the line, *The Generation Game* stopped being about the contestants, and instead became about Davidson, with the games delayed by extended mucking about. The most notable example came when Jim was joined by his son Cameron to croon 'Father and Son' at each other.

The contestants themselves often came across as little more than stooges, being gunged at every opportunity, even during the final conveyor belt round, as if Jim didn't even like them that much. Despite this, by 2002 he'd spent longer in the job continuously than either of his predecessors.

Yet by this time, regular appearances by the likes of Cannon and Ball left the show reeking of mothballs: what was this creaking old series still doing on telly in the twenty-first century? In the face of a rampant **Pop Idol**, *The Generation Game* was pulling in only around 3 million viewers – awful even by current standards. It was perhaps not surprising, then, that Jim finally decided to call it a day.

Even then, few at the Beeb could resist the evergreen format for long. At Christmas 2005, Graham Norton fronted a one-off version of the show, but with celebrities and their families as contestants, and fiendishly renamed *Generation Fame*. It looked as if this might be the cue for a new series, but poor ratings seemed to have stymied this. At the time of writing, one of the all-time-great Saturday night shows remains on the shelf, but it'll surely appear again soon. It'd certainly be welcome, not least so we could put Jim Davidson out of our minds.

Gladiators

LWT for ITV

10 October 1992 to 1 January 2000 (132 episodes)

It would be hard to imagine a programme screened on overnight ITV being promoted to a peak-time slot these days, but in the early Nineties *American Gladiators* became cult viewing among all those who came across the screenings at one o'clock in the morning (i.e. students). Here, members of the public who thought they were pretty fit had to take on the challenge of the former sports stars and bodybuilders who made up the titular Gladiators. This David versus Goliath concept struck a chord and a British version seemed a logical next step.

Gladiators was based in the vast National Indoor Arena in Birmingham, and the sheer scale was one of the most obvious

hooks. There was a huge audience, massive props and tacky but undeniably exciting bursts of pop music after each challenge. The Gladiators meanwhile, were all given names like Wolf, Warrior and Saracen, and each had their own cartoonish personalities to remind the audience to boo and cheer at the relevant points.

Hosting proceedings were Ulrika Jonsson and footballer John Fashanu, neither of whom were the slickest presenters (though Fashanu somehow managed to make 'Awooga!' a catchphrase) but they did inject enough excitement to convince us that something thrilling was going on here. John Sachs provided bombastic commentary and John Anderson was the dour harsh-but-fair referee.

At first glance, the idea of members of the public bashing former PE teachers around the head with giant cotton buds seemed bizarre, but there was something in the show that undercut the brashness. *Gladiators* succeeded because it pitched at just the right level – enough of a raised eyebrow to show they knew much of it was ridiculous, but not so much that the competition became pointless. So while part of the fun came from Wolf being billed as some sort of super-human yet unable to hold on to a full head of hair, the programme always made sure they emphasised that what the contestants were going through was actually a tough physical challenge, and that winning actually meant something.

Certainly, it was hard to resist the lure of the travelator or pugel sticks, and who could fail to be hooked in by the sheer excitement of the whole thing? *Gladiators* worked as the perfect example of a particular kind of Saturday night television: that which you can settle down in front of after a hard day's shopping and let the whole thing wash over you. It wasn't going to win any awards but, over the beans on toast, who cared?

The show's success led to umpteen spin-offs. A number of international editions saw contestants and Gladiators from the UK version do battle against their counterparts from overseas, while one-off shows saw Wolf and the gang take on celebrities or members of the armed forces. There was even a kids' version, *Gladiators: Train 2 Win*, playing up to its undoubted popularity among younger audiences – though this was a rather worthy effort with the emphasis, of course, on taking part rather than winning.

Meanwhile, the weekly series continued, adding new Gladiators and games each year, while John Fashanu was replaced by former rugby player Jeremy Guscott in 1997. Occasionally there was the odd bit of controversy, most notably when Gladiator Shadow was dismissed over drug use, but for the rest of the time the series didn't really have much to do with anything in real life and continued on its own merry way.

By the end of the Nineties ratings had dropped, and a four-part *Final Battle* rounded the whole thing off over Christmas 1999. Yet ITV seemed determined to replace it with a virtually identical show. The first, and most disastrous, attempt was **Ice Warriors**, a look-alike which, crucially, abandoned all the humour. A follow-up show from the old *Gladiators* production team, *Grudge Match*, went too far in the opposite direction. This took members of the public who had fallen out with each other and encouraged them to settle their differences via some *Gladiators*-style challenges, thus adding some light entertainment-style personality to proceedings, but the concept of warring neighbours having a fight to decide who should trim a hedge was just too daft to convince.

This shouldn't take anything away from the success of the original *Gladiators*. Sure, it wasn't the most cerebral of shows, but waving those oversized, pointy foam fingers in the air sure was a great way to spend a Saturday evening.

Hammer House of Horror

Cinema Arts International/Hammer Films/
ITC Entertainment for ITV

13 September 1980 to 6 December 1980 (13 episodes)

Although by 1980 Hammer may have been a fading force in the film industry, the notion of a mini-Hammer film playing out each Saturday night was still attractive to the audience at large, particularly as viewers pretty much knew what to expect before tuning in – horror stories served up with a twist in the tale.

Each episode of this anthology series would begin with a pre-title teaser, usually consisting of a point-of-view shot of that week's baddy breathing in a loud and malevolent way, while stalking some poor unsuspecting victim. After a freeze frame of said victim in mid-scream, we would then fade to the programme's evocative title of a spooky-looking house filmed at nightfall. Over this would play a tune that married a ponderously simple descending guitar line to a nicely chilling backdrop of lush orchestral music. Then in red text, as big as you like, would come the series title, before finally we were introduced to the name of that week's episode. If it was something exciting like 'The House That Bled To Death' or 'The Mark of Satan' then you knew you were in for a treat, just so long as you could persuade Mum that the mild but gratuitous nudity that popped up Most weeks wasn't sufficient reason to switch the telly off.

The first story, 'Witching Time', established the template that *Hammer House of Horror* would adhere to. Most of it was shot in and around the Great Hampden, Buckinghamshire area (that just so happened to house Hammer's headquarters), which meant that all the scenes of malevolence were played out in front of a very green and pleasant backdrop. The story itself featured Patricia Quinn as a witch who took a shine to trendy movie soundtrack composer David Winter (Jon Finch). As the episode unfolds, the witch attempts to destroy both Winter and his wife (played by Prunella Gee) and with the inclusion of a bit of cod-psychology, some blood and violence and extra-marital shenanigans we finally get to a quite silly finale which hinges around the line 'Water, so that's what you can't take – I should have known'.

Later episodes featured a number of similarly bizarre and equally poorly thought-out plotlines, including one in which Denholm Elliot turned up as Norman, an adulterous estate agent who seems to be caught in a recurring nightmare involving a strange house that contains an animated suit of armour and a dumb waiter that proclaims, 'You shouldn't have done it, Norman. You shouldn't have killed your wife.' The episode lumbers on in an utterly baffling manner, until Norman finally takes the hint and kills his wife, only to discover to his horror that he is no longer living in a dream and has unwittingly committed a murder in the real world.

The series performed reasonably well (peaking at 14 million viewers for 'Guardian of the Abyss') and a follow-up under the banner of *Hammer House of Mystery and Suspense* served up thirteen more chilling stories. But by then *Tales of the Unexpected* had well and truly exerted its pre-eminence as ITV viewer's twist-in-the-tale anthology of choice.

The Harry Secombe Show

BBC1

25 December 1968 to 29 December 1973 (31 episodes)

Harry Secombe is dressed as a policeman, and is directing traffic. His hands are waving in all directions and unsurprisingly bedlam breaks out on this particular stretch of the Queen's highway. Having caused a few motor vehicles to crash, Secombe removes the policeman's helmet and adorns a flat cap and scarf, before walking away from the scene with a giant smirk plastered across his chops.

This comedy quickie is typical of both *The Harry Secombe Show* and the wider comic output of the eponymous entertainer. But for a generation Harry Secombe's TV work conjures up images of straight-laced religious broadcasting. Secombe may have spent a decade visiting churches up and down the country on the Sunday teatime institution *Highway*, but this was only one part of a television life that spanned nearly fifty years.

Secombe's TV career harks back to the very early days of broadcasting – in fact, he was the first person ever to have a weekly show on ITV. However we're most interested in the series that ran on Saturday nights in the late Sixties and early Seventies.

Secombe possessed a versatility that made him the ideal host of a Saturday night variety series. He could tell a joke with the best of them, and his *Goons* training provided him with a thorough grounding in silly voices. But he was also an accomplished singer, and exercised this talent on numerous occasions – most obviously in the programme from April 1969 featuring the cast of *Oliver!*, including Lionel Bart and Ron Moody, performing numbers from the show.

Julian Orchard was Harry's sidekick throughout, and the likes of Dick Emery, Ronnie Barker, Arthur Lowe, Beryl Reid and, inevitably, Spike Milligan all put in an appearance. Although unremarkable, *The Harry Secombe Show* was swift and entertaining. Sketches were usually built round the silliest and slightest of premises (such as the routine in which Barker and Secombe play two men in a gentlemen's club who discover they each have ridiculous names), while the songs never strayed far from well-loved family favourites such as 'Bridge over Troubled Water' and 'On the Street Where You Live'. All in all, it was good, honest and inoffensive fare (albeit one episode did feature a sketch in which Dick Emery played a prostitute trying to drum up business, while one musical number saw Sheila O'Neill similarly dressed as a 'lady of the night').

After the series came to an end in 1973, Secombe starred in a number of other vehicles, including *Sing a Song of Secombe* for the BBC and *Secombe with Music* for ITV. Later telly work, however, was very much God-related, including that marathon Sunday afternoon stint, after which the Goon retired from our screens.

I Love the Seventies

BBC2

22 July 2000 to 23 September 2000 (10 episodes)

In the Seventies, any kid who ended up watching *The Generation Game* or *The Duchess of Duke Street* would be doing so under duress, annoyed they weren't allowed to go out with their friends instead. Twenty-five years on, exactly the same situation was no doubt taking place in homes, with exactly the same programmes – thanks to the rise of nostalgia television.

It seems bizarre that, with the oncoming of video, DVD and satellite TV enabling you to watch your favourite old shows more or less whenever you want, archive TV has only really flourished in the last few years.

Yet we can perhaps assign the start of the archive boom to Channel Four's *Top Ten*, a series that celebrated numerous musical genres via classic clips and interviews. Its warmly nostalgic tone made it a much-loved treat, but its success was undoubtedly down to being scheduled on Saturday nights. Those who had grown up with disco, punk or new romantic music were now likely to have kids of their own and hence be in the house on Saturday, nursing a mild yearning for their young-free-and-single days. *Top Ten* was a perfect way to revisit those glory years and was unsurprisingly lapped up by a receptive audience. Such was the series' success other broadcasters took to rummaging through their own archives in order to try and come up with something equally nostalgia-inducing.

I Love the Seventies was perhaps the most ambitious series yet, consisting of ten evenings of programmes, each devoted to a different year of the so-called 'decade that style forgot'. The centrepiece of each evening was an hour-long documentary where a star whose career peaked in the year in question (Britt Ekland in 1971, Roobarb and Custard in 1974) introduced items on the culture and crazes that had dominated the period. It made for enjoyable viewing – as well as a cheap way for the BBC to fill the schedules at the height of summer.

The Saturday night slot meant the emphasis here was very much on entertainment; this was the weekend, dammit, and a time to laugh at what we used to get up to. The likes of Stuart Maconie, Peter Kay and Johnny Vegas were regular contributors, passing on their anecdotes of a Seventies childhood, with the emphasis being as much on comedy as it was on analysing how we used to live.

The success of the series inevitably led to *I Love the Eighties* and *I Love the Nineties*. While the first was just as enjoyable, the latter series suffered from being broadcast at a time when there was simply too much nostalgia on telly. Inviting viewers to get nostalgic over 1999 less than two years after it had finished seemed a little pointless. Whatever the subject, though, the ability to find that evocative advert or TV clip made *I Love*, for the most part, hugely enjoyable telly. It proved that, yes, they don't make them like that anymore – in fact, sometimes they can do it rather better.

Ice Warriors

LWT/Julian Grant for ITV

24 January 1998 to 21 March 1998 (9 episodes)

Come 1998, *Gladiators* had been a hit for several years, but there were signs that the concept was running out of steam a bit. As such, ITV's big idea was to take its best bits – the goodies versus baddies, the over-the-top arena setting, the fantastical aspects – and apply them to a new show. This was *Ice Warriors*. A particularly ambitious commission, rumours had it that when one ITV executive first saw the giant ice rink set up at Manchester's Nynex Arena, he announced, 'This looks like a million dollars!', only to be informed that it had actually cost rather more than that.

The concept of *Ice Warriors* saw two towns battling it out against, not just each other, but the titular Warriors themselves. These Gladiators-by-another-name had silly monikers like Rax the Destroyer and Sharak the Avenger, while overseeing events was the Ice Warrior, who sat in a throne in the middle of the ice and exclaimed such things as, 'I award the city state of Milton Keynes one hundred credits!' The host of the show was Dani Behr, who had apparently lied about her skating prowess to get the gig. While it may have sounded pretty ridiculous, the faux-sporting antics of *Gladiators* had proven to be a smash hit, and there was no reason to suggest *Ice Warriors* wouldn't do the same.

Soon, though, it became apparent this wouldn't happen. The most obvious problem was an almost complete absence of humour. On *Gladiators*, the fact that Wolf was clearly a balding, ageing ex-PE teacher was all part of the fun, and if it sometimes appeared more like pantomime than a serious sporting contest, then that was all right too. On *Ice Warriors*, events were meant to be taken completely seriously, but it was impossible to listen to the Ice Master's references to 'the Island of Wight' with a straight face. Short-arse sidekick Schnapps was meant to provide the comic relief, running about and falling over, but just irritated the audience in a Jar Jar Binks fashion. Meanwhile, Dani Behr's contribution didn't really help, given all she did was repeat, word for word, the same lines every week ('While *Ice Warriors* is a fantasy world, the prizes are very real').

A basic lack of personality also hampered the series. The Warriors, despite their exciting names, were all very much interchangeable. The same could also be said of the teams of contestants. Unfortunately the show lacked the one-on-one aspect that had made *Gladiators* such a hit. Here there were too many people to get to know, and in the end viewers simply didn't care who won.

Yet these were problems that could have been ironed out given time. There was a more fundamental reason for *Ice Warriors*' failings – that being, you simply can't do very much on ice. Sure, you can skate around it really fast, and they could put obstacles in the way to slow you down, but there wasn't enough to justify an hour-long programme. In the end, all we got was a bunch of anonymous contestants being chased around the rink by a bunch of anonymous warriors, over and over again.

As the run progressed, *Ice Warriors* found itself moving earlier and earlier in the evening, eventually ending up in mid-afternoon. It was suggested that a second series might follow but in a reworked Saturday morning format (kids were the only demographic that seemed to consistently enjoy the show). This never came to pass, and the 1998 tournament proved to be *Ice Warriors'* only appearance on our screens.

It'll Be Alright on the Night
LWT for ITV/C4

18 September 1977 to 18 March 2006 (30 episodes)

A rather wizened-looking fellow holding a clipboard and standing around on a barely dressed set introducing the off-cuts from other television programmes might not sound like a great proposition, but *It'll Be Alright on the Night* was one of the most consistently popular British television programmes ever made. Helmed by Denis Norden (although entertainer Roy Castle was initially considered as host), these occasional compilations of 'cock-ups' (Norden's favourite phrase there) marked the first time that out-takes were considered of sufficient entertainment value to merit a show of their own.

Such was the programme's immediate popularity that, as Norden once memorably pointed out, 'if an actor makes a mistake and it gets into an out-take he will get paid wherever it is shown throughout the world. There can be repeat fees. With the paradoxical result that he will get paid more for not doing it right than he would if he had done it right. In fact, it's like running a farm where the manure is worth more than the cattle.'

Early editions gave a significant boost to the careers of Ulsterman protester George Cunningham (who on the back of his appearance found himself much in demand at pubs and clubs) and Richard Whiteley, then best known as a regional news broadcaster. Whiteley's famed tussle with a ferret provoked such a response from viewers that in a later interview Kenny Everett advised the *Countdown* host that he had 'always wanted to work with you – you're famous', and then bit the presenter's finger in an imitation of that notorious moment.

Recognising that the appeal of the show would soon wane if it was broadcast on a weekly basis, *It'll Be Alright on the Night* instead turned up as an occasional one-off. The third edition featured footage from America for the first time and these Stateside out-takes were particularly enjoyable thanks to the often hugely self-confident performances that preceded the blooper (including Christopher Plummer attempting to vouch for the enduring appeal of roulette while a ball pings off the roulette wheel and into the air). In 1985 Norden was given a partial respite from linking clips by comedian Rory Bremner who memorably delivered his links in the form of impersonations of famous people including, inevitably, Norden himself.

It has to be said that many viewers expressed irritation at having to sit through Norden's patter between clip packages (what do you want – Steve Penk?), but his role was important as it provided us with a chance to catch breath and recompose ourselves before the next batch of hilarious bloopers were unleashed. Anyway, after just a few years it became impossible to imagine anyone else popping up on screen straight after a clip of a dog dragging its arse down a hill (in an attempt to scratch an unreachable itch). Nonetheless it did become accepted practice when watching *It'll Be Alright on the Night* on video, to hit the fast-forward button every time the bespectacled presenter came into view.

The BBC, in the guise of Noel Edmonds, was quick to copy the idea for **The Late Late Breakfast Show**, using the conceit of awarding a 'Golden Egg' to the week's most entertaining bloopers. More substantially, the corporation later produced a long line of out-take programmes called *Auntie's Bloomers*. As with *It'll Be Alright on the Night*, these were only ever shown as specials, and a similarly mature presenter (Terry Wogan) was picked to link the footage. In fact that programme's title was actually thought up many years earlier by Denis Norden, when musing what he might call a BBC version of his ITV hit.

In recent years, *It'll Be Alright on the Night* became just one of several out-take programmes (including *TV's Naughtiest Blunders* and *Out-take TV*) and when in April 2006 Norden announced he was hanging up his clipboard for good, few really despaired that much. Still, while the competition might be able to serve up bloopers and blunders just as entertaining as those unearthed by Norden and his team, it was only ever *It'll Be Alright on the Night* that could boast a presenter willing and able to refer to 'the next VT package' as a 'cornucopia of cock-ups', and it was only Norden who could get away with prefacing a line of observational comedy with the phrase 'are you one of those people...'

It's Cliff Richard

BBC1

3 January 1970 to 28 September 1974 (46 episodes)

You'd had Lulu, you'd had Cilla, you'd had Dusty – you'd even had Kathy Kirby. Oddly, though, few male pop stars enjoyed their own Saturday night BBC1 series (and Rolf Harris and Val Doonican don't count as they come from a different musical direction altogether). Finally, in 1970, perhaps the iconic male solo artist of his generation had the honour of his own eponymous variety show.

By this point in his career, Cliff was well on his way from lively young pop star to national institution, so had no fears about selling out to the corporation. Joined by the Norrie Paramour Orchestra, and regular appearances by his mate Hank Marvin, the series was fairly indistinguishable from its Saturday night stablemates, although Cliff's 'in' into the pop world meant some notable names appeared – one of the few clips of Aretha Franklin in her prime that still exists in the BBC archives comes from Cliff's series.

The show also wasn't averse to giving the odd new act a break, and the 24 August 1974 edition is memorable for featuring what was billed as 'a TV debut for six sisters called "The Nolans"'. The Irish siblings went on to become something of a regular fixture on the last few editions. But that August show was also notable for being one of a few episodes that featured *Monty Python*'s Terry Jones and Michael Palin on scriptwriting duties.

A major part of *It's Cliff Richard* took the form of a search for the UK entry for *The Eurovision Song Contest*. Given Cliff's notorious failure to win the competion in 1968, it seemed like malice on the Beeb's part to foist this upon him; and not just once but three times, shepherding Mary Hopkin, Clodagh Rogers and The New Seekers on their way to the ever-popular pan-Europe croon-in. Fortunately for Cliff's ego, none of the three acts managed to go one better than him and actually win the thing, and presumably it inspired him enough to enter the contest once more in 1973 (and lose again).

Always relied upon to provide good clean entertainment for as wide an audience as possible, Cliff was a staple of Saturday evenings for four years, and when he called it a day, it seemed as if the whole concept of a singing star hosting their own show was coming to an end. Sadly, this meant we would never get to see 'The Johnny Rotten Variety Hour'.

Jim'll Fix It

BBC1

31 May 1975 to 24 July 1994 (287 episodes)

Anyone under the age of sixteen may well be baffled at the lengthy career of one of the most impersonated and most recognised TV stars in history. What is it that Jimmy Savile actually does? He doesn't tell jokes, he doesn't sing or dance, he doesn't act, he doesn't do impressions and he certainly isn't a slick TV host. Yet as well as enjoying twenty years as the leading face of *Top of the Pops* – despite having seemingly no interest in music – he also spent twenty years as a fixture of Saturday night TV on *Jim'll Fix It*.

The roots of *Jim'll Fix It* hark back to an earlier programme

Sir Jim fronted, *Clunk Click*, which owed its name to a series of public information films he was fronting at the time on the value of seatbelts. This was a mix of interviews and features – Jim claiming his dream guest for the show was Jesus – and such was Jim's personality that many of the items involved making dreams come true. One thing Jim could certainly do was persuade almost anyone to do virtually anything in the name of television. This bit was so popular it became a series of its own.

Although Jim was in charge in front of the camera, the main man behind the scenes was Roger Ordish, who produced every episode. It was Ordish who was responsible for choosing wishes from the sackloads of requests to make come true, relying on his maxim that the viewers at home should remark on how funny it was, how exciting it was, and how lucky the 'fixee' was. As children tended to come up with the most interesting requests and the best reactions, they appeared most of the time, though it was never officially a children's programme and there was almost always an adult winning a badge too.

As for Jimmy, unless it was specifically asked, he refused to take any part in the fixes themselves, as he felt it would detract attention away from the participant. Otherwise he simply showed up in the studio just before the recording and tried to get the petrified kids to say something during the post-fix interviews. Jim helped jolly things along with his whimsical approach, forever referring to the likes of 'Mr British Airways' pulling the strings, and Ordish himself as 'Doctor Magic'.

Jim'll Fix It's golden era was the early Eighties, when it was regularly at the top of the ratings and made numerous appearances on Christmas Day. By the early Nineties ratings were declining as the novelty wore off, though Jim said it was purely his decision to call it a day in 1994.

Since then, the concept of making dreams come true has been utilised a couple of times on Saturday nights, most obviously in *Whatever You Want*, which offered the chance to live out ambitions to the winners of various games and quizzes. With Gaby Roslin hosting, the show was rather cruelly referred to within the BBC as 'Dim'll Fix It'. Meanwhile, Sir Jim still continues to do, well, pretty much what he's always done – not much apart from smoke cigars and convince everyone to fix it for him to do whatever he wants. However, a long-overdue return to his famous Fix It seat in 2007 in the guise of *Jim'll Fix It: Now and Then* has been a timely reminder to those other would-be dream makers as to how fixing it is really done.

Johnny and Denise: Passport to Paradise

Celador/World's End for BBC1

3 July 2004 to 7 August 2004 (6 episodes)

Johnny Vaughan and Denise Van Outen were perhaps *the* TV double act of the late Nineties, with their quick wit and flirtatious banter managing to rescue *The Big Breakfast* from what looked like certain cancellation. Since their departure from that series in 2001, both had floundered somewhat. Van Outen's most notable telly work had been the depressing *Something for the Weekend*, the sub-*Word* late night Channel Four series. Vaughan, meanwhile, signed an exclusive deal with the BBC, the results of which had been a mediocre chat show and the critically slammed sitcom *'Orrible*. Teaming up again and replicating that *Big Breakfast* magic, therefore, was not only a way of brightening up BBC1's Saturday nights, but it also seemed to be an opportunity to get two careers back on track.

Passport to Paradise was a live mix of games and stunts with the climax being a quiz that would send one unsuspecting member of the audience on holiday to the titular paradise. Any similarity to **Ant and Dec's Saturday Night Takeaway** was, obviously, completely coincidental. Among the items were a look-alikes competition and a song from Denise where she was accompanied by the friends and relatives of a hapless member of the audience who would then be called on to identify these bit-part players.

Probably the best bit of *Passport to Paradise* came from the live link-ups to a public place, where viewers would be invited to phone up anyone who was present and get them to take part in a daft stunt to win a prize. Inevitably there would always be some hanging around while the duo waited for someone to join in, and the ad-libbing from Johnny and Denise was often particularly amusing.

Sadly, this sort of inspiration wasn't apparent in the rest of the show. It seemed as if the chemistry that came about during two hours of television a day was harder to come by in fifty minutes a week. It's also true to say that Johnny Vaughan was always something of an acquired taste and to package him as an all-round family entertainer seemed foolish.

After six weeks, *Passport to Paradise* came to an end and never returned. The items would probably have worked well enough on *Takeaway*, but with a tiny studio set and subdued audience, it came across as a sort of own-brand version of Ant and Dec's ratings juggernaut.

Jonathan Creek

BBC1

10 May 1997 to 28 February 2004 (25 episodes)

For those who didn't get it, *Jonathan Creek* was bafflingly silly. It looked like a serious crime drama, but the dialogue often resembled sub-Edgar Allen Poe witterings; the characterisation was, on occasion, totally hackneyed; and the investigations capricious in the extreme. Happily though, most people did 'get it', and recognised that this was a series that was meant to be watched as if you were (in the words of its creator David Renwick) 'snuggling up with a nice cryptic crossword'.

Each episode contained a familiar and reassuring framework; the intriguing impossible mystery and the comical B-story that bore only the slightest relation to the main plotline. The former was played out before the latter (which finished up every episode) and both ended with a twist in the tale. Although usually dealing with pretty grim subject matter (generally there would be a dead body or two per episode), humour was expertly used to set even the most baroque and macabre of storylines into some relief. All in all, as a template for a popular entertainment drama it was almost unsurpassable: it had a wonderful familiarity, sharp comedy, and a satisfying pay-off at the end of each episode.

Aside from the obvious strengths in its writing (David Renwick penned each and every adventure), *Jonathan Creek* also benefited from an excellent cast. Alan Davies's performance as the eponymous deviser of magic tricks turned detective struck the right balance between charisma and gawkiness, while his two assistants, Maddy Magellan (played by Caroline Quentin) and Carla Borrego (Julia Sawalha) were both pleasingly unpleasant without ever becoming downright loathsome (although Maddy came pretty close when she denied Jonathan the chance of finding true love at the end of 'Black Canary', the 1998 Christmas special).

Over the course of its twenty-five episodes, *Jonathan Creek* presented the viewer with a plethora of proper brainteasers. In terms of an out-and-out mystery, perhaps the best story was 'The Unreconstituted Corpse'. Not only was the puzzle itself highly ingenuous, but the introduction of an unrelated love interest subplot for Maddie cleverly wrong-footed the viewer into mistakenly believing that Maddy's lanky would-be suitor (Nigel Planer) was the mysterious tall observer intent on spying upon the ageing model at the centre of the main story. The trick here was to play upon the audience's preconception of TV murder mysteries, to whit: characters that at first appear unconnected and extraneous to the main story always turn out to be central to the resolution of the case – particularly if said character is played by a well-known actor.

Unfortunately, not all stories were as tight, and denouements that relied on, for example, the realisation that one of the characters was actually a bastard offspring of the monarchy (which happened in 'The Curious Tale of Mr Spearfish' – sorry if we've just ruined that episode for those readers yet to watch it) were a bit of a cheat. Given the appeal of *Jonathan Creek* was to show how a seemingly impossible feat could be achieved by a mundane, albeit complicated chain of events, episodes in which the impossible was instead shown to be the highly unlikely were a bit of a let-down.

Still, on the odd occasion when the plot wasn't quite up to scratch, the dialogue was always great. Be it insults ('Creek? As in "old and rusty or feeble little stream"?'), the set-up of that episode's mystery ('Shot through the heart in an empty room right under everyone's nose…somehow the murderer fired a bullet through a sheet of glass without breaking it') or, best of all, that one moment when a character walked into a scene with a wet patch on their trousers and made the wonderfully unselfconscious remark, 'Fortunately it's not urine so it won't stain.'

Juke Box Jury
BBC/BBC1/BBC2

1 June 1959 to 25 November 1990 (461 episodes)

One of the most untelevisual television programmes ever, *Juke Box Jury* was a staple of Saturday nights for nearly a decade, and enjoyed two subsequent revivals.

The premise was simple enough: a panel of four listened to some of the latest releases and offered their comments, suggesting whether they would be a 'hit' or a 'miss'. David Jacobs was in the chair throughout the original run, while almost anyone who was famous in the Sixties took a turn in the pundits' seats – appearances from The Beatles and The Rolling Stones were big news at the time.

In the pre-video days, there was obviously a requirement for

something to show while the records were playing, hence the cameras scooted around the audience to get an idea from the grins or grimaces as to their opinions. As it was teatime, the discussions were kept light, everything from Pinky and Perky to Joe 'Mr Piano' Henderson rarely getting anything more scathing than a 'Not my cup of tea, I'm afraid' – especially as there was a chance the artists would be lurking backstage, ready to surprise the panel.

After eight years, new ways of presenting pop on television, most obviously *Top of the Pops*, superseded the humble *Jury* and the show was cancelled. Such was its legacy, though, that in 1979 *Juke Box Jury* returned to Saturday evenings, with Noel Edmonds now in the chair. The new version kept many of the concepts from the original run intact – the shots of the audience, the mystery guests and the bizarre mix of panellists, from Tina Charles and Sting to Lesley Judd and Joan Collins.

The revival, however, is perhaps best remembered for the appearance of John Lydon, who managed to get into a slanging match with Alan Freeman by – gasp! – offering a critical comment. After referring to the comedy pretend-punk band Monks (performing 'I Ain't Getting Any') as, correctly, 'patronising rubbish', Freeman managed to patronise Rotten himself by requesting he 'Shut up, will you?', leading Lydon to leg it mid-show, to much uproar. Other than that, sparks failed to fly in much the same way as a decade previously and this most sedate of pop shows was dropped after one series.

The final revival, for now, came about in 1989 when Jools Holland resurrected the series for Sunday teatime BBC2. At least the rise of pop videos meant we no longer had to watch the studio audience sitting there like lemons. However only a slating of Glenn Madeiros by a panel who then had to meet him, leading the Hawaiian pop star to flee the set in tears, fire all his PR staff and cancel all future British TV appearances, lingers in the mind.

Juliet Bravo

BBC1

30 August 1980 to 21 December 1985 (88 episodes)

Juliet Bravo was in many ways the last of a dying breed of BBC 'cop shows with a conscience' that stretched back to **Dixon of Dock Green** and *Fabian of the Yard*. While ITV's *The Gentle Touch* took a vaguely sensationalist, hard-nosed look at crime through the eyes of a female copper operating in Soho, *Juliet Bravo* adopted a more sedentary pace. Yet, in their way, both series reflected the big issue of the day – unemployment. 'Baddies and goodies have gone,' explained Stephanie Turner (who played the programme's lead character – Inspector Jean Darblay). 'We have people with difficulties. For example, there's a strong emphasis on unemployment and the way poverty causes crime.'

    Juliet Bravo had a lot to say about contemporary society: 'The whole damn world's full of greed and corruption,' complained one would-be miscreant in an episode from the third series, later adding, 'You're chivvied and harried by so many tinpot officials. They turn people into criminals.' Rather wearingly, it wasn't just the criminals who would harp on about the decline of moral standards: the show's central triumvirate of Darblay, Sergeant Joseph Beck (David Ellison) and Sergeant George Parrish (Noel Collins) were happy to while away the time at the front desk of Hartley nick swapping comments such as 'What's the matter with the parents, I'd like to know. Don't they teach them any kind of decency these days?'

Although Stephanie Turner would claim that within the programme's first thirty episodes guns only featured twice, *Juliet Bravo* was able to weave a number of controversial plots into its usual mix of family-friendly storylines. In one episode, a woman who reported having been raped by a local ruffian (who we knew to be a baddie due to his penchant for drinking lager straight out of a can while sporting a sleeveless T-shirt) was asked point-blank by DCI Jim Logan (Tony Caunter) whether she thought the fact she wasn't wearing a bra might have provoked the attack.

After three years Stephanie Turner left and her character was replaced by the equally capable and ambitious Inspector Kate Longton (Anna Carteret). Surprisingly the replacement of the series' lead character didn't seem to have any detrimental effect on the programme's popularity and the formula remained much the same, only with Edward Peel (as DCI Mark Perrin) now adopting the Tony Caunter role of confidant and agitator to the series' central character. *Juliet Bravo* eventually came to an end in 1985 with, neatly, actress Anna Carteret having notched up forty-four episodes – exactly the same number as her predecessor.

Just Amazing!

Yorkshire Television Productions for ITV

4 June 1983 to 16 June 1984 (16 episodes)

With **Game for a Laugh** establishing itself as a major Saturday night series, it was little surprise that other programmes tried to recreate its winning formula. *Just Amazing!* (that explanation mark was optional it seems) was built very much in the *Game for a Laugh* mould and was presumably designed to get the viewer through those long summer breaks between bouts of Beadle.

The presenting trio of Barry Sheene, Jan Ravens (who was replaced in the second series by Suzanne Danielle) and Kenny Lynch presided over a pot pourri of studio and filmed items, all of which featured members of the public performing feats that were designed to provoke the viewing public into uttering, 'Just amazing!' The first show featured Stevie Starr (a regurgitator), Conrad Homer (a skydiver who filmed his own descent in which his parachute failed), Dr Arthur Lintgen (a man who could tell what was on a record by just looking at its grooves) and Hazel the Surfing Rabbit.

Unlike *Game for a Laugh* there was a lack of chemistry between the three presenters (not helped by Barry Sheene's extremely wooden presenting style) and the various joshing and leg-pulling that viewers had grown to expect from such programmes felt forced and contrived. Even worse, the patter was deeply unfunny ('I thought he was Finnish not Dutch'/'He will be finished if he fails to get this one right').

The series' credentials as a bona fide major Saturday night show were further undermined by its reliance on imported, or ancient, footage, such as the 1912 film featuring a man plummeting to his death from the top of the Eiffel Tower. It didn't help that each film was accompanied by a deathly dull voice-over complete with sound of bored members of the studio audience attempting to stifle a cough. That is not to say the programme didn't provide some memorable moments: the more idiosyncratic feats such as Creighton Carvello committing to memory 'the most boring book in the world' and Michel Lotito eating a Cessna light aircraft couldn't fail to grab the viewer's attention.

After just two series, *Just Amazing!* was no more. However, the notion of stunts on Saturday nights proved to be enduring, with shows such as **You Bet!** and *Don't Try This at Home* picking up the baton and providing a television home for people with odd and often mind-numbingly trivial skills for the next decade or so.

Kate and Ted's Show

Granada for ITV

4 July 1987 to 27 August 1988 (13 episodes)

'The biggest joke about ITV's comedy is that there isn't any,' claimed outgoing ITV Director of Programmes Nigel Pickard in 2005. This wasn't always the case, however, and in the Eighties you could be certain of seeing as much family-friendly comedy on Saturday night ITV as you would on the BBC. Never was this so apparent than on the evening of Saturday 4 July 1987, when the ITV schedules consisted of Gary Wilmot's gentle comedy show *Cue Gary!*, the gentle comedy sketch troupe *Five Alive* (who counted among their number Brian Conley), **Summertime Special**, featuring the gentle comedy of, er, Gary Wilmot and Brian Conley, and the gentle comedy of *Kate and Ted's Show*.

Kate and Ted were members of the Scouse showbiz dynasty, the Robbins family. The sister and brother duo had both established TV careers of their own, with Kate starring in *Crossroads* in the early Eighties and Ted co-hosting the forgettable **Game for a Laugh**-style series *Some You Win*. Then, alongside sisters Amy, Emma and Jane, they'd all appeared in one-off Granada special *Robbins*. The five siblings were adept stage performers, but Kate and Ted were the two whose talents lent themselves more towards comedy and were therefore awarded their own television series.

As one of the few brother–sister double acts, there was something of a unique selling point about Kate and Ted, but this was about as thrilling as *Kate and Ted's Show* got – it was a series that was about as imaginative as its title. Soap parodies, quickies and comedy songs abounded that could easily have appeared on any similar show – especially those it was surrounded by on Saturday evening ITV at the time. Perhaps the most notable aspect of the series was how it illustrated internal ITV politics; it was broadcast before *Five Alive* in every region apart from Granada, who swapped the two around so their own show got the slightly more prestigious slot a little further into peak-time

Despite the unexceptional nature of the pair's efforts, Kate and Ted returned for another series the following year. Unfortunately for Ted though, the show's title was truncated to simply *The Kate Robbins Show*, with Ted humiliatingly demoted to a supporting role. After their moment in the sun, Kate and Ted continued to work in comedy, with Kate a prolific voice-over artist, while Ted, thanks to his appearances in *Phoenix Nights* and *Little Britain*, no longer had to play second fiddle to his sister.

The Ken Dodd Show

BBC1

25 July 1959 to 21 June 1969 (35 episodes)

Ken Dodd is certainly one of Britain's most famous comedians, but strangely he has never enjoyed great success on television. It seems that Doddy's ideal home is the theatre stage. Perhaps his problem with television is that whereas most other comedians pick the material they think will be best for a specific show, Doddy always does all the material he's ever performed, ensuring his live shows tend to last around five or six hours.

Indeed, despite still tirelessly working the nation's theatres, his most prolific spell on television came early in his career, as *The Ken Dodd Show* ran throughout the Sixties. Each episode would come from a different theatre and consist of variety acts, sketches and some relentless gaggery from Ken, with his Diddymen puppets acting as stooges on numerous occasions.

Perhaps the most notable edition came in July 1966 when Wilfrid Brambell and Harry H Corbett appeared in a specially written *Steptoe and Son* sketch – at the time a real coup for the show. But most of the stars of Sixties comedy and music appeared at some point during the run.

Ken's co-writer for much of the series was Eddie Braben, at the time a bin man eager to get involved in comedy. Braben found Doddy's work a good training ground, as the high-speed delivery demanded more jokes per minute than anyone else. Indeed this was enough to convince Morecambe and

Wise to take him on as their scriptwriter when they moved to the BBC.

After *The Ken Dodd Show* came to an end as a regular series, Doddy appeared in numerous shows for both the BBC and ITV alongside his many stage appearances. It wasn't until 1982 that he returned to Saturday evenings in a new series, *Ken Dodd's Showbiz* on BBC1. Here Doddy was allowed to indulge his passion for the theory of comedy, welcoming guest stars from around the world. However it only ran for one series. Since then, besides two memorable appearances on **An Audience With**..., Doddy has concentrated on live work, and is probably still telling jokes as you read this. Even if it's four in the morning.

The Late Late Breakfast Show
BBC1

4 September 1982 to 8 November 1986 (79 episodes)

Noel Edmonds and Saturday night television are inextricably linked, and it all starts here. A bit like a BBC version of *Game for a Laugh*, only broadcast live and not quite as glitzy, *The Late Late Breakfast* also drew inspiration from the BBC's own popular Sixties chat show *Dee Time* (Noel was often referred internally at the Beeb as the 'new Simon Dee'). In addition to Noel, the first incarnation of *The Late Late Breakfast Show* featured John Peel (who seemed to spend most of his time looking sheepish perched at the end of a bar), and comedienne Leni Harper. With the promise of pop stars, interviews, stunts, celebrity bloopers and hidden-camera antics, this new series might have sounded like the place to be on Saturday nights, but for its first few years at least, that was far from the truth. Interviews with celebrity guests went on far too long, and Noel was too blatant in acceding to his interviewee's desire to plug their latest product ('It's a great book. Is it now available?').

The show also suffered from the amount of time it took to set anything up. The Whirly Wheel challenges, which featured members of the public participating in daring stunts, were supposed to be a high point but the build-up dragged on and on before anything exciting ever actually happened. To make matters worse, Noel would then spend ages cueing up the following week's challenge. The rest of the programme was given over to lacklustre pop performances of the ilk of Ryan Paris' 'Dolce Vita', plus the show's 'bloopers' strand – The Golden Egg awards ('it just might make you smile'), a dreary chat with someone of the calibre of the Bee Gees, and a couple of hidden-camera stunts screened under the banner 'The Hit Squad'.

Edmonds would later claim that the original *Late Late Breakfast Show* lacked confidence, and this was reflected in audience figures that dropped as low as 4 million. Rather than abandon the series, though, the BBC slung Harper and Peel out, and nixed the musical acts and dull interviews. Even the look of the show got an overhaul and the split-screen titles showing Noel doing lots of exciting things was replaced by an opening featuring a helicopter flying over a breakfast table. Meanwhile, the hideous set with horrible pink sofas was shipped out in favour of a set that had loads of superfluous steps.

Not that everything was discarded. The pun-laden viewer correspondence items remained, and on each episode Noel would run through the 'Stars of the Week' allowing him to sift through amusing news footage and poke fun at photographs and stories sent in by viewers. The Whirly Wheel stunt also remained, but it received a revamp at the hands of fellow Radio 1 DJ Mike Smith. 'Smitty' (as Noel referred to him) joined the series in 1984, and his arrival marked the moment at which the show got its act together. Now the various exchanges between Noel and the Outside Broadcast location for that week's Whirly Wheel stunt became a high point with the two presenters adopting a kind of elder and younger brother relationship. Noel would routinely complain 'oh get on with it, will you' while Smith would make regular cracks at Noel's sartorial elegance – or lack of ('we've tried to get as far away from your jumper as possible').

The Late Late Breakfast Show had found its confidence and was attracting massive audiences (reaching as many as 16.8 million viewers). It didn't even seem to matter when items went awry: Noel believed that you could make other programmes on telly look ten per cent less good simply by broadcasting your show live, and he realised that when items went wrong the audiences just loved the programme even more.

Such was the popularity of the series that *The Late Late Breakfast Show* not only defined BBC1's Saturday nights through the winter ('Oh gawd, it's you, it must be winter again!'), it also shaped the channel's Christmas Day running order too. Barely any expense was spared for these ninety-minute Yuletide extravaganzas as Noel broadcast the whole show from London's Telecom Tower, while Smitty, and the show's 'hollycopter' toured the length and breadth of the country threatening to gatecrash viewers' festivities. The Christmas specials also featured some notable firsts with live pictures beamed in from such faraway places as the Falkland Islands and Sudan (during which the charity Comic Relief was officially launched). Sadly, only two of Noel's Christmas shows would be broadcast under the *Late Late Breakfast Show* banner, with his Yuletide extravaganza in 1986 re-badged *Christmas Morning with Noel*.

That 1986 rebranding exercise came about due to a tragic accident that befell a Whirly Wheel contestant in November.

Michael Lush, picked out the previous week by the spin of the wheel, died while rehearsing a stunt in which he was to fall from an exploding crate. In January 1987, an inquest jury unanimously recorded a verdict of death by misadventure. Clearly, there was no way that *The Late Late Breakfast Show* could continue. Although Noel would receive offers to take over the popular series *This Is Your Life*, as well as host a pilot edition of a revived *The Generation Game*, it would take two years before he was ready to return to Saturday night television.

The Laughter Show
BBC1

7 April 1984 to 23 March 1985 (17 episodes)

The type of programme your gran would sit you down in front of as a supposed treat, ex-**Russ Abbot's Madhouse** inmates Dustin Gee and Les Dennis presided over a mixture of quick fire sketches and the odd musical number. In fact, it could be said that *The Laughter Show* was really just *Madhouse* minus most of the cast and all of the anarchy.

The first edition was originally scheduled for transmission on 3 March, but eventually made it to our screens five weeks later. In it Gee and Dennis were joined by future comedy stars Hale and Pace and the disturbing Roy Jay, described in the press as the 'Slither Hither, Spook Spook Man'. The music came from David Essex, and helping out with additional comedy business was David Copperfield, presumably kicking his heels since the demise of his own Saturday night comedy show, **Three of a Kind**. All things considered this was a pretty uninspiring line-up which was performed in front of sets that, due to a BBC strike, were used in six or seven other variety shows that year, including (according to Les Dennis) *The Eurovision Song Contest*.

Gee and Dennis' stock-in-trade were rather weak impersonations, and although Gee described Dennis as 'the best voice-impressionist in the country', in truth Les's Leonard Rossiter, Larry Grayson and Cilla Black were all broad-brush jobs that didn't really suggest any great powers of mimicry.

Undoubtedly the high point of the twosome's act was their take on the popular *Coronation Street* characters Vera Duckworth and Mavis Riley. These routines came about as a result of a sketch on *Russ Abbot's Madhouse* in which the eponymous host invited the studio audience to shout out which impressions they would like to see, and upon someone yelling *'Coronation Street'*, Dennis and Gee spontaneously adopted their respective personas. That first improvised run-through contained all of the lines they would later use in their endless scripted sketches (namely, 'Are you all right, kid?' and 'I don't really know').

By the third series, *The Laughter Show* was renamed *Les and Dustin's Laughter Show* in recognition of the duo's popularity; and their by now trademark end-of-show wrap-up (where they 'would like to say "goodnight" to each and everyone of you: "goodnight, goodnight, goodnight…"' accompanied by some dodgy special effects creating loads of Les and Dustins) had become as familiar as Cannon and Ball's 'Together, We'll Be OK'. In January 1986 tragedy struck, when after just one episode of the third series had been shown, Gee suffered a fatal heart attack. After a two-week break, the BBC recommenced the screening of the final series of *Les and Dustin's Laughter Show,* and 18 months later Dennis returned with *The Les Dennis Laughter Show.*

Given his success as solo comic and, later, game show host, coupled with the fact that his partnership with Dustin Gee lasted only three or so years, it's surprising that today Les Dennis is still so closely associated with his late comedy partner. Perhaps their work together, and in particular those aforementioned *Coronation Street* spoofs, hold strong memories for an entire generation – even if it is just of miserable Saturday evenings spent round your gran's house.

The Little and Large Show
BBC1

1 May 1978 to 20 April 1991 (76 episodes)

Without wishing to be too hard on Syd Little and Eddie Large, it's probably fair to say that their television career owes an awful lot to being in the right place at the right time. Ten years earlier the duo would have palled in comparison to the likes of Morecambe and Wise and ten years later their comedy would appear outdated in the extreme. Yes, for a run-of-the-mill, middle-of-the-road novelty double act looking for a career in television, the Eighties were the perfect decade.

Not that success came easily to the duo; they first met in 1964 and paid their dues working at Bernard Manning's World Famous Embassy Club and appearing on telly shows such as *Opportunity Knocks* (which they won with a

Photonews Scotland/ Rex Features

creditable score of seventy-seven), *Crackerjack* and *Three in a Bed*. They finally got their own ITV television series, *The Little and Large Tellyshow*, in 1977 only to hot-foot it to the BBC the following year.

Although far from groundbreaking or even original, Little and Large's comedy stylings were bafflingly popular, with their 1980 series actually ending up as one of the twenty most watched programmes of the year. Their appeal was due to the fact that they came across as nothing more or less than two daft but amiable blokes. Certainly, neither betrayed any hint of ego, and week in, week out they would kit themselves out in costumes that made them look totally ridiculous and (usually) deeply unattractive. Syd dressing up as a chicken feels like it must have been a regular occurrence, and Eddie's occasional forays into the realms of cross-dressing (including the time a slow lingering camera shot panned from Eddie's feet all the way up his torso to reveal a very burlesque imitation of Tina Turner) used the comedian's own physical inadequacies as a means to provoke laughter.

Little and Large were also quick off the mark when it came to identifying new targets to lampoon, and one of their most memorable sketches was the parody of the 1978 movie *Grease*. Apparently the boys were keen to work up something based on the film before their comedy competitors could get a look in. Their spoof of the track 'Summer Nights' in their 1978 Christmas special was both topical and entertaining and represented the high water mark of the duo's act.

Not that everything was plain sailing. In an era in which children's programmes such as *Grange Hill* were allowed to discuss issues such as contraceptives and drug abuse, the most innocuous Little and Large gags could provoke controversy. One sketch in which kind-hearted Syd bought ice creams from a seller (Eddie), for five children only to then discover that the seller was the kids' dad provoked irate letters to the BBC television show *Points of View*. Similarly, a sketch shown on the Saturday morning children's show *Saturday Superstore*, in which Eddie put a hot water bottle into a microwave, resulted in so many angry phone calls that the duo were obliged to appear later on in the show to warn of the dangers of putting unsuitable objects inside cooking equipment.

When not struggling with censorship, Eddie and Syd found themselves fighting with the BBC itself. On a number of occasions plans were made to scrap their show only for the decision to be overturned at the last minute. It is said that in 1989 the BBC's light entertainment department had finally pulled the plug, only for senior management to insist on its reinstatement thanks to high ratings. In 1990, the BBC went so far as to publicly announce they had cancelled the series, only for it to once again turn up the following year.

Indisputably, by the turn of the decade, *The Little and Large Show* was looking long in the tooth. In 1987, the duo had attempted to broaden their appeal by increasing their range of comedy characters, but by then the show had become a watchword for poor-quality comedy. Newspaper critic Nina Myskow famously laid into it without even watching an episode, and Syd himself recalls switching on rival comedians' shows only to be greeted by lines such as 'I'll make you watch Little and Large if you don't behave!'

By 1991 the game was well and truly up. Little and Large conceded that the quality of the scripts had deteriorated, and there was a realisation that finally this novelty double act's novelty value had well and truly worn off. With no repeats or commercial video releases forthcoming, Little and Large's contribution to British comedy has been allowed to atrophy. To this day, Syd claims that it was Eddie who invented the term 'brill' (the often-used abbreviation for 'brilliant'), and singer Robbie Williams is sufficiently enamoured by the twosome to have allegedly telephoned Syd Little in 2001 to thank him for making his childhood happier. However, with these two small legacies excepted, the fact that barely any of us refers to our punier associates as 'supersonic' suggests that Little and Large remain largely little remembered.

Look — Mike Yarwood!

BBC1

14 May 1971 to 7 February 1976 (48 episodes)

Cited alongside the likes of Simon Dee and Paul Gascoigne as a cautionary tale to those who find themselves in the glare of public adulation, Mike Yarwood's spectacular decline has overshadowed the period when he was one of the most famous people in the country. Indeed, while Morecambe and Wise's 1977 Christmas show is always cited as the high water mark of TV light entertainment, Mike's preceding programme actually pulled in 100,000 more viewers.

Yarwood could be said to have single-handedly changed the face of impressionism in the UK. He was one of the first to realise that you got your biggest laughs, not by impersonating the likes of James Cagney, but rather by taking off the public figures that everyone knew, from Harold Wilson (the jewel in his crown) to Vic Feather.

His early TV career came in guest appearances in variety, and then as one of the trio in the original Sixties version of *Three of a Kind*. His first starring series came from ATV, with *Will The Real Mike Yarwood Please Stand Up?*. It seems that he was already aware of being pigeonholed as simply a novelty act, and the second series, going under the shortened name of *The Real Mike Yarwood?*, scaled down the impressions in favour of emphasising Mike's all-round acting and singing talents.

In 1971, Yarwood defected to the BBC and appeared in

the first run of *Look – Mike Yarwood!* (accompanied by a radio series unsurprisingly entitled *Listen – Mike Yarwood*). This was the quintessential Yarwood series – solo stand-up, sketches parodying various celebrities of the day, a musical guest or two and, finally, Mike announcing 'and this...is me' and singing a song himself.

Getting laughs from public figures was an appealing diversion from the norm in light entertainment, with the chance to see union leaders (back when the public knew who they were) and politicians in unexpected situations. Don't think it was in any way controversial – most of the humour was simple ribbing at the stars' silly voices and unusual ways of speaking, *à la* Denis Healy's 'Silly Billy!' (which the Chancellor never actually said). The archetypal Yarwood sketch was probably the parody of *I Claudius*, retitling it *I Callaghanus*. Indeed, Harold Wilson enjoyed his send-ups so much he gave Yarwood an OBE, although in 1979 Mike was considered controversial enough for the repeat of his Christmas show to be cancelled during the election campaign.

By this point, Yarwood's series had been retitled *Mike Yarwood in Persons*, but the series remained much the same. Come the late Seventies, Mike was undoubtedly the biggest star at the Beeb, with the departure of Morecambe and Wise to Thames allowing him to bag the prime slot on Christmas Day. However, fate dealt him a cruel blow when on 5 May 1979, Margaret Thatcher was elected Prime Minister. Although Yarwood had plenty of other stars in his repertoire – and could farm out the Thatcher impression to Janet Brown –

he did admit to *Radio Times* in 1980 that 'My main wish for Christmas is a male Prime Minister'.

Nevertheless, the comic remained hugely popular, and was still on Saturday nights in the early Eighties. But, having profited from Eric and Ern's defection, in 1982 Yarwood inexplicably decided to follow them over to ITV. Despite the usual attractions (bigger budgets, more money), it's hard to work out why he decided to make the switch, and indeed why Thames wooed him when he was already past his peak.

Yarwood stayed with ITV for five years, but never seemed to find his feet. With the likes of *Spitting Image* and 'alternative' impressionists like Phil Cool stealing his thunder, and some well-publicised problems with alcohol, Yarwood fell out of favour and appeared in his last show in 1987 before disappearing from public life. A small comeback in the mid-Nineties saw him make a couple of TV appearances, most notably on *Have I Got News for You*. For a brief period there was even talk of a new BBC series, tentatively titled *Taking Off with Yarwood*, with appeals being made for members of the public to appear to show off their impressionism skills. But it never made it to the screens, and Yarwood returned once again to a life of semi-retirement.

The Man from Atlantis

Solow Productions [shown on ITV]

24 September 1977 to 14 January 1978 (16 episodes)

Whenever anyone discusses the classic Saturday night line-ups of the Seventies, it's virtually guaranteed that all the programmes they cite will have been on BBC1. So what were ITV doing during that time? Until the arrival of **Bruce Forsyth's Big Night**, not much – the evening was normally filled with films and shoddy imports, perhaps in recognition that the BBC opposition was just too strong. This is why such hokum as *The Man from Atlantis* could make it into ITV peak-time, and up against the BBC's successful **The Duchess of Duke Street** to boot.

Very much a footnote in American television history, given it ran for just one season on NBC, *The Man from Atlantis* nevertheless stuck a chord with Britain's kids. Half-man half fish Patrick Duffy had washed up, literally, in California where local doctor Elizabeth Merrill gave him the dynamic name of Mark Harris and put him to work for her Foundation for Oceanic Research, helping the government solve marine crime.

Mark's work would usually require him to make the most of his ability to breathe underwater, be it to recover an underwater probe, or to go on an undercover mission in a carnival as performer in a water tank. Whatever the mission, Duffy would handle it with a kind of otherworld serenity that many viewers could easily mistake for bad acting. In time, though, Duffy would take his acting in water skills to a new level, specifically during that infamous shower scene in *Dallas*.

Each episode of *The Man from Atlantis* took the form of vanquishing a villain-of-the-week (usually Mr Schubert played by Victor Buono), while the odd, spectacularly poorly realised sea monster would be on hand to offer Mark a quick grapple. Like other American action series of the time, *The Man from Atlantis* wasn't averse to throwing up some utterly fantastic plotlines. The episode featuring Mark travelling back in time to the Wild West to do battle with his evil doppelganger was only topped by the 'The Naked Montague' in which Mark found himself mixed up with none other than Romeo and Juliet.

With its 'don't drown!' messages at the end of each episode, *The Man from Atlantis* was clearly aware that its target audience had barely started shaving, and given the umpteen repeats during the summer holidays for the next decade, a generation of kids were suitably inspired. It's up there alongside the likes of *Automan* and *Manimal* as the kind of brainless import that, at the time, both the BBC and ITV seemed to have no qualms about screening. Indeed, given *The Man from Atlantis* pulled in over 14 million viewers at one point, it represented a valued success in an otherwise useless ITV Saturday night line-up.

Man O Man

Grundy/Anglia/LWT for ITV

4 May 1996 to 7 August 1999 (23 episodes)

Series such as *Tarrant on TV* had gained much mileage from mocking the excesses of foreign television, yet increasingly in the Nineties ITV seemed to be using these programmes as a mail-order catalogue. After **The Shane Richie Experience**, it was hard to imagine a less intellectual show finding its way onto Saturday night, but *Man O Man* managed to top it.

Man O Man came to the UK with meaningless name intact, and had been trailed in advance of its arrival on British screens as a smash hit throughout the world. The premise was almost insultingly simple – each week ten young men would parade in front of a three-hundred-strong, all-female audience, who would vote for their favourites over a number of rounds. Those who failed to come up to scratch would be pushed into the on-set swimming pool. Helming proceedings, and walking around with his hand in his pocket throughout, was Chris Tarrant.

The wafer-thin format failed to inspire much, with the hapless blokes attempting to charm the audience by essaying Frank Spencer impressions or just singing badly, while to ensure there was something to entertain any men who happened to be looking in, ten scantily clad ladies sashayed across the screen for several minutes before administering the duckings.

Appalling reviews and poor ratings suggested that the first

series would also be the last, and so it seemed until two years later when it surprisingly returned to the schedules for a further two weeks. The line was that after the World Cup, something female-friendly was required to offset a spell of laddish Saturday evenings. Remarkably, twelve months later it was back for a whole new series. At least second time around it was slightly more palatable, with the arrival of guest celebrities to offer their opinions adding some variety to the relentless voting and ducking. Yet not even the views of Vera Duckworth off *Corrie* could help this stinker of a show out.

Basically, *Man O Man* was the TV equivalent of a hen party – raucous and noisy with no one actually having a very good time.

Match of the Day

BBC2/BBC1

22 August 1964 to ongoing
(1998 episodes as of 9 May 2007)

Match of the Day must be one of the most famous programmes of all time, with even those who dislike football able to recognise the theme. It actually began on BBC2 in 1964 at the earlier time at 6.30 p.m. before it moved to BBC1 two years later and took up its familiar slot around 10 p.m. There it was soon pulling in enormous audiences.

This was partly because it was one of the only places you could actually see football on television – the Football League didn't allow live matches, fearing a detrimental effect on attendances, and permitted both the BBC and ITV (who shared the rights) to screen only one hour of highlights from a very small number of pre-selected fixtures, which could not be announced in advance. The standard *MotD* included just two matches, and if they turned out to be boring then it was tough luck. Furthermore, the programme was obliged to screen games from all four divisions of the league.

These conditions seem hugely archaic now, but they persisted throughout the entire Seventies. Jimmy Hill took over as presenter in 1973, moving across from ITV, and his opinions managed to infuriate fans of virtually every club throughout the season, but undoubtedly he gave *Match of the Day* an edge.

The first signs that the 'classic' *MotD* era was coming to an end came in 1978 when ITV announced that they'd signed an exclusive deal with the Football League, only for this deal to be quashed by the Office of Fair Trading. ITV did succeed in getting the BBC to relinquish their hold on Saturday nights, and in 1980/81 and 1982/83, *Match of the Day* moved to Sunday afternoons, with the regional ITV equivalents taking over the prime slot.

Yet at a time when more and more sport was being televised live, the highlights system was becoming increasingly outdated, and being forced to show unappealing lower-division games was hardly the best way to increase audiences. Eventually the broadcasters got what they wanted and, from 1983, the BBC and ITV were allowed to show league matches live.

From then on, highlights' days seemed numbered. If football wanted airtime, it had to provide what the broadcasters wanted to screen and what the audience wanted to watch – and that was live coverage from the top of the First Division. No longer would ten minutes of Rochdale versus Scunthorpe cut it as the main attraction. Saturday night highlights were now very much the exception rather than the rule.

In 1992, things changed once again. The new Premier League saw the big clubs who had made up the First Division go it alone, meaning they no longer had to share revenue and airtime with the lower leagues. The Premier League sold their live TV rights exclusively to Sky, but aware that taking football away from a huge number of viewers would be enormously unpopular, they also struck a highlights deal. *Match of the*

Day, now fronted by Des Lynam, was once more a regular Saturday night fixture. With camera crews at every Premiership match, and no need to screen the likes of Grimsby Town, this probably made for a better programme than in its pomp – albeit with the BBC paying substantially more for the privilege.

The enormous amount of live football has inevitably meant *Match of the Day*'s importance has diminished in recent years, and when ITV outbid the BBC for the rights in 2001, hapless attempts to make them a prime-time success illustrated that your average mid-table scrap did not make for attractive family viewing. But *Match of the Day*'s return to Saturday nights for a third time in 2004 was nonetheless greeted with delight by many football fans – proving there's still real affection for a programme that can round up everything that happened in half a dozen Premiership matches in less time than it takes to play one.

Mind Your Language

LWT for ITV

30 December 1977 to 15 December 1979 (29 episodes)

Back in the Seventies the ITV station LWT had developed a reputation for pioneering multicultural sitcoms (most notably *The Fosters*) and when it became known in 1977 that they were going to shoot a sitcom based on Leo Rosten's *The Education of Hyman Kaplan* (the classic 1937 book about immigrants trying to fit into an alien society), many thought it safe to assume that it was going to be another example of LWT's pioneering spirit.

It fell to the man who, somewhat ominously, had already given us the politically dubious *Love Thy Neighbour* to turn *Mind Your Language* into reality. Given *Love Thy Neighbour's* far from subtle exploration into modern-day multiculturalism, it was no doubt expecting too much for *Mind Your Language* to present any kind of insight into the lives of modern-day immigrants – particularly when writer Vince Powell drew upon his recollections of his bumbling au pair, and her gaffes with the English language, as inspiration.

A decidedly peppy title sequence with an animation of a teacher writing on a blackboard (done by future ident designer extraordinaire Martin Lambie-Nairn), belied the horror that awaited. *Mind Your Language* was supposedly about the trials and tribulations of a group of immigrants from different countries attending an evening class in an effort to learn English, but within the opening seconds of the first ever episode the low tone was set as Indian Ali Nadim (Dino Shafeek) responded to teacher Miss Courtney (Zara Nutley)'s mild chastisement of 'You're early' with the awful rejoinder 'Oh, no, I am Ali'.

And so on it went. Big studio audience laughs came from such notable gags as Ali declaring 'I am Sikh' only to be answered by the teacher Jeremy Brown (Barry Evans) with the predictable 'Oh dear, perhaps it's contagious.' The audience at home seemed to lap it up, with *Mind Your Language* becoming in 1978 LWT's most successful sitcom to date (with up to 18 million viewers tuning in). Clearly, beneath the veneer of casual racial stereotyping there was something about the show that appealed.

Perhaps it was that, although it was populated by a bunch of clichés, the characters were rather affable. Nevertheless, growing increasingly uncomfortable with the series' inability to move beyond stereotyping, LWT executives decided to pull the plug on *Mind Your Language* after three years. A new version followed some seven years later, but this time made by a completely different production company, and rather than propping up primetime Saturday nights, those ITV regions that did elect to broadcast it (and there were only four) were happy to bury it in the less hospitable climate of early Saturday afternoons.

The Moment of Truth

LWT for ITV

5 September 1998 to 29 September 2001 (36 episodes)

For almost the entire Nineties, it seemed as if ITV was continually trying to find something to curb its reliance on **Blind Date**. The show was still a huge success, but as the years went by, the ratings were gradually declining. In the autumn of 1998, ITV made their most concerted effort yet to find a replacement, albeit one that would still be fronted by Cilla Black.

This new show was an Anglicisation of a Japanese series that went under the baffling name of *Happy Family Plan*. For the UK, this became *The Moment of Truth*. Each edition would feature a couple of families who would select a series of prizes from 'Cilla's Dream Directory'. In order to win these, one member of the family (usually the hapless dad) would be selected to complete a challenge in the studio. These challenges would be staggering in their pointlessness (building giant houses of cards or memorising long lists of names or countries). To add to the excitement, the families would compile a video diary of their week's 'training' which was then screened for our viewing pleasure.

Come the big night, there'd be just one chance to complete the task, which could lead to some spectacular anticlimaxes if the contestant immediately cocked it up. In the event of a failure, the prizes were brought out onto the set and waved under the family's noses before being taken away. Needless to say, this 'look at what you could have won' act writ large was fairly controversial. Cilla being Cilla, was upset at the river of tears that the Japanese original had managed to generate and insisted that in the UK version the kids at least received consolation prizes.

The Moment of Truth wasn't much of a hit, with the *Radio Times* calling it 'fantastically dire'. In truth, the format really wasn't particularly inspired, nor did it seem that suitable a vehicle for Cilla in that there was little opportunity for the cheeky banter and piss-taking that had made *Blind Date* such a hit. Nevertheless, it continued for three more series, possibly because it wasn't seen as the done thing to axe a light entertainment legend. The show was continually tweaked throughout the run, with the original concept taking less of a role in proceedings. Instead team challenges and quickie games with the studio audience were introduced to add a bit more variety, but it could be said that this simply turned it into a mish-mash of ideas that lost the masochistic appeal the original show had possessed. Unsurprisingly, it still never threatened to become hugely successful, and quietly came to an end after its fourth run.

Twelve months later, a new series appeared on ITV1. This saw a celebrity move in with a family for a week to complete a challenge such as building giant houses of cards or memorising long lists of names or countries. A video diary of their week's 'training' would be filmed and then they'd come into the studio and have one chance to complete this challenge to win prizes for the whole family. No, it was a completely different programme, honest. It's rather obvious that *Celebrities Under Pressure* was a barely disguised variation on *The Moment of Truth*, but now celebrities were involved, all the problems were clearly solved. Cilla was also replaced by Melanie Sykes and, later, Vernon Kay, but it still failed to establish itself in the public's affections.

Indeed, the series is probably now only remembered for being used as a way to wind up John Fashanu during his 'Undercover' appearance on **Ant and Dec's Saturday Night Takeaway** – so at least it contributed one decent moment to the history of Saturday night telly.

The Morecambe and Wise Show
ATV for ITV

12 October 1961 to 31 March 1968 (67 episodes)

Perhaps the single most important date in British light entertainment is Christmas Day 1977. That night, over 20 million people watched a formidable trio of programmes – *Bruce Forsyth and The Generation Game*, *The Mike Yarwood Christmas Show* and *The Morecambe and Wise Show*. For those who cite the Seventies as the golden age of British television, it's an unbeatable line-up, and even now, over twenty years since their last series together, Morecambe and Wise remain the most famous names in festive television.

Eric and Ern weren't just for Christmas, though – they were hugely popular throughout the year. They famously made

something of a shaky start, however, and their first BBC series, 1954's *Running Wild*, was so unpopular they pleaded for the BBC to drop it mid-run. Several years spent refining their act meant that by the Sixties they were hugely popular and polished performers.

Despite their most

© Rex Features

famous association with the BBC, the magnificent two really rose to fame on ITV, making numerous series for ATV between 1961 and 1968 (indeed, this was the only time they were consistently on Saturday nights). Here their scriptwriters were Sid Green and Dick Hills, who also regularly appeared on screen, resulting in some memorable moments such as their famous encounter with The Beatles. Ernie fed the lines, Eric provided the gags and the duo were well established at the top table of British comedy. By the end of the decade the pair were after something new, and hopped over to the BBC, making their first programme for the corporation (originally on BBC2) in 1968.

Sid and Dick originally provided the scripts here, too, but when Eric suffered a heart attack shortly after their arrival the future of the act looked in doubt, and so the writers signed an exclusive deal with ATV. Happily, Eric recovered and he and Ernie continued to work – but now with Eddie Braben providing the scripts. Braben was selected due to his work with Ken Dodd and incomparable ability to hammer out gags at a rate of knots. Many fans suggest that at this point, the act was actually a trio, Braben being responsible for a lot of their most familiar catchphrases and running jokes (sharing a bed, the plays 'what Ernie wrote' and so forth). Certainly, with Braben on side, Morecambe and Wise were scaling new heights.

But it was the Christmas shows that really established Eric and Ern as Britain's favourite entertainers. Such was their appeal that virtually every big name jumped at the chance to appear alongside them. However the twosome were canny enough not to turn the show into simply a star vehicle. In the celebrated sequence featuring the likes of Eddie Waring and Frank Bough re-enacting *South Pacific*, for example, each famous face was on screen for only a few seconds. Better still, no matter how famous the guest star, they would each have to contend with Eric and Ern mistaking them for somebody else, or putting them in a stupid costume.

Sadly, it wasn't to last, and that momentous 1977 Christmas show (with Penelope Keith and Elton John, amongst others) was to be Morecambe and Wise's final programme for the BBC, as the duo signed an exclusive contract with Thames. ITV were obviously hugely excited by their new signings, chucking money and special guests (like Harold Wilson) at them, but it was obvious something was missing; namely Eddie Braben, who was still contractually bound to the BBC. Other writers, including Barry Cryer and John Junkin, failed to recreate the magic, while Eric's poor health and the 1979 ITV strike meant that after two shows there was almost two years before another *Morecambe and Wise Show* hit the air. So desperate were ITV to exploit their acquisition, the duo still appeared on Christmas Day 1979 even though the show consisted only of an interview with David Frost.

When they were able to finally put something new together in 1980, Eddie Braben was back on board and it looked as if the good times were back. Yet, while it was still good Morecambe and Wise, it wasn't classic Morecambe and Wise, and despite ITV's massive publicity, nothing was going to top their BBC work. Eric died in 1984, and since then, whenever anyone's wanted to illustrate their genius, it's the BBC archives they always turn to.

The Murder Game

BBC1

29 March 2003 to 17 May 2003 (8 episodes)

Billed as 'reality TV meets the traditional murder-mystery', *The Murder Game* featured ten contestants placed into the fictional town of Blackwater. Over the course of eight episodes they attempted to solve the murder of Catherine Prior by quizzing various suspects and turning up to specific locations to conduct searches for evidence. Each week, a suspect (there were nine to begin, all played by professional actors) and a contestant would be eliminated; the suspect through the uncovering of a piece of evidence that put them in the clear, and the contestant via 'The Killer's Game' – an extended *Blair Witch*-inspired sequence at the end of each edition where that week's two worst-performing investigators would be despatched to separate, but equally terrifying locations. For one, 'death' and exclusion from the game lay in wait, while the other would live to face another week of sleuthing.

The investigation was presided over by a real-life retired cop, DCS Bob Taylor, and it was his job to provide the would-be detectives with guidance and feedback. It was up to him, too, to keep a focus on the week's events to ensure that the audience had some chance of keeping up with what was going on. On paper this sounded like a grand wheeze, but it never really worked on screen.

One of the first surprises for the Saturday night viewer was the tone. Although broadcast after 9 p.m., the gruesome nature of Prior's death made this tough watching for the faint-hearted. Worse still, as the weeks went by, most viewers experienced a creeping realisation that what they were watching was actually pretty similar to the type of role-playing away days that you might expect a group of middle managers to indulge in – not really your idea of gripping television.

Through all this, DCS Taylor attempted to maintain a sense of solemnity and seriousness, yet it was clear that he was ill-equipped to deal with the rigours of heading up such a programme. Each week he would send the contestants off on their latest lines of inquiry with the strangely emphasised phrase 'Good luck – you are **going** to need it', and upon their return would grill them over their investigative shortcomings, spouting such silly lines as 'There are enough muppets in this room to make a movie', 'I can see the headlines tomorrow: "Bungling Police Know Nothing"', and best of all, 'I sent you off to find the murder weapon and all you've come back with is a jammy knife'.

All of these shortcomings contributed to the series' downfall, but easily the worst thing was the way in which the investigation unfolded. If contestants failed to find the vital piece of evidence that had been planted in the lake, or managed to miss the inconsistency within a witness's statement then Taylor's unseen back-up team would be called upon to reveal the clues for them. This meant the information needed to move the story along always came to the surface by the end of the episode, regardless of whether or not (usually not) the team were capable of uncovering it for themselves.

As if to add insult to injury, *The Murder Game* was billed as an interactive programme in which the viewer could take part in the investigation. There was even a special website laid on, containing additional clues, all of which promoted the idea that it was entirely possible for you to identify the culprit, even if the ten contestants were failing to piece the mystery together. Yet the series' denouement relied on the discovery of phone records that the viewer did not have any previous access to. For those who had swallowed the publicity that proclaimed 'Spot the clue, solve the case' this was hard to take.

With a group of contestants that proved difficult to warm to, plus a plotline that was a real challenge to follow, *The Murder Game* was unsurprisingly a ratings failure. By the time the last episode was transmitted at the ignominiously late time of 10.40 p.m., few people could remember who the victim was, let alone who the remaining suspects were, and *The Murder Game*, a brave, albeit flawed attempt by the BBC to bring something new to Saturday nights, was confined to the television casebooks.

The National Lottery Big Ticket

BBC1

28 March 1998 to 11 July 1998 (16 episodes)

Come March 1998, *The National Lottery Live* had been running successfully for three and a half years, but it was obvious that the novelty was wearing off a bit. It didn't help that the programme always ended with a massive anticlimax – you didn't know who'd actually won.

So a complete overhaul of the series was pioneered. The idea was to try and prop up sales of lottery scratchcards and add a bit of personality to the show by actually creating winners in the studio there and then. In the new programme, those who revealed TV-shaped symbols on their cards were guaranteed a big cash prize, but could also appear on the show to increase those winnings to a possible £100,000 – the biggest prize ever given away on the BBC.

Simple enough, but there were a mass of legal problems that had to be worked out. The first was that the links between the show and the scratchcards had to be played down, lest it seem too much like advertising, so there was no mention of the show on the cards, nor displaying of the cards on the show. A more pressing issue, though, was that lottery company Camelot's contract only allowed the company to run games of chance. As such, it was illegal to get the players to do anything that might have involved any skill. The fact that the contestants could therefore only cross their fingers to win prizes may, you'd have thought, put the dampers on the concept of a game show in the first place, but the BBC and Camelot tried their best to create a programme that didn't break any regulations.

Hence *The National Lottery Big Ticket* got other people to play the games on the contestants' behalf. Eight scratchcard winners were split into four teams, then each team was awarded two 'champions' – a Bobby Davro-esque celebrity, and a representative of a charity that was benefiting from lottery money. It was the two champions who would actually play the conventional games of skill, while the scratchcard winners would do nothing except sit down and root for 'their' team. As the game progressed, three teams would be eliminated (the members of the public in each team getting a couple of thousand pounds for their trouble) then the lucky surviving pair would spin a wheel to decide who would go for the really big prize. This final game involved selecting boxes at random to explode, with whatever cash sum inside being won by the contestant. So basically this was a conventional game show but one in which the prizes went to people who weren't actually playing the game. Anthea Turner was lured back to the BBC to compere, and she was joined by stand-up comedian Patrick Kielty.

What did these 'games of skill' involve then? On the whole, not very much. It was promised that the rounds would be 'spectacular', and they clearly were if you were playing them. Take the weekly 'Catapult Cars', for example, which, claimed *Radio Times*, 'has been developed by eccentric Belgian millionaire Hans Hollick. His degree in the

Psychology of Fun is put to good use when it comes to devising and designing the many games that his factory produces for theme parks all over Europe'. However what worked in a theme park and what worked on television were two completely different things. The 'Catapult Cars' saw the celebrities asked a question and then placed in a car on the end of a bungee rope heading towards a 'car wash'. If they'd got the question right, they stayed dry, and if they didn't, they wouldn't. But what did we care at home?

Indeed, this was the major problem – it didn't seem to matter who won. When you saw a contestant win thousands of pounds for simply sitting there, it couldn't help but fall flat. The original plan was to have ten contestants on each team instead of two, but this was changed at the last minute when too few scratchcard winners came forward. This turned out to be a stroke of luck, as trying to remember who forty people were would have been even less engaging. In the end, so few winners were volunteering to go on the programme that the rules were changed to let virtually anyone who'd bought a card appear.

As well as problems on screen, off screen things did not appear to run particularly smoothly. In addition to the regular draws, there was an extra lottery for the holders of the TV-based scratchcards which was presided over by a computer-generated virtual hostess named 'Bernie'. Kate Robbins provided the voice and on one episode had to use all her improvisational talents when the computer graphics spectacularly crashed live on air. Only the lottery draws were live, however, and during the run the *Daily Mirror* published a photograph of a deserted studio audience, with the majority of attendees apparently having legged it three hours into a marathon recording session. Challenged over this on an episode of *Have I Got News for You*, Patrick Kielty explained this away as having been taken during a recording break, where the audience had nipped off to the toilet. As Ian Hislop questioned, though, 'They'd *all* gone to the toilet?'

Ultimately, what *Big Ticket* learnt was that contestants have to be seen to actually deserve to win game shows, and watching someone win money for nothing was a ridiculous idea. There was something to be said for Dale Winton and a tombola after all.

The National Lottery Live

BBC1

19 November 1994 to 20 February 1999 (279 episodes)

Noel Edmonds, driving a truck around London containing a huge amount of cash, turns to camera and announces 'Someone watching this programme is going to be a millionaire – and it could be you!' A terrifically exciting way to start a TV show, but with the jackpot of the first National Lottery being claimed by multiple winners, nobody actually won a million pounds at all. Nevertheless, that didn't stop *The National Lottery Live* becoming one of the most talked-about Saturday night shows ever.

The UK was one of the last countries in Europe to get a National Lottery, but when John Major's government gave Camelot the go-ahead to run a weekly flutter, the BBC played on the idea that the National Lottery should be on the national broadcaster, and hence landed the rights to cover it. The BBC had to pay for the privilege, though many thought that, given the amount of publicity Camelot were receiving, it should have been them who were forking out. Mind you, the expectation was that the draw was going to secure massive viewing figures, so the Beeb weren't complaining.

Despite rumours that the draw would be included as part of **Noel's House Party**, it was decided that it would get its own dedicated programme. However, Edmonds did present the first draw on Saturday 19 November 1994. Of course, the draw itself only lasted a few minutes and so the rest of the hour-long show was padded out with a contest to decide who would have the 'honour' of starting it. This wasn't particularly inspired, but the promise of a massive cash dividend caught the nation's attention and millions tuned in to watch.

After the extravagance of the opening show, from week two the draw took place as part of a fifteen-minute programme fronted by Anthea Turner, then best known for *Blue Peter* and *GMTV*, and comedy actor Gordon Kennedy. Neither was a big name, but the BBC specifically decided on this approach to ensure that the draw was kept centre-stage, rather than the presenters.

This was certainly the case. The fifteen minutes of running time were devoted to lottery news and views, chatting to previous winners, and providing breathless updates on how much cash was in that week's kitty. For the first six months, the programme was out on the road, with the draw presented from a venue that would benefit from the lottery in some way. The first instalment came from the Rhondda Heritage Park in South Wales, and Turner would later refer to this as one of her worst experiences, with the autocue going down, an audience that wouldn't shut up, and the entire programme shot in the pouring rain.

Yet it didn't matter as in the early days up to 14 million people would tune in to see the draw. This was unlikely to be sustained, however, and after six months changes were made, which saw the departure of Kennedy and the permanent transfer of the show to TV Centre. Alan Dedicoat provided the voice-overs and the soon-to-be much lampooned Mystic Meg offered predictions of that week's big winners.

There was some respite from the previously ceaseless promotion for Camelot, though, as musical guests came into the studio to perform and start the draw itself. Such was the show's continuing high ratings, artists were queuing up to appear – although on one occasion Eddi Reader pressed the button with a resolutely off-message 'It could be you – it's definitely Camelot!'

Of all the changes the most pronounced was to the career of Anthea Turner. While she'd been selected as a virtual unknown, it was obvious that presenting one of the most watched programmes on British television meant she didn't stay that way for very long. Turner now dominated from start to finish, finally leaving in early 1996 to sign a 'golden handcuffs' deal with ITV and become one of the highest-paid people on television. In her place, a string of rotating presenters took over – including Dale Winton, Terry Wogan and, best of all, Bob Monkhouse. His topical monologues and endless gags meant that for the first time the programme was worth watching even if you didn't have a ticket.

The excitement of the lottery draw kept ratings up for some time, but eventually the novelty wore off and viewers grew increasingly happy simply to watch **Blind Date** and wait for the numbers to come up on screen on ITV. Hence from 1999, the lottery draw became subsumed into longer programmes, normally quizzes such as *Winning Lines*, *Jet Set* and the disastrous **Red Alert**. Throughout it all, though, Alan Dedicoat has remained a constant, breathlessly commentating on proceedings and referring to each ball's 'form' as if it were a greyhound.

The New Adventures of Superman

Roundelay/December 3rd Production
in association with Warner Bros Television [shown on BBC1]

8 January 1994 to 5 July 1997 (88 episodes)

One of the giants of popular culture, Superman has long been a favourite of TV and film, which every so often try and put a new spin on the Man of Steel. Back in the Fifties, George Reeves portrayed the archetypal square-jawed American hero in a long-running series, which thanks to endless repeats was a staple of British telly for some thirty years.

Christopher Reeve's portrayal in the Eighties movies reinvented him for a new generation, while the exploits of *Supergirl* were moderately popular (*Superboy*, which ITV showed on Saturday nights for a few weeks, was not). Come the Nineties, there was a new spin on the story – a touchy-feely look at the niceties of Clark Kent and Lois Lane's relationship.

In the US, the series went out under the name of *Lois and Clark*, as if to emphasise that this was just a normal relationship between two people, albeit one where the bloke would regularly save the world. In the UK, the BBC gave it a rather more descriptive title, and screened it in the Saturday teatime spot that had been home to umpteen imports before that.

The focus on characterisation ensured it appealed to a wider audience than just adolescent boys who could always be relied on to tuned into this sort of thing. The fact that Dean

Cain and Teri Hatcher, who played the couple, were fairly attractive was probably of some help too.

The series featured an additional fillip by being scheduled just before **Noel's House Party** (with the end credits accompanied by a bit of business with Noel eating his tea), and, if that wasn't enough, its phenomenal popularity with children was cemented by reruns on Saturday mornings.

The New Adventures of Superman proved to be successful for three years, managing to appear on the cover of *Radio Times* on two occasions – a rare feat for an imported programme. Alas the fourth year was a series too far, with plotlines stretching credibility to breaking point and the 'will they, won't they' factor beginning to pall. Viewing figures dipped on both sides of the Atlantic, and the BBC started screening the programme earlier and earlier in the evening. Unsurprisingly, the programme didn't make it to a fifth series.

Somewhat inevitably, for a time Cain and Hatcher seemed to fall foul of the so-called 'Curse of Superman', which in the past had seen George Reeves, Christopher Reeve and Margot Kidder (who played Lois Lane in the films) suffer what appeared to be terrible bouts of bad luck. For Cain and Hatcher, work post-*Superman* proved extremely difficult to come by, with Hatcher only being able to finally break the spell in 2004 when she won a role in *Desperate Housewives*.

New Faces

ATV Network/Central Production for ITV

7 July 1973 to 3 December 1988 (197 episodes)

While *Opportunity Knocks* was undoubtedly the most prestigious television talent show of the Seventies, pressing hard on its heels was the Birmingham-based *New Faces* – the series that shook up the talent-show formula by featuring a panel of judges who would say mildly rude things about the wannabe entertainers. So scathing was panellist Tony Hatch that he earned the epithet 'Hatchet Man' in the press. On each edition seven acts would ply their wares on a pretty minuscule stage. Linking the various comedians, musicians, singers, magicians and impossible-to-categorise novelty acts (such as the Ukranian Black Sea Cossacks who strutted their stuff on the show in 1975) was host Derek Hobson, a man who lacked the showbiz élan of Hughie Green, and instead looked as if he would be more at home reading out the football results on a regional news programme.

Yet for all its low-rent trappings, *New Faces* dealt squarely with the very Seventies aspiration of becoming a 'star' (as distinct from the twenty-first-century preoccupation with becoming a 'celebrity'). The rambunctious and anthemic theme tune sung by Carl Wayne encapsulated the dream perfectly in just five lines: ' Yesterday I was happy to play / For a penny or two a song / 'Til a fellah in a black sedan / Took a shine to my one-man-band / He said, "We got plans for you, you'd never dream"'. Then just to force the point home a little harder, each show was cued up by an unseen announcer pronouncing 'Yes, it's *New Faces*. Once again seven acts hoping for that big break into television stardom'.

Over its five years, *New Faces* was highly effective at unearthing acts that would go on to establish a successful career in show business: Michael Barrymore, Lenny Henry, Gary Wilmot, Jim Davidson and Victoria Wood all received an opportunity to test out their material in front of up to 7.8 million viewers. Yet the series was as equally defined by those performers who never achieved widespread fame. What, for example, came of the seven-piece act Abbott who appeared on a November 1977 edition? How about The Climax Band, or the exotically named four-piece Pacific? And one can only hope things turned out all right for the members of Blackpool-based Hareword Magna and comedian Bazz Harris.

New Faces finished in 1978 but was resurrected some eight years later with one-time contestant Marti Caine taking on the Derek Hobson part. The role of the judges was retained, but this time it was the likes of Nina Myskow issuing pronouncements from (literally) on high. The show also moved out of the dingy studio of yore to the Birmingham Hippodrome – a venue more in keeping with a Saturday evening light entertainment show. Yet despite travelling 26,000 miles in search of undiscovered talent, the revived series failed to uncover much in the way of new stars. The line-up for the 1988 final featured the likes of Stephen Lee Garden, Steve Womack, Domino, Tim Murray, Max Bacon and Stevie Riks – none of whom have gone on to become a household name. Of course, Joe Pasquale got his big break on *New Faces* (back in 1987), but the less said about him the better.

Night Fever

Grundy for Channel Five

5 April 1997 to 16 February 2002 (132 episodes)

Channel Five arrived on British TV screens in March 1997 with the promise of a 'modern and mainstream' schedule that would provide more choice for viewers, albeit on a microscopic budget. Saturday nights were something of a poser for the schedulers, though. If it was to provide a choice, it seemed pointless to offer light entertainment when BBC1 and ITV had the genre wrapped up. As a supposedly mainstream channel, and one that could ill afford to drive viewers away, it had to provide some competition.

In the event, most of Saturday evening was given over to films and imports, but one new entertainment programme was invented. This was *Night Fever*, which was perhaps the most accurate representation yet of how most of its viewers would spend their Saturday nights. Each week, five male celebrities took on five female celebrities in a karaoke sing-off.

It must be said that while they were 'celebrities' in the Channel Five sense, they were often completely unrecognisable, thanks to most of them being plucked from other Channel Five programmes. It comes to something when Jenny Powell is the most famous person on a celebrity show. Their 'performances' were supplemented with some slightly more professional numbers from the sort of tribute bands and over-the-hill singers who would normally be spending their Saturday nights performing in pubs and clubs.

Obviously, *Night Fever* was a cheap and cheerful hour that made no pretensions to be anything but raucous entertainment. It certainly wasn't likely to be challenging for BAFTAs, but it was curiously likeable, thanks mostly to the performance of host Suggs, and his barely disguised embarrassment at having to helm this shoutathon. As the series went on, it seemed to glorify in its tackiness, even providing Suggs with a co-host in the form of 'Pop Monkey'; a luckless bloke in an ape suit.

Viewing figures, unsurprisingly for Channel Five, were tiny, but the show managed to garner a loyal audience who stuck with it throughout its marathon runs. Such a wafer-thin concept had a limited shelf life and Channel Five finally called it a day after five years. Curiously, there was never any attempt to find a replacement show, either between series or indeed after it ended, making it Channel Five's only foray into Saturday night entertainment. Given the station's trek upmarket in recent years, don't count on a second attempt any time soon.

The Noel Edmonds Saturday Roadshow
BBC1

3 September 1988 to 15 December 1990 (48 episodes)

'The engines roar. The great adventure is on,' proclaimed the billing for the first ever episode of *The Noel Edmonds Saturday Roadshow*. 'Noel Edmonds and his crew travel the world to bring you a show brimming with new features from places that other shows cannot reach.'

It seems odd to think that, after **The Late Late Breakfast Show** was abruptly brought to an end, the Beeb were seriously considering bringing the programme back almost straightaway, albeit obviously minus one particular item. While *Late Late* never returned, two years later, Noel was back on Saturday nights with a new show.

The Noel Edmonds Saturday Roadshow was fairly similar to its predecessor, but in an attempt to keep it all a bit safer, the emphasis was far more on comedy. Noel teamed up with producer Michael Leggo to put the programme together, and the result was fifty minutes of shameless silliness that had very little to do with anything in real life. Nobody was going to get hurt here as nothing in the slightest bit serious happened. Even the name was taking the piss – the 'Roadshow' didn't actually travel anywhere outside the same TV Centre studio, which would be suitably redressed each week. The production made a virtue of the fact that nobody would be taken in by such deception and that it was all part of the fun.

Similarly Lisa Maxwell, in the regular role of the obsessed secretary of the Noel Edmonds fan club, played her part purely for laughs. However these comedy interludes became an increasing nuisance, as viewers who had tuned in to catch the latest Gotcha found themselves having to contend with the resolution to a half-baked comedy storyline involving sending a man to the moon in a milk bottle rocket. The idea of transmitting each show from a 'different location' certainly had its limitations, and quite apart from the unnecessary comedic intrusions there was the matter each week of having to transform the studio set into a pyramid in Egypt or a Venice station or whatever.

The *Saturday Roadshow* does not have much of a legacy, as it's been rather overshadowed by its successor, **Noel's House Party**, which it mutated into in 1991. But it should be noted that much of the *House Party* started life in this series – the Gotchas, the gunge tank, Wait Til I Get You Home and The Lyric Game were all *Roadshow* regulars that found a new home in Crinkley Bottom.

The *Roadshow* was a fairly successful, though unexceptional, series but it at least re-confirmed that Noel was undoubtedly a master of this kind of television. By 1990, having to devise a different concept each week was becoming too much for both the production team and the viewer, so it was time to try something a bit more adventurous. The results would be hugely impressive.

Noel's House Party

BBC1

23 November 1991 to 20 March 1999 (169 episodes)

Gunging, grabbing grands and getting one over on the unsuspecting presenter: in its prime *Noel's House Party* was just about the most exciting Saturday night television show ever to grace our screens. Like its immediate predecessor **The Noel Edmonds Saturday Roadshow**, *House Party* was broadcast from a fictional location, but this time all the action took place within just one setting – 'The Great House' located in the picturesque village of Crinkley Bottom.

This popular address would play host to all manner of guests (usually celebrities pretending to be a resident of Crinkley Bottom), who would turn up, deliver their scripted comedy banter with host Noel Edmonds and then go away again. These bits of business were usually corny in the extreme, but Dudley Moore did at least make a bit of television history, when part way through his sketch he inadvertently became the first person to say the 'F' word at six-fifteen on BBC1 on a Saturday night (albeit the utterance was largely smothered under the audience's laughter at the preceding joke).

As planned, many aspects from *Saturday Roadshow* appeared in *House Party*, however, as *House Party* was broadcast live, there was scope to include some exciting new ideas within this freewheeling show that capitalised on the programme's immediacy. NTV (reputedly standing for 'Now

The Viewer' although some reckon it's short for 'Noel Television') was easily the most memorable of these new segments.

Each week Noel would click his fingers and an unsuspecting viewer would find him or herself broadcasting live from the comfort of their own sitting room, via tiny cameras secretly installed in their television set. Given the nature of the item, NTV was extremely risky business and on at least one occasion provoked strong language from the intended target. It also proved a big challenge for Noel, who was required to keep his eye on a monitor broadcasting live from the victim's house for up to ten minutes before the item actually began.

It was carefully planned too, and to ensure Noel had enough embarrassing material the production team would actually conspire to meet the target under false pretences (such as 'bumping' into them in the pub and pretending to be a 'friend of a friend') so they could surreptitiously pump them

for information. But it wasn't only people's homes that could end up on *House Party*; one particularly memorable NTV required Noel to interrupt a film showing at a cinema. The idea was to cut seamlessly from a scene in the movie to a similarly dressed shot in the *House Party* studio.

The scripted scene that Noel had to perform was designed to sync up with thirteen separate moments in the film – it took until the thirteenth before the programme was in a position to spring the trap.

While undoubtedly *Noel's House Party*'s greatest success, NTV wasn't the only element of the programme that got viewers talking. The Gotchas (in which a celebrity would unwittingly become the focus of a hidden-camera stunt) provided a suitably entertaining conclusion to each week's show. One memorable stunt featured Noel and his cohorts pretending to be members of rival pub quiz teams taking part in disc jockey Dave Lee Travis' 'Double Top' radio quiz. The complete inability of either team to answer a single question correctly drove DLT to ever increasing levels of rage, so that when Noel carried out the big reveal, the vitriolic response ('You are a dead man!') was trailed for about ten weeks before the item was actually shown.

Not all Gotchas were as good value, and a 'hit' on presenter Carol Smillie became better known for what was omitted (footage of Smillie undressing in front of the hidden camera) than for what was shown. Even worse, one Gotcha was abandoned completely when the target proved to be so obnoxious that the production team chose to junk all the footage and send him home without carrying out the reveal. Undoubtedly, though, the Gotcha's most significant (one would hesitate to use the word 'greatest') contribution to popular culture was the introduction of the comic character that would later come to symbolise the public's antipathy towards *Noel's House Party*.

Having just 'got' presenter Eamonn Holmes (during which Edmonds surreptitiously dressed up as an ape-like creature), it became evident that the introduction of a costumed character provided a way for Noel to get closer to his targets without arousing their suspicions. And so on 24 October 1992 Mr Blobby made his television debut in a sting on dancer Wayne Sleep, and from that point on things changed for ever.

Although Noel felt uncomfortable at becoming a foil for a character that had only ever meant to be a conduit to hidden-camera hilarity, it was difficult to deny Mr Blobby's burgeoning fame and increasingly episodes of *House Party* were given over to Blobby arsing about in the studio supposedly causing 'anarchy', but actually irritating long-term viewers patiently waiting for the next item to start.

By 1996, *House Party* had notched up an incredible one hundred episodes, but was beginning to look tired. New items were tried out (some of which never made it to the screen including an ill-judged idea that involved rolling giant hay bales) and the show was given a revamp. But by 1999 viewers were no longer that interested in the goings-on at Crinkley Bottom (and even Noel would later concede that he should have called it a day after five series) and in February of that year the show was cancelled.

Its spirit lives on in the shape of **Ant and Dec's Saturday Night Takeaway** and pretty much any modern entertainment show. As a number of observers have commented, *Noel's House Party* remains perhaps the last ever television programme to truly unite the TV-watching nation and for that reason our memories of it should be kind.

One by One

BBC1

29 January 1984 to 2 May 1987 (32 episodes)

Saturday night is no stranger to 'me too' television, and with the vets of *All Creatures Great and Small* having seemingly closed their practice for good some four years earlier, the similarly themed set of autobiographical books by David Turner provided an obvious source material for a new drama.

One by One portrayed the progress of lead character Donald Turner (Rob Heyland) as he attempted to establish himself as a freelance international vet. Much like *All Creatures Great and Small*, the action took place within the recent past (in this case the Sixties). However, while James Herriot and his partners worked the Yorkshire Dales, Turner's stomping ground was far smaller, focusing on zoos and safari parks. Sure enough, idiosyncratic and eccentric characters were as likely to appear in *One by One* as they were to be found wandering the dales around Darrowby (most notably James Ellis as the cantankerous liquor-drinking, animal-loving Paddy Reilly), but in *One by One* the emphasis was less on community and more on the function of the veterinary practice.

By and large the series seemed to fare well, although some viewers took objection to what they way felt was a tacit approval on the programme's part for the practice of keeping animals in captivity. The episode 'End of an Era' broadcast on 2 February 1985 proved to be particularly memorable though, if not a little harrowing, as it featured the slaughtering of two big cats, the death of a gorilla who had pined for its absent mate and, worst of all, a long and lingering demise for Donna the elephant, a popular animal in the show.

After the conclusion of the second series, and despite decent ratings (peaking at 14.9 million), it was announced that there were no plans to make any more, but *One by One* turned up again for one final run in 1987. By the time the show finally wrapped up, Rob Heyland was sporting an unruly beard that rather undermined any aspirations he may have had to become a well-loved, clean-cut quiet hero in the mould of James Herriot. But that difficult beard somehow suited *One by One*. While forever stymied by its obvious similarities to that more auspicious vet drama, it did at least try and go its own way, and if nothing else it got the audience warmed up for the return of the real thing the following year.

OTT

Central Production for ITV

13 February 1982 to 3 April 1982 (12 episodes)

Any show that features the audience en masse spelling out the letters that make up the programme's title has to be great, surely? *OTT*'s animated title sequence (featuring an inflatable lady flying through space towards what can only be described as a scene of indeterminate naughtiness) was the just the sort of thing we had come to expect from the masterminds who created the anarchic but superb Saturday morning kids' show *Tiswas*. However, while *OTT* (short for 'Over The Top') looked as if it was going to be brilliant, it somehow fell far short of its potential. In fact, if you were looking for a neat way to sum up *OTT* then a moment from the first episode featuring John Gorman in full fowl costume opining 'a duck-billed platypus is more entertaining than that, pal' proved to be pretty spot on.

The show was originally going to be called 'The Big Tis' in reference to its Saturday morning origins until a comment by comedian Michael Palin prompted lead *Tiswas* man Chris Tarrant to adopt the name 'OTT' instead. In addition to the usual *Tiswas* crew, *OTT* provided very early television exposure to up-and-coming comedians such as Helen Atkinson-Wood and Alexei Sayle. The Scouse comic in particular would prove to be a very striking, although not always that funny, component within the show and his weekly diatribes against the 'Habitat-bean-bag-hessian-wallpaper brigade' were something new for Saturday nights ('Social Democrats are the K-Tel of British politics. Same old shit – different package').

However *OTT*'s main stock-in-trade was the kind of saucy humour that might have once felt like the natural extension of the *Tiswas* brand, but by the Eighties was pretty outdated and a bit grotesque. A sketch featuring bikini-clad models and whipped cream attracted the ire of many, as did a sequence in which a man was shown to kick a rat live on television (after his stuffing-a-pair-of-trousers-with-rodents act went frighteningly awry). *Tiswas* had gained a reputation for being somewhat naughty, yet that which was deemed risqué on Saturday morning came across as pretty passé by Saturday evening and *OTT* was forced to think up ever more mischievous ideas in order to support its counterculture credentials.

Such supposedly 'anarchic' material included an attractive girl who, each week, promised to remove her bra but never actually did, and the infamous 'balloon dance' sketch in which three puny, but still a little bit flabby, naked fellas jiggled along in time to some music, with nothing but a diminishing number of balloons to protect their modesty. Although gratuitous nudity was actually kept to a minimum in this routine, viewer complaints still flooded in. Yet with material this poor (not to mention an overlong *That's Life!* skit entitled 'That's Tough!', and a terribly dull segment in which Chris Tarrant tried to recount a feeble anecdote from his childhood), the viewers should have been complaining about how unfunny the show was instead.

Throughout the series regular slots came and went including 'Beat Your Brains Out' in which members of the studio audience attacked each other for no good reason; 'Tanks for Dropping In' – a quiz played by contestants dangling over a tank full of gunk; and something called 'Weekend Wind Up'. Just a few weeks in, Alexei Sayle quit and was replaced by Bernard Manning, who though no less offensive was at least more in keeping with the style of the show. Yet still the critics and the general public poured scorn on the programme and presenter Lenny Henry had to endure the ignominy of unwittingly overhearing his own family giving it a right good slagging.

After the final episode was transmitted, you could almost hear ITV's sigh of relief. Chris Tarrant was allowed another stab at Saturday night television the following year but *Saturday Stayback* was pretty similar to *OTT* and therefore not very good. After *Stayback* the notion of transferring a Saturday morning kid's show onto Saturday evenings was something ITV steered well clear of for another twenty years.

Parkinson

BBC1/Granada Television for ITV1

19 June 1971 to ongoing
(536 episodes as of 16 June 2007)

You know you've become famous when you can be referred
to simply by your surname. Apologies to Lord Cecil, but
Parkinson has always meant the Barnsley-born chat show
curmudgeon.

Michael Parkinson started his career on television in the
early Sixties as a reporter at Granada. His Yorkshire accent –
clear enough to understand, but distinctive enough to suggest
northern grittiness – and encyclopaedic knowledge of sport
and show business saw him gain a reputation as a first-rate
interviewer, and after a brief stint at LWT (during its first,
disastrous months on air) he moved on to report for the BBC's
24 Hours. Then in 1971, a gap opened in the late night

Saturday schedules, and Michael was asked to fill it for a few weeks with a cheap chat show. Eleven years later, he was still there.

There was little gimmickry about *Parkinson*, it was simply Michael, two or three guests, and some incisive chat. This straightforward approach meant it was possible to entice big-name guests to appear; Orson Welles was the first major star, followed by the likes of Peter Sellers, James Stewart and, most famously, Muhammad Ali. Billy Connolly made his name on the programme, though the most repeated encounter was undoubtedly with Rod Hull and Emu; somewhat amusing given he was probably the least prestigious guest in the series' history.

Parky's no-nonsense approach meant he soon became the first choice for any big star. For his part, Parkinson was lucky to be operating at a time when most of the major names of the Hollywood golden era were still alive. Such was the show's success, by the end of the Seventies plans were made to broadcast the show every night of the week. This was vetoed by the BBC governors, although a Wednesday episode was established in 1979.

Michael interrogated the stars six months a year for eleven years, but called it a day in 1982, leaving for Camden Lock and the brave new frontier of breakfast television in the shape of TV-am. This proved to be a bit of a mistake and throughout the Eighties and much of the Nineties, Parky found himself fronting virtually any show going.

Then in 1995, Parky was lured back to the BBC to front a series of his most memorable interviews, to massive critical acclaim. Eventually, in January 1998, *Parkinson* came back. Virtually nothing had changed, with many of his most famous guests (including, of course, Billy Connolly) returning alongside newer names from the world of entertainment. It was as if he'd never been away, and as before Parky's credentials continued to attract major names, including the first interview with a post-arrest George Michael.

That's not to say this new *Parkinson* was entirely faultless; there was a crankiness about the older Michael that occasionally overshadowed the interviews, most obviously during a notorious exchange with Meg Ryan that couldn't have been more stilted if they had been in different studios. But it was still a major shock when, in 2004, Parkinson announced he was quitting the BBC and taking the show lock, stock and barrel to ITV. The reason for this, apparently, was that the eponymous host felt he needed to be on at 10 p.m., but with the return of *Match of the Day*, *Parkinson* on BBC1 would be scheduled earlier in the evening. Parky claimed this would make it 'a different show', but failed to explain what these 'differences' might be, or why being scheduled at nine o'clock would be such a disaster.

Parkinson remains an important part of Saturday night telly more than three decades on, though in its ITV incarnation it would difficult to suggest that Joe Pasquale and Shane Richie are quite at the same level as Richard Burton and Robert Mitchum.

The Paul Daniels Magic Show
BBC1

9 June 1979 to 18 June 1994 (125 episodes)

The thing about magicians is that the very nature of their act makes them hard to like. While you stand there looking like a fool, perhaps with your watch surreptitiously swiped from your person, they go ahead, reveal the card you were thinking of all along and win all the applause. But, crucially, they always look a bit smug too. Perhaps this explains why the general public at large have never really shown Paul Daniels an unequivocal warm embrace. His conjuring skills and the quality of his patter may not be in question, but over the course of his fifteen years of Saturday night telly success, his relationship with the viewer was always slightly brittle, as if Paul was waiting for the next crack to come from the audience about his toupee.

In fact the kind of attention that Daniel's hairpiece has attracted down the years has been quite revealing, with the jaundiced cheers that erupted on his eventual admittance to wearing a wig carrying a far nastier aftertaste than any of the joshing Bruce Forsyth and Terry Wogan have endured regarding the pedigree and recent history of the follicles sitting atop their bonces.

The Paul Daniels Magic Show (or 'Small Daniels Tragic Show' as some wags renamed it) featured magical acts and nothing but, with the onus being on the eponymous man of magic himself. This meant that Paul was required not only to devise countless tricks per series, but had to come up with new and interesting ways to present them. On any given edition you could expect to see Paul silently working through a little close-up magic with only the gentle tones of a lounge bar jazz guitarist to accompany his prestidigitation, dressing up as the Jack of Hearts and recounting a little story while performing a standard three-card trick, and awkwardly asking a member of the audience for a loan of his handkerchief, before then enquiring whether it had previously been used or not ('can you imagine borrowing one on television and it's all rotten?').

A trademark of the series was how ill at ease most of the studio audience seemed to be in Daniels' company, mainly because Paul would happily berate his volunteers if he felt they were being too slow ('preferably today' being one of his most often used phrases, but for some reason rather less celebrated than 'say "Yes Paul"', 'You're going to like this – not a lot!' and 'Now that's magic!'). A more memorable brush with the public came in the shape of a very simple but elegant sequence in which Daniels, accompanied

© Sten Roselund/ Rex Features

by a young girl called Blue, ran through a routine involving three rings. The climax of the performance required a clearly nervous and embarrassed Blue to swallow an invisible substance given to her by Paul. Informing her she had just consumed some confidence, Paul attempted to effect a touching moment by telling her 'confidence is the most magical thing in the world, Blue. Once you have that you can do anything.'

Similarly entertaining were Daniels' routines featuring two chimps decked out in bright yellow T-shirts with the legend 'That's Magic'. But undoubtedly everyone's favourite part of *The Paul Daniels Magic Show* was the Bunco Booth in which our host would contrive to con a member of the public using only the techniques and games of America funfair hustlers. Although Paul (ably assisted by his later wife Debbie McGee) had to bear the burden of entertaining the viewers at home for most of the episode, each edition featured a few guest artistes. Over the years *The Paul Daniels Magic Show* played host to a number of truly superlative and original novelty acts, the two best remembered are the frankly nuts Hans Moretti (who was so skilled at hyperbole that he could even manage to oversell the seriousness of shooting a crossbow bolt at his own head), and the wonderful Tommy Noddy's Bubble Magic (which combined nicotine and soap suds to form a truly enchanting act).

Equally essential were the grand illusions that formed a climax to each episode. These would often be recorded outside, and might feature Paul escaping from a garden hut before a series of giant concrete slabs could crush him to death, or even re-enacting a favourite Houdini stunt. Unlike most of the rest of the show, the tone here was usually very sombre, with Paul talking an independent witness (generally in the shape of some celebrity or other) through the intricacies of the stunt, continually accentuating the risk to his personal health.

By the time the series was cancelled in 1994, television magic had entered a period of doldrums and Daniels had fallen out of fashion with programme makers. Yet, you can't escape the fact that *The Paul Daniels Magic Show* proved to be remarkably durable, and in notching up fifteen years on primetime Saturday nights, Paul succeeded in performing a feat as miraculous as any of his illusions.

Pets Win Prizes

BBC1

16 July 1994 to 3 August 1996 (22 episodes)

'It's your licence fee at work!'

When it was announced, the concept for *Pets Win Prizes* was met with, to put it mildly, some scepticism. This really must have been the silliest idea for a game show yet. Members of the public brought their animals into the studio to participate in a number of games – snail races, cockerel crowing and so forth – to win prizes for both the humans and the pets.

On paper, it sounded absolutely awful, and some would say in actuality it was absolutely awful too. However, there was something more to it, as the presence of Danny Baker as host illustrated. Baker revelled in the ludicrous nature of the series, and sent up the whole affair something rotten. In a way it was tailor-made for Baker's love of the bizarre. One game sums it all up; a pair of shire horses battled it out to be the first to pull a pint a beer. Baker's commentary consisted of little more than repeating, in incredulous tones, 'It's shire horses pulling pints of beer!' Even the host couldn't believe how demented this programme was.

There was an obvious delight in the bizarre nature of proceedings that managed to make *Pets Win Prizes*, perhaps surprisingly, rather an appealing affair. It was transmitted at a time when Danny Baker seemed to be presenting every other programme on TV, and many viewers failed to buy into his rather unique presentational style. As such, when the series returned the following year, it was with Dale Winton in charge.

Winton's work on the likes of *Supermarket Sweep* had shown his genuine love for old-school light entertainment, and he certainly brought bags of energy to the screen. However, without Baker's subversive edge, *Pets Win Prizes* failed to convince quite as much as before. Basically, it was almost being taken seriously, which wasn't right. The arrival of celebrity guests in the final series suggested the show was losing its way somewhat – it was hard to argue that Garry Bushell umpiring a dog tennis match was particularly ground-breaking television, no matter how much irony was involved.

Nevertheless, with Danny Baker in charge, *Pets Win Prizes* was certainly one of the strangest series ever shown on Saturday night television; but one that wasn't without its charms.

Pop Idol

Thames/19 TV for ITV1

6 October 2001 to 20 December 2003

After the first series of **Popstars**, producer and judge Nigel Lythgoe talked about it with his friend, the music business executive Simon Fuller. Fuller suggested that an even better idea was for the public to actually decide upon the band's members. Lythgoe said that wasn't *Popstars*, but, undeterred, Fuller realised there might be some mileage in his idea. He devised a concept through his company 19, and asked Lythgoe if he would like to produce it. The tagline – 'This time, you decide'.

Pop Idol was, at first glance, simply *Popstars* 2, only aiming to find a solo artist rather than a group. The early episodes were fairly familiar, with hopefuls attending auditions, music industry professionals casting their verdicts, and a mix of the exceptional and the embarrassing making the final cut. So far, so ordinary, but there were some changes. The most notable was that, rather than the voice-over, there were now presenters in the shape of Ant and Dec. They attended each audition and hung around with the judges and hopefuls, asking them their opinions and jollying things along.

The show's judges were also more flamboyant. 'Nasty' Nigel stayed behind the camera this time around, but Nicki Chapman stayed on board. She was joined by legendary record producer Pete Waterman, Capital Radio DJ Neil

'Doctor' Fox and someone who they'd tried to land for *Popstars*, Simon Cowell. This was a heavyweight line-up, and the auditions were changed so that the hopefuls entered the room one by one and faced all the judges – hopefully heightening the tension and causing more conflict.

The big difference came when the hopefuls reached the last fifty. At that point, it became a more traditional entertainment show, as each auditionee performed in front of the cameras, and it was down to the viewers to phone in and choose their favourite. The judges were still on hand to offer their opinions, but it was us who had the final say in cutting the field down to ten. At this point the series had been running long enough for the viewers to get familiar with the contestants. Gareth Gates and the enormous Rik Waller had, for obvious reasons, caught the eye very early on, while one Will Young had snuck through almost unnoticed.

By the time the final ten had been found the programme had become a huge hit. The next stage was different again, with the action relocating to the massive Fountain Studios, and the final ten now performing live each week, with the hopeful with the fewest votes being eliminated each time. This could have made for pretty boring viewing, watching the same people over and over again, but the production team worked hard, and cleverly used a different theme for each episode. The happy side effect was that we could see the likes of Will and one-time *Popstars* reject Darius Danesh improve, and get to know them much better. By the time we'd got to the final five, everyone had a favourite.

The final episode, on 9 February 2002, received more

column inches than more or less every other Saturday night show of the previous decade put together. The series had been a huge hit, and seemed to prove that light entertainment was very much alive and well. But this was a very twenty-first-century take on the idea. One episode took time out from the singing to allow the audience to ask questions of the judges, one of which involved a discussion as to how the programme had dealt with Rik Waller's throat problems and his subsequent withdrawal. In the past, a knotty problem such as this may have been swept under the carpet, but *Pop Idol* spent time debating how to deal with this, which seemed refreshingly honest.

Despite Will Young being voted winner, there were in fact numerous victors of *Pop Idol*. There was Ant and Dec, finally stars of a successful primetime series. There was Simon Cowell, now a hugely famous face after two decades of success behind the scenes. And there was Simon Fuller, the pop svengali who had invented the show and was soon to see it span the globe in a **Millionaire** fashion.

Indeed, by the time the series returned to British screens in August 2003, the *Idol* franchise had become a smash hit in numerous countries. Most notably, *American Idol* was a huge ratings winner for Fox, thanks mostly to the performance of outspoken judge Simon Cowell. His comments were completely new to American audiences and ensured he became one of the most famous people in the world.

The second series of the original UK version stuck with the winning format. There seemed to be fewer memorable participants in this run and eventual winner Michelle

McManus was more notable for her weight than her voice or personality.

The last British viewers saw of *Pop Idol* came at Christmas 2003 when *World Idol* invited the winners (and the judges) from the now numerous international versions to a mass sing-off, won by gap-toothed Norwegian Kurt Neilsen. Such is the nature of American television, Cowell continues to appear in yearly series of *American Idol*, despite the fact he was involved in legal proceedings against Simon Fuller over claims that his next series, **The X Factor**, was too similar to the *Idol* franchise. The dispute was later settled out of court, but *The X Factor*'s rather contrived nature was certainly no match for the excellent simplicity of *Pop Idol*. With ITV committing themselves to *The X Factor*, it looks as if *Pop Idol* is unlikely to return to the country it began in – making for a premature end to one of the most popular Saturday night shows of recent times.

Popstars

LWT for ITV

10 January 2001 to 22 December 2002 (28 episodes)

Pop music has always played a part in Saturday night television, but it took an Australian company to spot the potential of turning the wheelings and dealings of the music industry into a TV show. It's perhaps obvious, as the whole business of putting a band together is very much like a game show. You have wannabes battling it out through auditions, with much potential for tears and excitement along the way, and as the process continues the numbers are narrowed down until we get the 'winners'.

Popstars began life on Australian TV, as the girl group Bardot was put together with the cameras following every step of the way. The country was hooked on the concept, as was LWT Head of Light Entertainment Nigel Lythgoe, who chanced upon the series while on holiday. When Lythgoe found himself making sure he was in front of the TV the following week, he knew that he was watching a hit, and snapped it up for ITV.

Popstars was a major step in Saturday night TV as it was, essentially, a documentary. There were to be no hosts, with an anonymous off-screen voice passively narrating events instead, and there was no studio, with all the action filmed on location in various conference rooms and offices.

The three 'faces' of *Popstars* were the judges. Nicki Chapman, former Spice Girls publicist, and Polydor A&R man

Paul Adam were booked, but Lythgoe wanted somebody more outspoken to take a lead role. Eventually, someone came up with the idea of Lythgoe himself as a judge. This made sense given his previous role as frontman of Seventies Saturday night regulars The Nigel Lythgoe Dancers.

The judging panel assembled, the tour of the country began, with open auditions held to try and find untapped talent. Here, absolutely anyone would be invited to sing a few lines from a choice of songs, with the best progressing and the rest sent on their way home.

In these early shows there was just as much time spent on the tone-deaf and out-of-tune hopefuls as there was on the impressive. Indeed, the montages of half a dozen hapless individuals all murdering Westlife songs fast became a staple of the show, as did Lythgoe's continual putdowns.

Week by week, the contestants were narrowed down further and further through a number of workshops. By this time everyone was picking their final five. When the decision was made, Noel, Kym, Suzanne, Danny and Myleene became five of the most famous people in the country.

After this, *Popstars* continued for a few more weeks, following the newly named Hear'Say while they recorded their records, filmed their videos and made hundreds of personal appearances. Along the way, this meant that the band would be interviewed on other programmes about being on the programme, and then *Popstars* itself would be a programme about them appearing on other programmes talking about being on the programme.

The final show was broadcast live, with Davina McCall

joining the band to find out whether their debut single 'Pure and Simple' had made it to number one – and not only was this the case, but it had become the fastest-selling debut single in history. This was the perfect end to what had been a hugely successful series, and one that had changed the whole concept of the talent show. No longer would simply finding a good singer and then putting them on the telly suffice.

The autumn of 2001 saw *Pop Idol* refine the concept of the pop talent show further, which meant that when *Popstars 2* finally arrived, major changes were required. Hence LWT came up with *Popstars: The Rivals*. Instead of finding one pop group that the nation was expected to root for, the new show would create both a boy band and a girl band, and at the end of the series both their singles would be released at the same time. The act who charted higher would therefore be the official series 'winner'.

By this point the make-up of the judging panel was one of the major selling points. For this show Pete Waterman was kept on from *Pop Idol*, while Westlife manager Louis Walsh was also appointed. Finally, ex-Spice Girl Geri Halliwell was hired to add a bit of glamour to the show. This meant that none of the original *Popstars* personnel appeared in this new run. Unlike the first series, too, there was a presenter, the apparently ubiquitous Davina McCall.

It soon became obvious that this was not really *Popstars 2*. It was, in fact, *Pop Idol* 2. The early instalments followed the *Pop Idol* principle to the letter – hopefuls performed in front of the judges, one at a time, before being congratulated or comforted by Davina in the corridors. Various rounds followed to separate the tone-deaf from the talented until we got to the final ten in each gender. Then it was into the studio, where the acts would sing each week with the loser in a phone poll going out each time. Even the judges sat in the same place on the *Popstars* set as they had on *Pop Idol*.

Yet Davina's insistence on everyone sticking to the marks — and, worse still, the prolonged bouts of crying — made it rather irritating viewing, while the uninspired song choices ('I Just Called To Say I Love You' again?) meant it was hard to tell anyone apart. In the end ITV got what they wanted when the girls got to number one for Christmas while the boys languished at number two.

While the run of *Popstars: The Rivals* was going on, Hear'Say announced they were splitting up. Less than two years after having a smash hit with 'Pure and Simple' it was reported that the abuse they received from members of the public was so extreme that they simply couldn't carry on. Yet despite this warning thousands of young people were still desperate to get involved in television talent searches, obviously believing that stardom still beckoned.

The Premiership

Central/ISN for ITV1

18 August 2001 to 16 May 2004 (286 episodes)

Seven o'clock, Saturday 18 August 2001. Des Lynam looks at his watch. 'Better for you, better for all of us,' he crows. The transfer of Premiership football highlights from the BBC to ITV had been a major coup for the commercial channel, but it had come at a high price. At a cost of £60 million a season for three seasons, the largest amount of money ever lavished on non-live football, ITV needed to make the most of their investment. Hence, for the first time in decades, football highlights were to be pre-pub, rather than post-pub, television.

Placing an hour and a quarter of football in peak-time television seemed a brave move, possibly alienating much of the existing audience, but ITV were bullish. Director of Programmes David Liddiment heralded it as 'a once-in-a-lifetime opportunity to change the shape of Saturday evening viewing. The assumption that football is a male preserve is not borne out by the facts – for many women and children it is the national game.'

Yet despite Head of Sport Brian Barwick, a former *Match of the Day* editor, pointing out 'The best stuff will still be the action, but at a time when we're not half asleep', it seemed that many of the production team decided that Premiership needed a bit of help to entertain the prime-time audience.

Terry Venables got his hands on ProZone, a much-hyped computer program that was apparently used in all the top clubs to help with training, but which translated into a dull set of diagrams on screen. Ally McCoist selected his top three goals of the day to much banter from Des and Terry, while Andy Townsend commandeered the 'Tactics Truck' and parked up at a match to lecture a player on what he'd done wrong. Managers were interviewed at half-time as well as full-time, match reports followed players off the pitch and the biggest match was kept to the end of the show to increase the excitement. It was certainly a packed programme – which meant that only twenty-eight minutes of the first episode was actually spent showing football.

This inevitably attracted the ire of football fans, but worse still it failed to interest the general audience. The first programme was soundly beaten by BBC1, pulling in under 4 million viewers, while the following week, despite an increase in the amount of match highlights, ratings sunk still further; the 3.2 million audience contributing to ITV's worst-performing Saturday night for five years.

ITV claimed that as the nights got darker viewing figures would rise, but there was one factor that meant *The Premiership* was never going to hit the heights – it was a football programme. Sure, big England matches broadcast live would pull in big audiences and get many casual fans tuning in, but highlights of goalless draws between Middlesbrough and Southampton were less likely to. Football fans hated *The Premiership* because it wasted time that could be spent showing matches on whimsical fillers, and non-fans hated it because there was football in it, full stop. Hence, almost from day one, it became a case of when, rather than if, it would be moved from its prime-time slot.

Viewing figures bumped along around 4 million for a few months and eventually, ITV waved the white flag and announced that, from November, *The Premiership* would be rescheduled to 10.30 p.m. Replacing it at 7 p.m. was a new series of **Blind Date**, and ratings for its first show were some 2 million higher than anything Des and the gang had achieved.

Eventually the 10.30 p.m. *Premiership* fell into something of a groove. Late at night, the pressure to entertain was nowhere near as great, and viewing figures in this late slot were pretty similar to those it had attained in peak-time. For the expense, ITV had clearly expected more, and when the rights came up for renewal for the 2004/5 season onwards, they returned to the BBC – who actually paid less than ITV did three years earlier. *The Premiership* therefore came to an end – and as if to emphasise ITV's commitment to football, the final programme was delayed to make way for **Stars in Their Eyes**.

The Price Is Right

Central Production for ITV

24 March 1984 to 8 April 1988 (100 episodes)

For the unsuspecting viewer, switching on the first episode of *The Price Is Right* must have been a bit like opening an oven door only to be greeted by the very fire of Hell itself. Loud, crass and completely unapologetic, it's safe to say that British television had never seen its like before.

Based on the American game show of the same name that had been running Stateside since the Fifties, it took until 1984 before *The Price Is Right* made it to our screens.

Michael Crawford was the first person approached to present the show and when he turned it down *Game for a Laugh*'s Matthew Kelly and actor Mike Reid were briefly considered. Russ Abbot was in the running for a while too, but his vision for the programme (which featured a number of changes to the proposed running order, as well as a major role for his *Russ Abbot's Madhouse* sidekick Bella Emberg) fell foul of the American producers who held the rights to the format. As history will attest, after much to-ing and fro-ing eventually entertainer Leslie Crowther was the man who landed the job.

The Price Is Right was most famous for its studio audience that each week somehow whipped itself up into a frenzy. Bussed in from all over the country, the television viewer was left only to speculate whether or not there was some kind of hallucinogenic drug piped into the studio, such was the manic reaction whenever Leslie Crowther uttered the show's immortal catchphrase 'come on down'.

In the original American version it had actually been an unseen announcer who uttered those three famous words, but over here each and every show would begin very simply with Crowther bellowing out the name of the lucky audience members chosen to play followed by that 'come on down' command. As soon as those select few had made their way down the steps onto Contestants' Row (all to wildly rapturous applause) we were off and running with no further preamble required.

The show was devastatingly simple: the opening round featured contestants trying to estimate the cost of various items without exceeding the actual value. The best-performing contestant would go on to play a further game, and would then be either disqualified or placed on 'hold' in preparation for the big finale. This process was repeated until six people had been chosen to compete in *The Price Is Right*'s end game, 'the Showcase Final'. Here the contestants were allowed to choose a prize of their choice from a bevy of big-money items presented before them. All that was required to win was to successfully estimate the total value of the Showcase.

While all the hype was reserved for the end game, the middle rounds featured some brilliant challenges. 'Cliffhanger' (which was accompanied by some wonderfully upbeat yodelling music) featured a cheapo-looking model mountaineer who made his way up a slope in accordance with the contestant's overestimated value of various prize items. 'Plinko' was another well-liked, if rather more straightforward challenge, in which contestants got to play a game of what was essentially bagatelle. Although little skill was required beyond placing a token into the top of the Plinko board, there was something strangely mesmerising in watching the little chip's progress down between the pins.

Although an instant hit with the audience at home (within a matter of weeks *The Price Is Right* hit the top of the ratings with 16 million viewers), critics were repulsed by the show, with the *Daily Mail* lambasting its 'unspeakable vulgarity, ghastly materialism and unedifying greed'. A consensus was reached pretty quickly that the studio audience were either sourced from the most vulgar sections of society, or were somehow put under a mysterious spell in the studio that resulted in them behaving in such a riotous manner. Yet neither was the truth. In fact the recording of the first episode was momentarily stymied when the first-ever contestant, Mary Brown (chosen because her surname rhymed with 'Come on down'), became instantly paralysed with fear at the sound of her name being read out and refused to leave her seat.

The show was finally axed in 1988 in what remains mysterious circumstances (the first Crowther heard of it was when a reporter turned up at his house to get a comment about its demise). After a period in exile (well, on Sky Television), *The Price Is Right* turned up on ITV screens again almost ten years later. It has remained an occasional presence since then with various hosts down the years girding their loins and steeling themselves to take on the scariest audience in television.

Public Enemy Number One
BBC1

5 September 1992 to 17 October 1992 (7 episodes)

One of the BBC's curious affectations in the Nineties was their continual snapping-up of past-their-best ITV personalities. Signing Jim Davidson for **Big Break** proved a success, but hiring Jimmy Tarbuck, Marti Caine and Hale and Pace definitely wasn't. The same was true for Bobby Davro.

Davro turned up at the corporation in 1992 requiring a new home, as the ITV company TVS, who'd made all his shows to date, had just lost their franchise. On the BBC he wasn't hired as a comedian and impressionist, but instead as a game show host, put in charge of the new show, *Public Enemy Number One*. Each week, he would welcome four celebrities who would attempt to predict how many people would fall for various pranks. If they got it wrong, embarrassing clips and forfeits would be forthcoming.

With hidden-camera stunts involved, it was no surprise that the word 'Beadle' loomed large, someone Davro was keen to distance himself from, as he told *Radio Times*: 'the humour of Beadle – and it can be funny – comes through humiliating people, which can be cruel. This show is not like that.'

Maybe so, but a little savagery might have helped a series that completely failed to stick in people's minds. Perhaps it was the Z-list nature of the celebrity panellists (with the likes of Paul Shane, Peter Stringfellow and Keith Chegwin involved) or the witless nature of some of the stunts (such as Davro dressing as a sheepdog and attempting to round up a flock), but after seven episodes the programme was swiftly cancelled.

Those newspaper critics who bothered to pass comment seemed to reflect the public's attitude in suggesting that there should be no period of great mourning at the show's passing. Davro himself came in for a fair amount of stick, with his effervescent and decidedly 'peppy' demeanour coming across as irritating, and not a little dated. It is perhaps no surprise that he has since referred to the series as 'Public Enema'.

Public Enemy Number One only really had two lasting legacies. The first came at the end of the series when the celebs got their own back on Davro by placing him in stocks. Unfortunately, these were rather shoddily assembled and Bobby plunged to the floor and broke his nose (this moment is actually preserved for posterity on BBC internal health and safety videos). But perhaps the series' most significant contribution occurred with the hiring of a local radio DJ to take part in some of the stunts. Yes, it's thanks to *Public Enemy Number One* that Dale Winton received his first exposure on Saturday night television.

Punchlines

LWT for ITV

3 January 1981 to 22 December 1984 (80 episodes)

Punchlines was bawdier than **Celebrity Squares** (although the set, and in particular the manner in which celebs were stacked on top of each other, closely resembled that show) and somehow even more ridiculous than *Blankety Blank*. But this was the game show that had a catchphrase that was also a piece of advice: 'Remember what you heard, and where you heard it!'

Today, the series' pleasingly robust three-dimensional logo wouldn't look out of place on the front of a Franz Ferdinand CD, but that aside *Punchlines* is a relic from an era that has long since passed – the primetime non-ironic, middle-of-the-road game show. It featured a number of celebrities, each of whom would read out a punchline that the contestants would have to match to the correct opening line of a joke. Of course the programme worked best when the contestant chose the wrong celebrity, therefore allowing a comic talent of the stature of, say, Dave Wolfe or Bernie Winters to milk their answer for all its worth (particularly if the juxtaposition led to something that sounded in anyway mildly risqué). The other highlight of any edition occurred when the celebrities were required to swap positions. This meant leaving their little box and scurrying up or down stairs in order to occupy a vacant space. As you can imagine, when the likes of Rod Hull and Emu were on the show, this was a recipe for much supposed hilarity.

Punchlines was notable for the relatively low level of celebrities (or 'star guests' as the series referred to them) featured on each edition. Favourites on the show included Bobby Davro, Melvyn Hayes, Madeline Smith and Matthew Kelly (in fact, *Punchlines* proved important for Kelly, as it was on this programme that he first caught the eye of the producers of **Game for a Laugh**). Of all the celebs there is no doubt that the most memorable was Irish folk singer Rose-Marie. Her husky tones (think Phyllis off *Coronation Street*) and banter with Bennett were all very entertaining; but the inescapable question remained: who actually was Rose-Marie, and what had she done to merit a central performance on a primetime ITV game show?

Slightly rubbish, but never offensively so, *Punchlines* was just one of a number of new game shows that ITV launched in the early Eighties, and while not as long-running or well loved as, for example, *Play Your Cards Right*, presenter Lennie Bennett's huge grin, silly curly hair and willingness to kid himself that he was having a great time were infectious enough to keep audiences tuning in week after week.

Randall and Hopkirk (Deceased)

Working Title for BBC1

18 March 2000 to 24 November 2001 (13 episodes)

Are Vic Reeves and Bob Mortimer the most unsuccessful successful comedy duo of all time? The likes of *Vic Reeves Big Night Out* and *Shooting Stars* may have received massive critical acclaim and a fanatical following, but, despite numerous attempts, the twosome have yet to translate their cult appeal into a genuinely popular success. **Families at War** had been a little-watched stab at making them primetime stars, but just a year later came another attempt to crack Saturday nights.

But things were different this time. First of all, Vic and Bob abandoned the game show genre in favour of drama; and secondly for the first time in their careers they were to feature in a series that wasn't of their own invention. Actually, Reeves and Mortimer's second Saturday night offensive had been in gestation pretty much since the duo had signed to the BBC in 1993. They had been asked what they'd like to do next on TV and out of the blue had suggested a remake of *Randall and Hopkirk (Deceased)*, the ITV series from the Sixties that is perhaps best summed up by the title it adopted in America, *My Partner the Ghost*. As luck would have it, the rights for a remake were available, and Vic and Bob were offered the lead roles. Reeves would don the white suit of the late Marty Hopkirk, leaving Bob with the role of Mike Randall. Bob seemed happy enough with this arrangement, and spoke excitedly of becoming 'the new Nick Berry'.

The next job was to find a writer – step forward Charlie Higson. Having worked with Reeves and Mortimer for many years, Higson had achieved fame in his own right as a star of *The Fast Show*. He also maintained a sideline as a writer of serious thriller novels, so had the literary credentials, as well as comic touch, to pen a drama suited to Vic and Bob. Unsurprisingly, the humour content was increased, and the result was a show that seemed to take its lead from the already popular ***Jonathan Creek***, mixing (sometimes broad-brush) comedy with proper serious drama (albeit writ in an adventure mould).

The revival struck a chord with audiences, with a whopping 10.5 million people tuning in for the first episode – comfortably the biggest audience Reeves and Mortimer had garnered in their entire career. But it didn't last, and the series shed almost half its viewers over the run. Nevertheless, it was still a qualified success, thanks largely to Reeves and Mortimer's successful transition into serious acting, backed up by decent special effects and sharp scripts (Higson's *Fast Show* colleague Paul Whitehouse co-wrote one of the episodes, ensuring that at least the jokes were up to scratch). One story featuring an emotional reunion with Marty Hopkirk's dad (also played by Vic Reeves) could almost be described as a minor classic.

In retrospect it was a brave decision to run the series on Saturday evenings (apparently the BBC advised Higson that the show was to be first and foremost a detective drama because audiences knew the genre and wouldn't be too frightened by something new) and we can perhaps view it as a dry run for the revival of **Doctor Who.** Indeed, *League of Gentlemen* star Mark Gatiss was involved in both programmes and Higson's role as writer and producer draws comparisons with Russell T Davies' 'showrunner' position on *Doctor Who*. Of course, that's not to mention the regular show-stealing cameos by Tom Baker.

Sadly, once the novelty of the revival wore off, *Randall and Hopkirk*'s enthusiastic fanbase proved to be a lot smaller than the BBC had hoped. The series' long-term fortunes weren't helped by some ropey scheduling of the second series, and after thirteen episodes *Randall and Hopkirk (Deceased)* was deceased...pending future revival.

Red Alert

Ginger Television for BBC1

13 November 1999 to 1 April 2000 (14 episodes)

With *Noel's House Party* having called it a day in 1999, the BBC needed a big new show for Saturday nights that could deliver the same huge audiences and run for as many years. Hence *Red Alert*, which, it was hoped, would take light entertainment into the twenty-first century. Big things was expected from it, as the production company behind it was Chris Evans's Ginger Television, which had already revolutionised the genre with *Don't Forget Your Toothbrush*.

Indeed *Red Alert* owed a lot to *Toothbrush*, specifically the edition where the entire audience were taken away to Disneyland Paris. At the end of each episode of *Red Alert*, the residents of an entire street would be whisked away on an exotic holiday, while daft games and musical guests would jolly things along while we got there. Add to that the National Lottery draws, and you had a sure-fire hit. Didn't you?

It's perhaps tempting to guess the thought process that went into choosing *Red Alert's* main host – with Cilla Black undoubtedly the queen of Saturday night telly, why not hire one of her contemporaries? Lulu had in her Sixties pomp fronted her own BBC1 Saturday night shows, yet thirty years on she seemed to have forgotten everything she'd learnt and brought little warmth or humour to her presentation. She also had a distinctly frosty relationship with co-host Terry Alderton, who just seemed overwhelmed – unsurprisingly for a comedian whose only previous TV experience had been short bursts of his stand-up act.

Yet it would have been hard for anyone to make *Red Alert* work. Broadcast live from an enormous studio, the show was massively overambitious, with four streets battling it out to win a holiday, leading to some four hundred people all angling to get into shot. This meant the viewer could never understand who they were supposed to be watching and rooting for. It just wasn't possible to care who won because you didn't know who anyone was.

The games themselves also left a lot to be desired – the most notable being 'Pump Up Your Postie', where the entire crowd were demanded to jump up and down on their seats to blow up a giant inflatable, the sort of thing that even *Noel's House Party* would have considered 'a bit stupid'. The games almost always went wrong in any case, thanks to the set being too big for anyone to hear anything and Lulu and Terry going to pieces.

Meanwhile darts commentator Sid Waddell was hired to voice-over the lottery draws. His Geordie accent and ludicrous turns of phrase were clearly supposed to subvert the conventions of light entertainment, but hearing him greet the balls with such expressions as 'Twenty-one! That's seven double seven!' was just a waste of time, especially as massive sound problems rendered him completely unintelligible. Sid was dropped after just one week.

Everything else staggered on until Christmas, when the series took a break. When it returned, pretty much the only things that remained were the name and the hosts. The studio set had been completely changed to a virtual replica of the old *Toothbrush* setting. Lulu was confined to a sofa and did little more than introduce that week's musical guests, while Terry was on the other side of the studio and ran the games. Now it was a battle between two streets, both of which nominated three people to take part – so at least it was easier to actually get a grip on who we were supposed to be watching. The programme was also now pre-recorded and this ensured it was far more professional than the shambolic first attempt.

However, it was equally useless as a piece of entertainment. The mechanics of the game had been simplified, but to a ludicrous extent. There were rounds of general knowledge questions, there was a round of observation questions based on a film clip and, unbelievably, a round where the two streets' hardest residents took part in an arm-wrestling bout. This was hardly the future of entertainment, and *Red Alert* was unsurprisingly axed at the end of the series. At least the first version's endless cock-ups had been quite funny.

Robin of Sherwood

Goldcrest/HTV for ITV

28 April 1984 to 28 June 1986 (24 episodes)

Robin of Sherwood was a thoughtful reinterpretation of the classic story, only with added magic. The series' pagan allusions (including references to Herne the Hunter, a pre-Christian god) and occasional political subtexts may have provoked complaints from some viewers, but there was a sense of immense grace about the show, helped in no small part by the tranquil title sequence that featured Robin of Loxley (Michael Praed) adopting a number of 'Man from C&A' catalogue poses to the haunting and murky tones of the BAFTA-winning soundtrack provided by Irish folk group Clannad.

To be sure, it was a beautiful-looking programme, from the luxuriant hair products obviously but rather incongruously used by Robin (but less so by his band of followers) to the wonderfully lit woodland locations in which dark shadows were contrasted by angelic shafts of light piercing through the deep undergrowth. All in all, this was a British drama with a lustre that was unfamiliar to most Saturday evening viewers.

The series was a conscious attempt to do the original legend justice, but the downside to this 'back to basics' approach was an almost total absence of humour; and whereas the earlier *Dick Turpin* (by the same writer) had added a pleasing sense of the absurd to the fight scenes, with

Robin of Sherwood it was heavy grunting and hands gripping faces all the way.

The second series culminated in the death of Robin, a move that was brought about by Praed's desire to try his luck in America. In stepped Jason Connery, who assumed the title role for the third and final year in a move that left most casual viewers utterly perplexed. Perhaps then it's not altogether surprising that the final run is generally regarded as inferior to the first two. Many cite Connery's performance as wooden and lacking the charisma which Praed had brought to the part. In addition the new writers (including Anthony Horowitz who some years later would pen **Crime Traveller**) were said to be unsympathetic to the programme's archetypal content. Unsurprisingly, there was to be no fourth series.

Like many cult programmes, rumours have surfaced on a regular basis about *Robin of Sherwood*'s revival. In 1991 Praed, along with Nickolas Grace (who played the Sheriff of Nottingham), appeared on *Good Morning Britain* to discuss a mooted new production. For whatever reason, this fell through and it was left to the BBC to bring the man in Lincoln Green back to Saturday nights after a gap of twenty years.

The Rolf Harris Show
BBC1

21 January 1967 to 23 January 1971 (56 episodes)

Rolf Harris must own a gatefold passport. Over fifty years on British television he's been involved in loads of different types of programmes, and assumed lots of different roles. There's Rolf the artist, enthusing about the great painters and attempting to produce something in their style, and Rolf the animal lover, comforting blubbing adults watching their pets being put down.

There was also Rolf the children's entertainer, joined each week by a different school's worth of hyperactive youngsters for games, stories and stylophones, and of course Rolf the singer, getting out his wobbleboard and didgeridoo and essaying another novelty song like 'Tie Me Kangaroo Down Sport'.

However, we're most interested in the late Sixties, where the most versatile man in show business was Rolf the light entertainer. *The Rolf Harris Show* ran for several years, and saw Rolf, in a nippy Italian suit, joined by almost all the big names in music and comedy for songs and sketches.

It's a format that was not unusual at the time – the likes of Cilla Black and Lulu had helmed their own variety shows and, as a noted musician himself, Rolf was the natural choice to follow them. His series used as its theme, somewhat inevitably, 'Tie Me Kangaroo Down Sport', although in a rather jazzy arrangement with subtly altered lyrics for each week's episode and added accompaniment by The Young Generation. This toothy dance troupe were a fixture of Rolf's shows and the great man would regularly join in on their routines; although we're sad to report that dancing is perhaps one of the few things Rolf didn't excel at.

Rolf's first series saw Sandie Shaw appearing every week to showcase the finalists for the UK entry to *The Eurovision Song Contest*, with Rolf travelling to Vienna to commentate on the triumphant performance of 'Puppet on a String' in the contest itself. The rest of the series continued along this musical bent, with the likes of Dudley Moore, Dusty Springfield, Cleo Laine and Ray Stevens guesting.

Throughout the run, Rolf was never less than versatile, performing in any musical style and able to deliver the all-important gags. Whereas most of the other musicians who landed their own BBC variety show were transfixed to the autocue when they weren't belting out their hits, Rolf's professionalism meant that he felt entirely at home in front of the cameras.

The series came to an end in 1971, and for the rest of the decade, although Rolf was still a regular on Saturdays, he tended to be on rather earlier in the evening with shows aimed at a much younger audience. However those kids of the Sixties turned into the TV executives of the Nineties and ensured the owner of perhaps the world's most famous beard never remained out of favour for long.

Russ Abbot's Madhouse

LWT for ITV

12 April 1980 to 5 August 1985 (45 episodes)

If you were looking for comedy heroes back in the Eighties, they came no bigger than Russ Abbot (real name Russ Roberts). During those whirlwind ten years of television ubiquity Russ won countless awards, found himself described as 'the hottest comedy property since Peter Sellers' and was even named Comedian of the Decade. All of this, from a gangly-looking bloke with a propensity for dressing up in Fifties gear.

Russ's success is based almost entirely on *Russ Abbot's Madhouse*. Yet that show wasn't devised with him in mind and actually began in 1979 under the name of *Freddie Starr's Variety Madhouse*. According to Abbot, three pilot

shows of that series were made, each with different casts before a supposedly workable formula was hit upon. However it was far from a happy production, with Freddie Starr in particular causing a rumpus and complaining about what he felt was poor material ('You are a complete idiot!' / 'No I'm not, I've got a tooth missing'). When Starr walked off the set in protest a new team was put together with Russ, a supporting artiste in the original series, promoted to leader of the gang. Comedy actors of the calibre of Jeffrey Holland were brought in to provide a better balance to the line-up and although Tracey Ullman was considered for a part, the female roles went to Susie Blake, Sherrie Hewson and the soon to become iconic Bella Emberg.

The humour was, by and large, rather silly and perhaps not a little surreal ('My mother never understood me – she was Japanese'), but it was also timeless in nature. The show's regular characters sought not to reflect or comment upon modern society and instead drew inspiration from the well of popular fiction: Boggles was a spoof on the stiff-upper-lip RAF pilots of wartime fiction, while Cooperman was the point at which American comic books and well-loved British comedians met. Other memorable creations included Barratt Holmes, Fritz Crackers ('Ladies and gentleman my name is Fritz Crackers and I come from Switzerland, but unfortunately I don't speak a word of English. So for the benefit of any people in the audience from Switzerland: "Good Evening"'), Basildon Bond, Vince Prince, Wilf Bumworthy, the Fat Man, Val Hooligan and most famously, Jimmy McJimmy (or CU Jimmy as he later became known).

Bizarrely, the incomprehensible Jock owed at least some of his appeal to the Thin White Duke of Pop, David Bowie. Apparently fellow inmate Dustin Gee had been working himself up to impersonate Bowie when he decided that the red wig ordered as part of his costume looked out of place. Spying the discarded hairpiece, Abbot decided on a whim to try it out with his new character (apparently Abbot was often told he had an excellent face for wigs), and the rest – as they say – is history.

Each edition of *Russ Abbot's Madhouse* featured a vast array of comic characters and the sheer speed of the programme meant that many of these were reduced to simple, repeatable catchphrases, almost all of which found their way into schoolyard vernacular. Big musical numbers were also important and the cast's performances as fictional acts such as Vince Prince and the Tone Deafs injected a youthful energy that few other shows of the time could match.

For six happy series, *Russ Abbot's Madhouse* attracted big Saturday teatime audiences and provided fast-paced inoffensive comedy that was never too proud to pick on the most obvious of comedy targets. In 1986 Russ brought the *Madhouse* to an end, and took his act to the BBC.

His show on BBC1 ran until 1991 when allegedly a BBC bigwig was heard to announce at the Montreux Television Festival that Abbot no longer represented what the audience wanted to see on their screens. But Russ remains proud that his show proved to be an important launch pad for a number of successful entertainers (chiefly Les Dennis, Dustin Gee and Michael Barrymore) and Abbot's influence can still be detected in today's popular alternative comedians (after all, what was Steve Coogan's Tony Ferrino if not an updated version of Julio Doubleglazias?). Whether or not there will ever again be a place on Saturday nights for Abbot's particular brand of comedy remains doubtful, but maybe some kind of revival, if only in the form of a DVD release, is now due.

Sale of the Century

Anglia Television for ITV

19 February 1972 to 13 November 1983 (374 episodes)

'And now,' proclaimed John Benson on voice-over, 'from Norwich, it's the quiz of the week!' Each week *Sale of the Century* brought us three contestants who would fight it out in a quick-fire quiz to earn varying sums of money (in the first round questions would be worth £1, before rising to £3 and eventually £5 as the game progressed). At the end of each round, host Nicholas Parsons would try and tease the contestant who had acquired the most cash into making a purchase from one of the many goods the show put on offer at knock-down prices.

In this role, Parsons was at his oleaginous best, forever enticing old ladies to part with their winnings in return for impractical-looking fur coats. In fact as a game show host, Parsons managed to be both accomplished and idiosyncratic, in one memorable edition peppering the introductory chat with the nonsensical question 'so do you know a lot of information?' directed at each of the contestants.

The first edition featured a playgroup supervisor from Salisbury, a stock controller from Sudbury and a schoolteacher from Allesley battling it out for prizes such as £1,000 sports car (that could be purchased on the show for just £95 of the contestant's winnings); a £333 colour television set (a snip at £30); a £720 continental bedroom suite (just £70), and a fortnight's family holiday in Cyprus, worth £560 (for only £55). Clearly this was an aspirational show, and it is probably of no surprise to learn that on at least one occasion *Sale of the Century* fell foul of the Independent Television Authority who believed the programme 'gloated over the high value of its prizes'.

Although the contestants were mainly drawn from the rank and file of the general public, on occasion *Sale of the Century* would invite celebrities in to play. The first such edition took place on 2 January 1981, and the exercise was repeated again the following year. Yet by the early years of the Eighties, *Sale of the Century* was looking old hat. True it did hold the title of ITV's longest-running game show, but after the conclusion of the 1983 series the show was wrapped up. The timing of the cancellation was probably just about right given that its trademark avaricious streak was to be completely superseded the following year by the introduction of **The Price Is Right**.

Saturday Live

LWT for C4

12 January 1985 to 11 April 1987 (19 episodes)

'This beats poncing around on *The Late Late Breakfast Show*. This beats *The Two Ronnies*. This is what they want: anarchy!' Ah, the Eighties – a decade in which a sketch consisting solely of a member of Margaret Thatcher's government appearing before a Commons Select Committee with a gag tied round their mouth could pass for biting satire. These were truly exciting times, but although the performers and camera trickery of *Saturday Live* endure, stripped of its live energy, much of the show's material now seems rather weak and, worse still, irritatingly overconfident of its own humorous merit.

Saturday Live was a conscious attempt to do a traditional Saturday night entertainment series, but one featuring new performers, many of whom had never previously appeared on television. The show was originally planned to run from 8 p.m. to 11 p.m. on Saturday evenings, but this ambitious idea had to be scaled back when it was pointed out that *Hill Street Blues* (which showed at 10 p.m. on Saturdays) was really popular with viewers.

An initial edition was broadcast in 1985. It was presented by Lenny Henry and featured comedians such as Robbie Coltrane, Rik Mayall, Adrian Edmondson, as well as music from old-time rockers Slade, and The Style Council. Although a highly polished and fast-moving show, it wasn't without its problems; the biggest one being that the entire audience were seated on a row of benches, meaning that when the action moved from one stage to another they all had to get up and turn round.

Although it may have launched the careers of innumerable comedians, *Saturday Live* is almost as well remembered today for its use of giant inflatables. Although visually impressive, these lumbering bits of set dressing could be problematic as the heat of the studio caused them to wilt. On one edition the musical act Fascinating Aida were part way through a particularly serious number, when the trunk of an inflatable elephant began to very visibly deflate, causing a lot of laughter from the audience. Given how noisy the air pumps were, the production team had to wait until a commercial break to take corrective action.

In the early days, each show would consist of a guest presenter, a token American comedian, a variety of bands and a roster of established regulars such as Fry and Laurie, The Oblivion Boys, The Dangerous Brothers and, of course, Ben Elton. Of all the performers in those early days, it was Elton who attracted the most interest. His stand-up offered a kind of overtly politicised comedy that hadn't been seen on television before. Routines might begin with an observation on the humble instant noodle, but would wind up with proclamations such as 'Every newspaper is made out of a squirrel's home – that's why they're full of crap'. Famously, his favourite target was the Prime Minister, who at the time was entering the middle years of her premiership and seemed ripe for satirical attack.

Not that Elton had a monopoly on *Saturday Live*'s political comedy, far from it. The programme's disaffection with

Margaret Thatcher and her government may well have been representative of the beliefs of its target audience, but at times you wished they'd give it a rest. The newsflash items (that were mercifully dropped from the show after just a few editions) featured such clunking one-liners as 'Mercedes-Benz have announced the introduction of a new model that steers itself and has a mind of its own – Mrs Thatcher has banned it from the Cabinet'.

By the end of its second year, *Saturday Live* was on a roll and attracting masses of press coverage. However, for some reason the ratings remained stuck around the 1.5 million mark. Reasoning that fewer people were out on a Friday night, the show was moved from its customary slot, and a final series was broadcast under the banner *Friday Night Live*. But still the ratings remained stuck at the same figure and so Channel 4 wisely decided to give the whole thing a rest.

Eight years later ITV, very unwisely, decided to resurrect it. The new *Saturday Live* was broadcast each week at 10 p.m. amidst a hope that this new version would become as much of a must-see as its predecessor. Lee Hurst was selected as host and regular guests on the revised version included Harry Hill, and Armstrong and Miller. Many other big names from the stand-up circuit and album chart also appeared, but by 1996, stand-up shows were all over TV, and there was nothing on the new *Saturday Live* to make it stand out. Hurst also made for a rather uninspired host and when he invited the audience to 'join us next week for the last ever *Saturday Live*...er, well, maybe not the last ever', no one shed any tears when his verbal fumble proved to be correct.

Saturday Night at the Mill
BBC1

6 March 1976 to 11 July 1981 (94 episodes)

While **Parkinson** generally occupied the winter months, Saturday late night chats in the spring and summer were presided over by the likes of Bob Langley from the foyer of the BBC's Pebble Mill studios. *Saturday Night at the Mill* was, in truth, just a jazzed-up version of the daytime magazine show *Pebble Mill at One*. It featured a house band in the guise of Kenny Ball and his Jazzmen and guests primarily pulled from the entertainment firmament. The first ever edition included Michael Bentine, Elaine Delmar, Buddy Greco and Mary Malcolm, all who were able to deliver a low level of pleasantly diverting chat and entertainment.

Although Langley remains the figure most closely associated with the series, one-time *Magpie* host Jenny Hanley took a turn in presenting, as did US political columnist Arianna Stassinopoulos (although she left after just four episodes amidst a volley of complaints from viewers that they couldn't understand her Greek accent). The show also dabbled with guest presenters, but the likes of Jackie Collins weren't really suitably equipped to provide other guests with even a mild grilling.

Aside from the usual chat, *Saturday Night at the Mill* also indulged in more conventional Saturday night entertainment, with acts such as The Shadows quite happy to come on and play a few numbers. One of the most memorable moments featured Bruce Forsyth gatecrashing a performance given by his daughter's band Guys And Dolls. Although this interruption was in fact scripted (and included Bruce disposing of Guys and Dolls' lead singer Paul Griggs by telling him he was 'wanted on the phone'), a later musical tour de force, in which a drunken Oliver Reed dropped his trousers while encouraging Kenny Ball and his Jazzmen to strike up some 'joke music', obviously wasn't.

Over its six series *Saturday Night at the Mill* managed to achieve a good haul of celebrity guests ranging from Terry Thomas to Peter Ustinov. In the main, it steered clear of Hollywood celebrities, presumably in the knowledge that Parky had got them all sewn up for his show, but nonetheless it regularly served up the kind of agreeable chat that ensured your Saturday night in ended on a satisfactory, if sort of unspectacular, note.

Saturday Showtime

ATV for ITV

24 September 1955 to 18 August 1956 (26 episodes)

It's fair to say that, for those of a certain age, *Sunday Night at the London Palladium* is the epitome of light entertainment, striding over the weekend schedules like a colossus for over a decade in the early days of ITV. Yet it certainly wasn't the only example of the genre and, for the first year of the commercial channel, the stars who weren't making their way to the Palladium on Sunday could be found at the Wood Green Empire appearing on *Saturday Showtime*.

This series was something of a catch-all title for that week's big entertainment spectacular, and started so early in ITV's life (its third day on air, in fact) that producers ATV were still known as ABC, before they changed their name to avoid confusion with the imminent franchise holder for the north of England.

Saturday Showtime was really an umbrella title for a number of otherwise unconnected series. The first six shows were hosted by Harry Secombe, 'the Goon with the Golden Voice', and consisted of gaggery with sidekicks Fred Nurke and Johnny Vyvyan, as well as variety acts and the *Saturday Showtime* Tiller Girls – who were presumably some relation to the Tiller Girls who were doing the same job at the Palladium the following evening.

The strand then took on the name 'Wakey Wakey!' and was a showcase for some 'boisterous fun' with Billy Cotton and his band, joined each week by Alan Breeze and Doreen Stephens. This part of the series was directed by Bill Ward, who forty years later was still involved in television, directing the kids' drama *Wavelength*.

Richard Hearne's Mr Pastry helmed the series to see it into 1956, with The George Carden Dancers now providing the hoofing, before Ruby Murray took over for the final stretch, accompanied somewhat further down the cast list by an aspiring comedian called Tommy Cooper. Then that was it, although the name was resurrected for a few one-off variety spectaculars in the next few years.

That was until 1978, when ITV decided to revive the *Saturday Showtime* brand to link a series of one-off specials starring Leslie Crowther ('Leslie Crowther's Scrapbook'), Dave 'Lee's dad' Evans ('An Evening with Dave Evans') and Dickie Henderson, who starred in the brilliantly titled 'I'm Dickie – That's Showbusiness', something of a companion piece to the same year's equally brilliantly titled 'I'm Bob – He's Dickie', where he starred alongside the equally venerable Bob Monkhouse.

Saturday Spectacular

An ATP/ATV Network Production for ITV

10 November 1956 to 18 March 1961 (202 episodes)

Theatre impresario Val Parnell is a big figure in the early history of ITV. His role as managing director of The Moss Empires theatres (which he took on in the mid-Forties) put him in a crucial position when ITV began broadcasting in 1955. Not only did he have access to almost all of the biggest variety stars in Britain, but he also had control over the iconic and prestigious London Palladium.

Sunday Night at the London Palladium was his first major television hit, and it wiped the floor with the BBC's opposition, forcing the corporation to broadcast its own variety special, *We Are Your Servants* which nominally existed to celebrate ten years of post-war service, but featured at least one musical plea to encourage viewers to continue paying the then £3 licence fee. But up against the best contact books in the business there was little the BBC could do against the onslaught of top-quality variety acts on ITV.

Val Parnell's Saturday Spectacular was launched just over a year after *Sunday Night at the London Palladium*, and offered a different take on the world of variety. Each week, the entire running time (ranging from forty-five to sixty minutes) would be given over to just one act, such as Gracie Fields, Max Bygraves, Johnny Ray or Bob Monkhouse. While many of the shows took on the form of a standard revue, the likes of Sid James used his appearances (in 1961) to present to the audience a collection of sketches that reflected a move away from simply broadcasting variety performances, towards material that was specifically tailored for the small screen.

With the same acts returning again and again (Arthur Askey notched up six appearances between 1959 and 1960), in many ways *Saturday Spectacular* (the abbreviated title that the show took on from 1958 onwards) became less a distinct programme in its own right and more of a merry-go-round of different series, with each entertainer patiently waiting before the spotlight fell on them again. It performed reasonably well though, occasionally making it into the list of that week's ten most-watched programmes.

With the exception of the showcase *Sunday Night at the London Palladium*, ITV's variety programmes were actually quite difficult to distinguish from one another. *Val Parnell's Startime*, *Val Parnell Presents Young and Foolish*, *Bernard Delfont Presents* and *Sunday Night at Blackpool*...and the rest all did much the same thing, but to great acclaim from audiences. In fact, for a time in the late Fifties and early Sixties, it really did look as if ITV's star-studded line-up could actually sink the mighty BBC.

Search for a Star
LWT for ITV

8 December 1979 to 4 September 1982 (21 episodes)

While **Opportunity Knocks** relied on its clapometer and **New Faces** on some fiercely complex voting system based on points awarded by a group of judges and a special studio audience panel, *Search for a Star* (not to be confused with the series of the same name that ran for fourteen episodes on ITV in 1964) selected its top acts via an overly complicated collection of regional voting panels. This method was obviously designed to eat up a fair bit of airtime (as presenter Steve Jones had to flit from region to region to collect the scores) and bring to the programme a degree of stature and importance somewhat belying the fact that *Search for a Star* was, in essence, just another talent show.

But then *Search for a Star* billed itself not as a talent show as such, but as a platform for 'working professionals who need a break on television'. This distinction meant that the series was, happily, relatively free of the rather sickly aspirational overtones of its more famous forebears, with the acts coming mainly from the pool of professional stand-up comedians who were working the clubs and pubs of Britain.

The first series was won by Dave Wolfe, a no-nonsense comic who managed to beat off the opposition and land the much coveted star prize – a sixty-minute television special all of his very own (well, Dustin Gee, Faith Brown, Preston and Syreeta, The Supremes and Mary Wilson all appeared, but

Wolfe did get top billing). Other comedians who launched their careers off the back of *Search for a Star* included *Tiswas* presenter Fogwell Flax and Paul Squire (who was very big for a brief spell in the Eighties, before unfathomably slipping back into relative obscurity).

The second-series winner, Lenny Windsor's subsequent career was equally muted, with a stint on *The Cut Price Comedy Show* marking his only significant television work. Given this was the era in which comedians of the questionable calibre of Little and Large were flourishing, it was something of a poser why none of the *Search for a Star* graduates made more of an impact. But the show did at least provide early television exposure for future *Countdown* presenter Richard Whiteley and *Good Morning Britain*'s Nick Owen. Unfortunately, though, neither appeared as an act; instead they were two of the many presenters who turned up each week to deliver the voting scores from the regions. But it was good to see that at least a few careers benefited from an appearance on the show.

Seaside Special

BBC1

5 July 1975 to 29 August 1987 (60 episodes)

The variety show broadcast from some British seaside town or other has been a common staple of Saturday night television down the years. But it has to be said that the various big top, or pier end productions from Jersey, Blackpool or wherever tend, with only memories to rely on, to become indistinguishable from one another. However there are one or two seaside-based extravaganzas that stand apart.

Featuring a galaxy of shiny faces that had caught just a bit too much sun, *Seaside Special* was entertainment at its lightest in the mid-Seventies. Broadcast each week from locations such as Jersey, Torbay, Weymouth, Poole and, of course, Blackpool, each show assembled a selection of the cream of seaside-based acts. Series one kicked off with Ken Dodd, Dana and Wild Honey, while popular acts such as Little and Large, Cilla Black, Rolf Harris and even ABBA turned up during that first year. The likes of Noel Edmonds, Tony Blackburn, Lulu, David Hamilton and Dick Emery all took a hand in presenting and each edition was introduced by an adrenalin-pumping piano and sax theme tune called 'Sunshine Saturday'. This upbeat number featured lyrics that provided a thorough account of each weekday, before pronouncing 'I just can't wait for Sunshine Saturday / the kids in the street know the weekend's come'. Incredibly the song got to number four in the charts.

By 1979 *Seaside* Special, buoyed by a blackout at ITV, was being watched by an astonishing 19.2 million viewers. However the show was wrapped up at the end of the series. Although the BBC would launch the altogether similar *Summertime Special* a couple of years later (complete with theme tune that protested 'I'm tired of fighting / I've had enough / I need some blue skies to lift me up'), the *Seaside Special* brand wouldn't be seen again for another eight years.

Renamed *Seaside Special '87* and broadcast each week from the same spot in Jersey, the revived version featured Radio 1 DJ and one-time Noel Edmonds sidekick Mike Smith as resident host. Over six weeks acts such as A-ha, Shane Ritchie, Val Doonican, Little and Large, Roger De Courcey, Keith Harris, Joe Longthorne and the Roly Polys all plied their wares in front of a relaxed crowd of Jersey holidaymakers, while Smith shepherded contestants through a game of 'Beat the Clock'. *Seaside Special '88* was conspicuous by its absence as instead the series was dropped in favour of *Michael Barrymore's Saturday Night Out*. Again this offered much the same kind of mix of entertainment, allowing the seemingly never-ending production line of summertime beach-side bonanzas to roll on.

The Shane Richie Experience

Granada for ITV

26 August 1995 to 30 August 1997 (17 episodes)

'Deep within the recesses of Granada, once one of Britain's proudest ITV companies, a highly paid team of executives is working on a £1 million series which marks a depressing nadir, even by the often-lamentable standards of light entertainment.' This may seem bad, but the *Daily Mail*'s review of *The Shane Richie Experience* was actually one of the kinder notices this notorious series received.

In the early Nineties, Shane Richie was developing into a familiar face on British television. With an act of singing, dancing and comedy served up with bags of energy, he came across as something like Brian Conley's little brother. He moved up from the summer seasons onto television, hosting the BBC's *You've Been Framed!* rip-off *Caught in the Act* and the Saturday teatime sketch show *You Gotta Be Jokin'*. But an extended stint on *Live and Kicking* annoyed Richie, who felt the BBC thought he was only a kids' entertainer, so he quit and signed an exclusive deal with ITV.

The first fruit of this contract was the cheerfully awful bingo quiz *Lucky Numbers* which can be summed up by Richie's catchphrase, 'Show me your balls!' The main focus, though, was on a new Saturday night show. Shane was hopeful, as he later recalled in his autobiography: 'It was like *TGI Friday* [sic] meets **House Party** meets *Lucky Numbers* meets **An Audience With**… and I was really excited about doing it.'

The show took advantage of the new marriage laws in the UK that meant weddings no longer had to be conducted in churches or register offices, and offered as a prize the chance to get married there and then on national television. To get that far you had to participate in a number of games including, unforgettably, the 'Laundrette of Love' where the brides-to-be had to identify their partners from their backsides. Musical guests sung a few songs, as did Richie himself, and the nation's TV critics exploded at the crassness of the whole thing, claiming it trivialised the entire concept of marriage.

Regardless of the ethics, it was certainly a rum affair, with Richie proving rather resistable as the smug host. Even Shane said he was disappointed with the show, saying that the singing and sketches got in the way of the games, and it was aimed at too young an audience to be a big hit.

Remarkably, despite low ratings (under 6 million) and critical ire, the following year Shane returned for a new series. There were, however, major changes – the songs were dropped, as were the bottom-related games, while the top prize was the chance to get married anywhere in the world, all expenses paid, as opposed to in a shed round the back of Granada Studios. The idea was to make it a bit nicer and more romantic, and to complete the revamp – and to perhaps distance itself from the bad press – the name was changed to the less phenomenal *Love Me Do*. The show was toned down to such an extent that it lost any sort of curious appeal it might have had, and nobody seemed to notice when, eight weeks later, it was axed for good.

Simply the Best

Carlton/Channel for ITV1

17 July 2004 to 4 September 2004 (8 episodes)

Despite **Gladiators** having been axed several years previously, it always seemed as if ITV were desperate to revive it. Certainly the idea of a huge spectacle on a Saturday evening was something that appealed, and *Simply the Best* was yet another attempt to recreate the high-energy family entertainment provided by Wolf and the gang.

Simply the Best was notable from a telly perspective as being one of the few ITV shows ever made by tiny regional company Channel TV. Their involvement came about because the show was broadcast from an open-air arena in Jersey, acting as a 'neutral venue' for cities around the UK to do battle and find out which one was, yes, 'Simply the Best'. The prize on offer was a cash award to be spent on community projects within the winning city.

Despite being billed as a new series, *Simply the Best* was based on a very old series indeed, the French show *Intercities* that had been running since the year dot. The only difference was that, unlike its Gallic parent, a live bull didn't roam around the arena. Fronted by Kirsty Gallacher (or 'Kirsty Gallacher in a bikini' as the trailers pointed out, suggesting the target audience) and Phil Tufnell, each week two cities would be represented by two celebrities and six members of the public in a number of hugely embarrassing *It's a Knockout* style games, most of which seemed to involve carrying around buckets of water and falling over and were normally hideously overcomplicated. A number of musical guests added an element of summer cabaret to proceedings and helped pad the show out to a whopping ninety minutes.

Again, *Simply the Best* fell foul of the same problems as **Ice Warriors**: each team was recklessly overmanned, making it impossible to remember who was who. Celebrity team captains were an attempt to solve this problem, though they were hardly better known, with former *Blue Peter* presenter Stuart Miles and glamour model Leilani as the big names in one show. Where the series really fell down, though, was that the show was simply crass and brainless. The hope, it seemed, was that the open-air location would provide a summery setting for Saturday evenings. But this was stymied as at least one episode was recorded in torrential rain, in the grand *Knockout* tradition.

It was as if the last twenty years of Saturday night telly had never happened. It didn't help that *Simply the Best* was broadcast just shortly after BBC1, with **Strictly Come Dancing**, illustrated exactly how to bring old ideas into the twenty-first century, updating the original concept in a far more subtle way than just filling it up with dolly birds. After weeks of poor ratings and critical derision ITV took action – and actually extended the show to a mammoth two hours. The grand showpiece final, however, found itself relegated to that hallowed slot of half past three in the afternoon – not quite the time you'd expect to see an earth-shattering clash of the titans.

Sin on Saturday

BBC1

7 August 1982 to 21 August 1982 (3 episodes)

In the Seventies and Eighties BBC1 churned out an almost constant diet of vaguely high-minded late night Saturday talk shows that attempted to emulate what they thought was a better class of intellectual dinner party. *Saturday Night at the Mill* and *Saturday Matters with Sue Lawley* managed to just about get away with it, but there was one attempt at a TV dinner party that has since become infamous in the annals of broadcasting

Described as 'eight discussions, interspersed with music and comedy that is thoroughly sinful', the high concept underpinning *Sin on Saturday* was a weekly discussion of one of the seven deadly sins (given the series had been scheduled to run for eight weeks, an additional sin in the shape of 'getting caught' was added to the list). Each week, we were told, guests who had some direct connection with the sin in question would be invited to join host Bernard Falk in a stimulating, free-for-all discussion. Well, that was the plan anyway.

The first programme covered the sin of lust and porn actress Linda Lovelace, ex-nun Karen Armstrong, a representative from the Salvation Army, novelist Charlotte Lamb and actor Oliver Reed were all brought together to give the subject a good airing. Undoubtedly this was an eclectic bunch and Falk visibly struggled to create a decent, structured argument. A question to a line of beauty queens in the audience asking them to 'define lust' resulted only in nervous giggles, and even the most straightforward line of debate went nowhere thanks to the intractable opposing viewpoints of the guests and their obvious disinterest in the conversation. Realising what a stinker the show was turning into, Oliver Reed even tried to walk off the set just as his interview was beginning.

The press reaction was almost universally hostile, with headlines such as 'The Sins of Falk', 'Hell Bent', 'The most deadly sin – just not good enough', 'Bummer of the season', 'A nasty and incompetent piece' filling the papers. BBC1's own Controller went on record to claim that the programme had 'committed the most deadly sin in television of being both boring and banal'.

The second programme featured a discussion on covetousness and included a similarly eclectic selection of guests, but there was a sense that everyone concerned recognised *Sin on Saturday* was a sinking ship. Disgraced Walsall MP John Stonehouse (who in 1976 faked his own death and was jailed for fraud, theft and deception) responded to a question about his return to public life by explaining, 'I do it because you invited me. I think you're a great guy... Bernard here has a great idea for a programme and it's a live programme and I think we should all help live programmes because that's what TV should be about.' But despite Stonehouse's defence for the series, the knives remained out and sharpened.

The third programme (envy) proved to be the last. This time Alan Whicker, the Duke of Argyll and veteran anti-royalist

Willie Hamilton were forced to artificially mutate their life stories into treatise on the pitfalls of coveting someone else's ox. As the final *Sin on Saturday* drew to a close Falk advised us to tune in the following week, where he would be discussing gluttony with 26-stone bounty hunter Tina Boyles, Fanny Craddock, George Best and chef d'humeur Patrick Barlow. But there was to be no 'next week' – *Sin on Saturday* was pulled from our screens after just three episodes.

Slap Bang with Ant and Dec

Blaze Television for ITV

12 May 2001 to 16 June 2001 (6 episodes)

Ant and Dec are perhaps the biggest draw of all on Saturday nights, with *Saturday Night Takeaway* one of the most successful series in recent years. Yet its roots actually belong in a rather less popular show that was an excruciatingly embarrassing flop.

By the start of 2001, Ant McPartlin and Declan Donnelly were being wooed by both of the major channels. They'd presented two series of *Friends Like These* for the BBC, and the corporation was prepared to offer them an exclusive contract. Meanwhile, on ITV, the duo had managed to end the BBC's twenty-five-year domination of the Saturday morning audience with *SMTV Live*, a hugely popular children's series that, thanks to daft features and big star guests, had managed to pull in a sizeable audience of both kids and adults. The series even won the viewers' vote at the 2000 British Comedy Awards – beating off other 'grown-up' shows.

Slap Bang (so called because it was 'slap bang' in the middle of the weekend) was a *Don't Forget Your Toothbrush*-style miscellany of features. Some of these were taken wholesale from *SMTV Live*, including 'Challenge Ant' (only this time with pensioners rather than children asking the questions) and the pun-laden sitcom 'Beers' (which was simply a relocation of the popular *SMTV Live* 'Chums' sketch).

If *SMTV Live* had been the new *Tiswas*, here was Ant and

Dec's *OTT*. The programme was soundly beaten by the BBC1 opposition – which was, horror of horrors, *Friends Like These*, doing just fine under new host Ian Wright. In fact the final episode of *Slap Bang* found itself going out at the hugely hallowed time of 5.35 p.m., just before a repeat of *Catchphrase*.

So what went wrong? The most obvious factor was that, despite Ant and Dec's obvious wit and charm, they still needed a decent premise, and nothing here sparkled. Even the concepts that worked so well on Saturday morning failed to shine – 'Challenge Ant' had simply been done better on *SMTV*, while 'Beers' didn't have the charm of 'Chums', possibly because what had started as simply messing about was now 'proper' light entertainment, and the outrageous puns and crap jokes just seemed juvenile and half-arsed. Despite big-name guests like Helen Mirren and Ricky Tomlinson, there seemed little reason to watch the show because, in essence, nothing of any real consequence happened.

Ant and Dec went back to the drawing board and started from scratch to find out what worked on Saturday nights. In the meantime, *Slap Bang* is probably the greatest example of the belief that people would watch their favourite performers read the phone book. Although at least the phone book has a point.

Stars in Their Eyes

Granada for ITV

21 July 1990 to 18 March 2006 (197 episodes)

Everyone seems to love *Stars in Their* Eyes now, but back in 1990 the idea was greeted with absolute amazement. Members of the public dressing up as their musical heroes? Then attempting to sound like them? And all presided over by Leslie Crowther, former host of *Crackerjack*? This was surely the most bizarre and downmarket Saturday night concept yet.

This could well have been the case, but there was something in the execution that made *Stars in Their Eyes* pretty special. The contestants would enjoy the full attention of the make-up and costume department and singing live on stage was clearly wish-fulfilment at its most exciting. Indeed, during the early days, this 'dream come true' element was particularly emphasised, the contestants chatting to Crowther in front of a backdrop representing their profession, such as a builder being interviewed surrounded by a pile of bricks, as if to point out how unglamorous his real life was.

In the days before tribute bands became a familiar sight in pubs and clubs, the idea of a member of the public expending so much effort on looking and sounding like their favourite artist was unusual enough to stand out. Hence the show was successful enough to run for a few years.

After three series Crowther was involved in a serious car accident that led to a severe deterioration in his health. Russ Abbot stepped in for a Christmas special (an Elvis-themed edition, with Fat Elvis duetting with GI Elvis and so on), before Matthew Kelly hosted the 1993 series. This was only supposed to be temporary but Crowther never got well enough to return, so Kelly took over full time. This turned out to be a blessing, as the replacement took the series to new heights.

Kelly's greatest asset was his determination to treat the contestants with absolute respect. There was an overall decency and politeness about his manner with the punters (always referred to, without irony, as 'star guests') that made for likeable viewing. Add to that the quality of the transformations and the overall sense of spectacle and you had a Saturday night banker.

Added fun came from the wide range of artists represented, and you could argue that while the real Elvis Costello probably wouldn't be invited onto a peak-time ITV show someone doing an impression of Elvis Costello on *Stars in Their Eyes* would. If you removed the competition aspect, you were left with an old-fashioned variety show, with Kelly's enthusiastic introductions adding to the fun.

Such was Kelly's determination that the contestants were the stars, he originally refused to have anything to do with a planned celebrity version. He was eventually convinced and these made for equally entertaining viewing, thanks to the sight of the stars clearly absolutely petrified of singing in front of a live audience.

At times in the past decade and a half it has seemed as if *Stars in Their Eyes* was ITV's only reliable audience winner. Matthew Kelly finally left the programme in 2003 to return to acting, and Cat Deeley took his place. The series remained popular, but overexposure, especially far too many celebrity specials, with seemingly the entire cast of *Coronation Street* taking a turn, meant the show lost some of its appeal. Nevertheless, at a time when reality TV was in vogue, it was still a treat to see a programme that consists of people being really nice to each other.

Starsky and Hutch

Spelling-Goldberg Productions/Columbia [shown on BBC1]

23 April 1976 to 27 October 1979 (92 episodes)

'Tough and rough – but likeable and friendly. Two young cops walk a tightrope in the world of crime.' So began the *Radio Times* billing for, it appears, every single episode of *Starsky and Hutch*.

Surely the acme of Seventies American television, it's intriguing to remember that, despite its huge appeal to children, *Starsky and Hutch* was always a post-watershed series and regularly featured storylines concerning drug-pushers, pimps and rapists. Shown in 1976, the first series was number one in the ratings (having been watched in 8.5 million homes) and proved to be an even bigger hit in the UK than in its native land.

Paul Michael Glaser (Starsky) and David Soul (Hutch) were the

© Rex Features

archetypal 'chalk and cheese' cops. But, while derivative in the extreme, the series was produced with such panache it was hard to sneer. A large part of the credit must go to Aaron Spelling, who through the likes of *Charlie's Angels*, *Hart to Hart* and *Dynasty* would go on to confirm himself as the king of unchallenging but fiercely popular American television.

Although *Starsky and Hutch* is virtually carbon-dated in the Seventies, the Beeb saw fit to repeat it through almost the entire Eighties – in fact *Starsky and Hutch* was still being screened in primetime (pre-watershed now) in 1985, and, what's more, on one occasion 13 million people tuned in (although that particular episode was opposite a three-hour documentary about the miners' strike on ITV).

Even after the repeats finally came to an end, *Starsky and Hutch* enjoyed an almost immediate second wind, with nostalgia ensuring the twosome's adventures became cult viewing. Indeed, come 1999, Channel Four devoted an evening to celebrating the programme, including screening the episode entitled 'The Fix' for the first time in Britain (the BBC having missed it first time round due to its plot involving Hutch becoming a heroin addict).

Such is the series' enduring popularity in the UK, that in recent years both David Soul and Antonio Fargas (the jive-talking Huggy Bear) have relocated to Britain. Indeed, Soul is perhaps busier now than he was in the Seventies, with a stint on *Holby City* being followed by the lead role in the notorious *Jerry Springer – The Opera*.

Steve Wright's People Show
BBC1

1 October 1994 to 22 July 1995 (14 episodes)

Until its mid-Nineties revolution, Radio 1 was popular mass entertainment on a huge scale. Pulling in millions of listeners a week, the big name DJs were major stars, and Noel Edmonds proved that skills learnt on air could easily be transferred onto screen. Steve Wright was the biggest name on Radio 1 at the time, with his afternoon show being one of the most listened-to programmes on the airwaves. Wright's array of comedy characters and silly features was a major departure for the form, and as Alan Yentob, then-controller of BBC1, suggested, 'If we can translate that humorous nerve he touches onto the screen, we have a winner.'

For his part, Wright pointed out he was still something of a newcomer to television, and simply wanted to have a go to see if he could do it. He described *People Show* as nothing more than an experiment, seemingly more able to describe what it wasn't than what it was – it wasn't a chat show, a consumer show, a music show, or a comedy show, but apparently all of them at once. He couldn't even decide on the programme's title, wondering if and where his name should appear.

What we eventually got involved Wright sitting at a desk, looking ill at ease, in a rather extravagant studio set including umpteen staircases and water features. In the first series Wright was joined by co-presenters who sat on a sofa alongside him (clearly an attempt to recreate his Radio 1 'posse'). However, they would jabber on to little effect and by the second series Wright was on his own to interview dull celebs (John McCririck, Michelle Collins) and set up in-studio stunts (meeting people who ate catfood, inviting audience members to put their hands in boxes of spiders, and so on). All in all it was rather like a low-rent *Game for a Laugh* or *Noel's House Party*.

Throughout two series, Wright never seemed very happy on telly, acting as if he'd been asked to hold the fort for someone else at the last minute. He wasn't helped by the quality of the material he had to work with – getting three members of the studio audience to dress up like characters from soap operas was not exactly 'high concept' Saturday night television. Similarly, who really wanted to kick off their Saturday evening watching *Coronation Street* actor Bill Roache (Ken Barlow) going on about a new board game he'd invented?

Less than a year later Wright joined Radio 2, reverting back to exactly the same type of features and music he had used to great effect on his Radio 1 show. He was also back with a moustache, having shaved off the beard he had grown for his great TV adventure. Never has one man been so desperate to be Noel Edmonds.

Strictly Come Dancing
BBC1

15 May 2004 to ongoing
(41 episodes as of 25 December 2006)

For a man so associated with Saturday night, it's surprising to realise that by 2004 Bruce Forsyth hadn't appeared regularly there for nearly a decade. Having left *The Generation Game* to return to ITV in 1994, Bruce spent the next few years fronting a revival of *Play Your Cards Right* and a new version of *The Price Is Right*.

But by 2004, the BBC were looking for a way to ride the popular wave of celebrity reality television series. The combination of Brucie plus a revived celebrity-hued version of the old show *Come Dancing* looked like a winning formula.

As such, in the renamed *Strictly Come Dancing*, eight professional ballroom dancers were teamed with eight celebrities, who each week would be challenged to learn a different dance. A panel of judges and the voting public would then decide at the end of the show which pair would be eliminated. Obviously the show owed a lot to *Pop Idol* and the like, but added an old-school variety element to it that stopped it appearing derivative. And who better to take away the cynical edges than the newly hip Bruce? As usual he sent up the contestants ('You've got nothing to beat!') and everything else, with his warmth and old-school charm.

It was Brucie's first live series since the *Big Night* a quarter of a century earlier and, in fronting the show alongside Tess

Daly, Bruce was enthusiastic about the show – unsurprising given it let him sing and dance at every opportunity. The public soon took to it and viewing figures topped 7 million, making it the BBC's most successful light entertainment launch on a Saturday night for over a decade. It even inspired *The Times* to note, 'As reality TV plumbs new depths of vulgarity, it's refreshing to see something so sweetly arch and antique on the up'.

Strictly Come Dancing was immediately recommissioned for a second series in the autumn, where it went head to head with the much-hyped **The X Factor** and managed to beat it most weeks – despite the ITV series enjoying about ten times the column inches. Such was its impact that the commercial channel attempted to replicate its wonders with *Dancing on Ice*, which proved equally successful. The BBC, too, filled the gap between runs with *Strictly Dance Fever* where members of the public took to the floor.

Despite the umpteen spin-offs, however, the original show remained a charming and entertaining Saturday night series of the old school. But it also ensured that, nearly fifty years after his television debut, Bruce Forsyth was just as popular and successful as ever.

Success

Granada Television for ITV

8 May 1982 to 19 June 1982 (7 episodes)

Having produced the talent show *The Video Entertainers* the previous year, legendary television producer Johnnie Hamp was keen to develop another nationwide forum for new talent. His track record in this field had been excellent, with Bernard Manning, Cannon and Ball and Paul Daniels figuring amongst his discoveries, and countless more receiving television exposure thanks to Hamp's earlier series **The Wheeltappers and Shunters Social Club.**

Success wasn't just another ordinary talent show; instead it was a platform for new discoveries to perform their entire act, rather than having to shoe-horn their best work into a three-minute spot as demanded by the other common-or-garden talent shows.

Each of the seven episodes devoted its thirty-minute airtime to a different performer, with Stan Boardman, Lisa Stansfield, Dustin Gee, Roy Walker, Tammy Cline, Mick Miller and Gerard Kenny all headlining. Although none of these acts were new to television (Stansfield had been discovered on *The Video Entertainers*) this was the first time they had been afforded a whole programme of their own within which to strut their stuff. In particular Roy Walker, today best known as a comedian, was able to stretch his wings and even belt out a song (apparently much to the delight of his mother) in an episode specially written for him, and better still, all about his life.

Lisa Stansfield appeared on *Success*'s 15 May edition and represented *Success*'s greatest, ahem, success. But not everyone who performed on the show went on to bigger and better things; Tammy Cline appeared on the 5 June edition, and had already been hailed as 'Britain's best female country singer, as decided by two major polls in the music press'. This reputation had been forged in part thanks to an appearance on the talent show **Search for a Star**, but sadly Cline's career post-*Success* showed little signs of a promotion into entertainment's premier league.

Yet given five out of seven of the acts have since gone on to become if not household names then at least no stranger to primetime television, *Success* achieved a far better success rate than just about any other talent show on telly.

Summertime Special

TVS for ITV

19 July 1986 to 27 August 1988 (20 episodes)

Over the course of the first thirty or so years of ITV's existence it had become customary for most of its programmes to be supplied by just a few of the ITV companies (referred to as the 'Big Five') that made up the network. By the turn of the Eighties this 'consortium' consisted of Granada, LWT, Thames, Yorkshire and Central. However, the company serving the affluent south and south-east of England was keen to muscle in on the action, and over the course of the decade stepped up production of more and more mainstream series. Light entertainment was a particular strong suit and, with the likes of Bobby Davro on their books, by the mid- to late Eighties TVS were knocking out a load of programmes for the network such as *Bobby Davro on the Box*, *Five Alive* and *C.A.T.S Eyes*.

Yet given the sway the Big Five retained over the ITV schedule TVS found themselves mainly having to plug the gaps the others left behind. The accepted wisdom was that the really big audiences were to be found in the autumn and winter time, and so that's where the likes of LWT and Granada concentrated their efforts. This meant that TVS's main focus was on the period running from the end of Easter through to August. Unsurprisingly they decided that a series that made a virtue out of the good weather was the logical way to go.

Obviously based on the BBC's *Seaside Special* as well as

Auntie's own early Eighties variety show called *Summertime Special*, ITV's own version adhered to the tried and tested template, a seaside resort (in this case the Bournemouth International Centre) and a dazzling but relatively inexpensive line-up of acts. The first edition was hosted by Bobby Davro (who seemed to be turning up on everything TVS put out on Saturday nights at around that time), and included acts such as Richard Digance, Five Star, Brian Conley (who introduced a regular section called 'Kopy Kids' which featured young children impersonating pop stars) and 1980 *Search for a Star* champion Dave Wolfe.

Later editions of that first run saw Michael Barrymore and Les Dennis host, while *Copy Cats*' Aiden J Harvey and The Nolan Sisters all showed up to run through their acts in front of ice-cream-addled holidaymakers. All in all this rather bland concoction managed to attract an audience of 10 million viewers, but there was no denying it was much of a muchness.

The second series brought a similar mix of performers, with Jim Davidson, *Five Alive*'s Kevin Devane, Nino Firetto, Five Star, Johnny Logan and Hazel O'Connor all turning up at the Bournemouth International Centre. For series three Lulu was installed as a regular singing act and Chris Tarrant was asked to mix with the holidaymakers, but beyond that very little had changed. Thankfully, though, by the end of the Eighties viewers were turning away from such creaky fare, and, given that an increasing number of families were now holidaying abroad, *Summertime Special* came across as both outdated and a little bit parochial.

Tarby and Friends

LWT for ITV

24 November 1984 to 17 May 1986 (13 episodes)

In the Nineties, Janet Street-Porter famously suggested that 'comedy is the new rock'n'roll'. Thirty years previously, Jimmy Tarbuck managed to become a star thanks partly to a vague connection to The Beatles.

However, after the Merseybeat explosion had died down Tarby enjoyed continued success. There wasn't anything particularly exceptional about his comedy routines, simply the usual mix of normally clean, though occasionally risqué, one-liners. Tarby forged a career thanks to his exuberant personality and the fact he seemed to play golf with everyone in the business.

After making an early impact as one of the comperes of *Sunday Night at the London Palladium* (which had already elevated Bruce Forsyth to stardom) Tarby spent the rest of the Sixties and most of the Seventies as the star of numerous sketch shows and stand-up specials for both the BBC and ITV, under such names as *Tarbuck's Luck* and *Tell Tarby*. In 1975 he got sidetracked into quiz shows and spent over a decade as the host of Yorkshire TV's schedule staple *Winner Takes All*.

In the Eighties those golf-course connections came good with the first in a series of variety shows for ITV. *Tarby and Friends* was about as straightforward as you could get – Jim told a few gags and welcomed his comedic peers, the likes of Russ Abbot, Michael Barrymore and Bobby Davro, to the studio to swap anecdotes and give them space to do their routines. Tarby held court over the show as he would over the nineteenth hole, engaging in ribald banter and reminding all and sundry what great mates they were.

Concurrently, Jim spent many Sunday nights fronting LWT's long-running variety shows *Live from Her Majesty's/The Piccadilly/The Palladium*, which took much the same idea and featured most of the same people. Tarby had the wit to keep proceedings running smoothly – most obviously when he had to continue an edition of *Live from Her Majesty's* after Tommy Cooper had died.

By the end of the decade, the new breed of alternative comedians were making their mark on television and the old guard spearheaded by Tarbuck were becoming unfashionable. Hence, when it expired, it was decided not to review Jim's contract, and he followed the likes of Cannon and Ball out of the door after presenting his final Palladium show in December 1988.

He wasn't idle, though, and has remained busy enough since with game shows, guest appearances and after-dinner engagements. Besides, it gave him more time on the golf course.

Thank Your Lucky Stars
ABC for ITV

1 April 1961 to 25 June 1966 (249 episodes)

For over forty years, until it was axed in 2006, the BBC owned pop telly with *Top of the Pops*. However much of that programme's success was attributable to the fact the opposition was always frittering away the advantage at the last minute.

Thank Your Lucky Stars was a perfect example; pretty much every major pop act of the time made an appearance. What's more the show provided the first television break for The Beatles (the Fab Four appeared in January 1963 performing 'From Me To You'). Yet ITV axed it in 1966, as they did stablemate *Ready Steady Go!*, ensuring that the Beeb had primetime pop all sewn up for the next four decades.

Thank Your Lucky Stars was the commercial channel's attempt to rival **Juke Box Jury**, and its centrepiece was a shameless rip-off of that evergreen series. 'Spin-A-Disc' invited celebrities and members of the public to rate the latest singles (marks out of five rather than hits or misses, mind). The slot was most famous for the regular appearances of Brummie teenager Janice Nicholls, who would invariably award her favourite platters 'foive'. Indeed, the most notable aspect of the show was that, rather than swinging London, *Thank Your Lucky Stars* came direct from glamorous Birmingham. Happily, given the limited number of outlets for pop music on television in those days, there was never any problem enticing acts up north.

For the most part Brian Matthew hosted, fresh from playing the platters that mattered on the Light Programme's *Saturday Club* that morning. Jim Dale took over later in the Sixties. He'd previously hosted legendary Fifties pop show *Six-Five Special*, and the incestuous nature of these early pop telly series was further illustrated by the fact original presenter Keith Fordyce hosted both *Lucky Stars* and *Ready Steady Go!*.

When British pop stopped booming quite as much as it had in the days of Merseybeat, the series came to an end, and from then on all pop stars looking for a spot on telly were diverted to Dickinson Road, Manchester where Jimmy Savile and the *Top of the Pops* audience lay in wait.

Three of a Kind

BBC1

1 July 1981 to 8 October 1983 (17 episodes)

A woman who went on to develop a curious mid-Atlantic accent, a funny man who became a staple of BBC light entertainment, and an unknown who fell back into obscurity. No, not the people you're thinking of – Lulu, Mike Yarwood and Ray Fell all appeared in the first incarnation of *Three of a Kind* on BBC2 in 1967.

Spool forward to the early Eighties, and the BBC is putting together a new variety show, all big production numbers and ensemble sketches. *Six of a Kind* was led by Don Maclean, with Pearly Gates, Karen Kay and other light entertainment staples, but the pilot didn't amount to much. Two members of the cast did impress, though – club comedian Stanley Barlow, aka David Copperfield, and *Tiswas* star Lenny Henry. They survived the decision to focus on comedy and slim the cast down to a more manageable number.

When Tracey Ullman became the third member of the trio, *Three of a Kind* was born. With a youthful line-up in place, the series adopted a similar ethos to *Not the Nine O'Clock News*, focusing on fast-moving and contemporary sketch-based humour. Yet while the BBC2 show had enjoyed the credibility and freedom of a post-watershed slot, *Three of a Kind* was broadcast on peak-time BBC1 and had to appeal to the widest audience possible. This meant an emphasis on corn rather than cutting-edge stuff ('I arrested a librarian –

and I booked him!' 'I arrested an explosives expert – and I let him off!') but the matter was delivered with so much energy it was hard to sneer for long, and the show appealed to adults and kids alike.

All three stars brought something to the mix: Ullman's stage training meant that she was the best performer, but Henry had bags of charm and was a genuinely funny man. Even Copperfield's working-men's club training meant he could make a decent fist of the slapstick. Added to the mix was GAGFAX, a now-risible attempt to surf the zeitgeist by displaying one-liners on screen via the wonders of Ceefax.

With Tracey and Lenny's stars on the rise it was never going to last, and after just three series *Three of a Kind* came to an end. Tracey later moved to the USA and went on to enjoy phenomenal success, while Lenny graduated to his own show, taking many of the *Three of a Kind* production team, as well as most of the characters he'd created (Fred Dread, Rev Nathaniel Westminster), with him. David Copperfield, sadly, failed to capitalise on the success and within a few years could be found on kids' TV, in the likes of *Lift Off! With Coppers and Co!*. While Copperfield wasn't too concerned about this, his agent advised him that appearing on kids' TV was causing the adult work to dry up. Copperfield duly turned his back on the juvenile only to find he fell between two stools (something he'd probably had to do in a sketch) and was no longer welcome in prime-time.

Effect-heavy presentation and endless jokes about Space Invaders and British Rail have ensured that *Three of a Kind* has aged somewhat, and unsurprisingly the series hasn't been repeated for some twenty-five years. Nevertheless, it's still fondly remembered by a generation – for a time when Ceefax wasn't only confined to misspelt weather forecasts.

Thriller

ATV Network Production / Yorkshire Television for ITV

14 April 1973 to 22 May 1976 (44 episodes)

It begins with a pleasant shot of a seafront, with some nice music, but within seconds we've already faded to Robert Powell looking shifty in the foreground of a hotel reception and straightaway we know shenanigans are afoot. Then it's just a matter of seconds before the creepy oboe and glockenspiel music kicks in as Powell rifles through some belongings in a guest room that is clearly not his. Before we know it he is back out in reception and on the phone to someone called 'Paul'. 'Yes, she's the one, no doubt about it,' he proclaims with approaching menace. 'A lonely girl...yes, I'm about to fall desperately in love with Jenny Frifth: single, dress size twelve, shoe size eight.' Then all it takes is for Powell to hang up the receiver and mutter into the close-up the following refrain: 'lonely girl' and we're hooked.

This is the opening scene of *Thriller*, perhaps the best ever suspense series shown on British television. Over the course of six series it amassed a body of high-quality, self-contained mystery stories and, week in, week out, guarantee the audience a gripping story with a satisfying twist in the tail. Although the characters in *Thriller* could sometimes be pretentious, the series itself was a good Saturday night pot-boiler, nothing more, nothing less, and if it might have been overly formulaic, you had to admit it was a great formula.

Given that so much of the writing stemmed from the pen of one man (Brian Clemens) it's unsurprising that various motifs developed throughout the series. More than one episode featured relocated newly wedded urbanites getting their comeuppance in a country idyll. Similarly, drinks decanters were a common sight, as were elaborate breakfast trays brimming with toast, tea and orange juice. Such props signified that our characters, while possibly deeply malevolent, were at least civilised and well cultured on the surface.

Couples slept in separate beds and sported sensible night apparel, meaning any investigations they might need to make as the result of an unexpected sound in the night were at least undertaken appropriately attired (even if they were most likely to end with a bang over the back of the head). In the main though, this was a series in which the men were men and the women were frightened. Moreover, the villains hid their derangements underneath suave personas that would become increasingly frayed over the course of the episode. In fact, psychological disorders featured in a great number of the plots, and while over the years we have grown increasingly used to psychopathic killers in our suspense stories, here the notion that a man who is haunted by a mysterious killer could discover that the murderer is in fact himself operating under some kind of split personality was cutting-edge stuff.

Filmed with one eye on the American market, *Thriller* attracted some notable guest stars such as Hayley Mills, Jeremy Brett, Patrick McGee, Denholm Elliot and Bob

Hoskins. But then surely any actor worth his or her salt would be unable to resist the chance to gaze knowingly into the camera while hiding a wicked smile.

Trick or Treat

LWT for ITV

7 January 1989 to 25 March 1989 (12 episodes)

'A game show where Mike Smith and the Joan Collins Fan Club lead their contestants up the garden path to windfalls or washouts.' So read the listing mag blurb for one of the strangest Saturday night game shows of them all.

By the late Eighties there was a large section of the audience that saw Saturday night television as 'naff'. Yet the viewers who were turning their backs on TV were the very ones that ITV (and its advertisers) most wanted to attract; they were young, intelligent and, more importantly, had access to disposable income. ITV tried to entice this disenfranchised section of the populace back in front of their television screens by putting on programmes that were supposedly 'edgier' and more intelligent than those that had gone before.

In 1989, for 'more intelligent' read 'post-modern'. Basically anything could be made up to look smarter than it actually was by adding a smattering of self-awareness. Certainly, that's what the producers of *Trick or Treat* attempted to do. The show featured presenters Mike Smith and Julian Clary (then under the guise of 'The Joan Collins Fan Club') inviting members of the studio audience to participate in a range of silly games to win a place in the grand final at the end of the programme. So far, so ordinary. But the prizes ranged from the genuinely good (a brand new car or a caravan) to the amusingly awful, such as a broken-down Mini or 24 carrots (get it?). The show's so-called 'dolly birds' weren't quite what they seemed either, and in a move that was seen as a satire on traditional game shows they would 'accidentally' knock a prize off a trolley, or look sullen and miserable.

Clary's liking for double entendres and predilection for referring to contestants as 'punters' were both designed to bring an edge to *Trick or Treat* and establish the series' modern, 'with it' credentials. Conversely, Mike Smith was from the mainstream school of TV, and was presumably deemed a safe pair of hands, able to keep the show moving in the right direction. Although this arrangement sounded entertaining enough it didn't really work, and when it was revealed that most of the 'dolly birds' had previously appeared in soft-core pornography such as *Electric Blue*, the press sensed their opportunity to bury the series.

In retrospect, *Trick or Treat's* attempt at bringing an alternative comedy 'edge' to a mainstream game show did little more than prove how difficult it was to blend the two together. However, its creators – at least – still look back at the series with some fondness, citing *Trick or Treat* as the future of game shows and the precursor to series such as Vic Reeves and Bob Mortimer's *Shooting Stars*. Whether that comic duo would concede such an influence on their own series, though, seems pretty unlikely.

The Tripods

A BBC production in association with Fremantle International Inc/The Seven Network, Australia for BBC1

15 September 1984 to 23 November 1985 (25 episodes)

To start one of the most expensive drama series ever made by the BBC with a caption reading 'A village in England, July 2089 AD' seems a remarkably foolhardy move, and although the futuristic date is mildly tantalising, the prospect of a drama set in a 'village', let alone one that feels it necessary to announce its arrival via on-screen captions, just seems all wrong, particularly when ITV are showing **The A-Team** at the same time, and any minute now there's going to be massive car crash.

Yet *The Tripods* arrived on our screens amidst a level of hype (it has to be said primarily orchestrated by the BBC) that marked the series out for intense scrutiny right from the outset. Based on a trilogy of books by John Christopher, the series offered up an intriguing recipe of science fiction, history and travelogue; seemingly ideal raw material for a television drama.

The Tripods wasn't really a traditional science-fiction story at all. While the notion of giant three-legged aliens taking over planet Earth has distinct echoes of conventional sci-fi stories such as *The War of the Worlds*, *The Tripods* was less about fighting bug-eyed monsters and more about following the growth of the adolescent lead characters as they embarked upon their quest to find 'The White Mountains'. It also didn't help that the future world as envisaged in the series had devolved to a pre-industrial state thanks to the dominance of the Tripods ('How is it done?' asked one character when he was shown a functioning railway line. 'It's called electricity' was the seminal response).

None of this would have been much of a problem had the show's promotion not relied so heavily on the impressive-looking Tripods as a means of engaging viewer interest. Notoriously, the Tripods rarely featured in the first series. Worse than that, the storyline unfolded at a chronically slow pace, such that by the end of the first episode the lead character Will Parker (John Shackley) had only just come to the realisation that he should probably leave his home village. As the story wound its way across the first thirteen parts the pace barely quickened. A crucial interrogation scene in the final episode of series one perfectly summed up the programme, as Will's cousin Henry (Jim Baker) advised his captors that for much of the preceding few weeks he had been engaged in picking grapes and making wine. For those tuning in late it was hardly likely to encourage you to watch out for the repeats.

Admittedly the second series picked up the pace a little and introduced the Tripod's City of Gold. This impressive model apparently took fifteen months to construct and was certainly worth the effort. However, by this time *The Tripod*'s episodic nature was working against it. In terms of ratings, the first year was pummelled into the ground by the ITV competition. Then in 1984, notorious science-fiction cynic Michael Grade became Controller of BBC1 and cancelled the series while it was in pre-production for its third and supposedly final run.

The Two Ronnies

BBC1

10 April 1971 to 25 December 1987 (94 episodes)

One of the most comforting series on television, *The Two Ronnies* remains the nearest small-screen equivalent to a cosy old pair of slippers – warming, familiar and the perfect cue to put your feet up and unwind.

Right from the first episode *The Two Ronnies* featured many of the aspects of the series that would become familiar over the next sixteen years. The pair introduced and closed the show from behind a desk, Ronnie B essayed some elaborate wordplay, Ronnie C delivered a monologue and there was a long musical parody at the end. Some parts of the programme took some time to fall into place though, and at the start sketches mingled with variety acts (a man climbing a mountain of chairs, for example), while Ronnie C delivered one of his monologues seated at a piano. The audience even chuckled at 'It's goodnight from me...and it's goodnight from him!', though it's hard to remember that this was once a new joke.

As the series progressed, most of the variety trappings were ditched, bar the single appearance from a singer (Elaine Paige and Barbara Dickson seemed to turn up more than was healthy) each week. By the end of the Seventies *The Two Ronnies* had perfected a never-changing routine: 'in a packed programme...', news stories, Ronnie B's spoonerisms, a dinner party sketch, musical guest, long serialised sketch, couple of quickies, Ronnie C in the chair, the musical parody, more news stories, 'goodnight from him'. A mechanical approach, maybe, but it always worked, helped by wonderful performances and contributions from all the leading comedy writers of the day (all the Pythons, Barry Cryer, David Renwick, Spike Milligan, David Nobbs and dozens more).

The Two Ronnies was a Saturday night staple for many years and, in addition, the pair found great acclaim working independently of each other. By the Eighties their show had become part of the establishment, reaching the status of being parodied by the next 'new wave' of comedians via 'The Two

Ninnies' in *Not the Nine O'Clock News*. Yet even without the subversion or social comment of the new breed, the series was still very funny.

Come the mid-Eighties, Ronnie B decided the time was right to call it a day. Apparently he simply wasn't enjoying it as much as he used to (the final straw seemed to be when he was offered a major role in the West End and found himself turning it down because he couldn't be doing with the commuting). It did mean The Two Ronnies avoided the risk of being humiliatingly dropped by a new broom at the Beeb who decided they were no longer fashionable, as befell their peers Little and Large.

The Ronnies' final show was broadcast on Christmas Day 1987, yet they remained part of the schedules with endless compilations – starting with *Twenty Years of The Two Ronnies* in 1986 – running almost as long as the original series. Then in 2005 *The Two Ronnies Sketchbook* saw the pair selecting and linking their favourite routines. Barker's death the same year, however, meant this was a once-only reunion. But it was wonderful to be with them again. Wasn't it, Ronnie?

Ultra Quiz

TVS Production in Association with Action Time Ltd for ITV

9 July 1983 to 17 August 1985 (24 episodes)

Dubbed 'The Kamikaze Mastermind', *Ultra Quiz* was a game
show played out on a massive canvas. The first series was
presented by Michael Aspel (from the studios of TVS),
Jonathan King and Sally James (both on the Outside
Broadcast). For the first round alone (which took place on
Brighton beach) 2000 contestants lined up to take part
requiring twenty coaches to ferry them around and twenty
policeman to deal with crowd control.

For this first set of challenges contestants had to endure a
number of rounds involving a piano-smashing karate team, a
parachute jump by a member of the Royal Green Jacket's
Parachute team and a stunt featuring Eddie Kidd and jet-
propelled water skis. Each competitor was provided with a
coloured balloon that they were meant to release as and
when they became eliminated from the game. However a
small number cheated and got through to the next round
simply by keeping a tight hold on their balloon. Those who
made it through were decamped to Hampshire's Watercress
Line (a steam railway run by a group of enthusiasts) where
further games awaited them.

Next there was a trip across the Channel, where the
remaining two hundred or so players were subjected to a very
long quiz, during which they all had to display their own
scores on their head. For those who continued to escape

elimination, there was a luxury coach ride to the heart of France's Champagne region, then trips to Amsterdam and Bahrain. All the while, the field was whittled down and down until only eight contestants remained.

The final location was Hong Kong, where the series ran into the worst rainstorm Hong Kong had endured for seventeen years. One of the games was to be set at the summit of Victoria Peak, but as soon as the contestants embarked upon the journey to the top it became apparent that there was a risk of rock falls. A barricade of police cars and ambulances blocked their route but, undeterred, the decision was taken to conquer Victoria Peak via tram instead.

The final episode of the first series took place in the TVS studio. Throughout the run, astrologer Russell Grant had popped up at various points to try and determine who the eventual winner would be. David Manuel, a computer boffin, used statistical analysis and data to discern the same information. These two 'experts' only finally agreed who the series victor would be when it came down to the final two – and they were both wrong! After eight gruelling weeks, though, there was one last sting in the tale for the eventual winner: the prize of £10,000 (then far and away the biggest cash prize given away on a British television programme) was delivered in one-pound coin denominations.

With games devised by Jeremy Beadle, an impressive budget and some superb stunts, the first series of *Ultra Quiz* made quite a splash, and its return was inevitable. However, series two never quite managed to replicate the scale and panache of the first year. Aspel was replaced by David Frost, and the tasks allotted to the contestants were less ambitious. A final run followed, this time with Stu Francis presiding, but now *Ultra Quiz* didn't even leave the shores of the UK. Given its USP was its ambition and scale, this seemed like absolute folly, and it was no surprise when the series failed to return the following year.

The Val Doonican Music Show

BBC1

26 December 1976 to 24 December 1988 (89 episodes)

The cardigan-clad crooner, sitting in a rocking chair and essaying songs about Paddy McGinty's Goat or declaring in music that 'Some of My Best Friends Are Songs', should have been the epitome of unsophisticated and dreary variety. And yet, there was something about Val Doonican that was always curiously likeable.

The entertainer started his marathon stint on British TV in the early Sixties, having first arrived from Ireland as a member of folk group The Ramblers. His easy charm and pleasant voice made him a staple in variety, and landed him a starring show. Here he was joined by special guests to sing songs and participate in sketches, and there was also a comedy slot, which provided some of the earliest TV exposure for Dave Allen.

Having established himself as a Saturday night regular, in 1971 Val was lured over to ITV. Here he enjoyed some of his highest ever audience figures, but soon regretted the move, and switched back to the Beeb in the mid-Seventies. His admission that he'd made a mistake in defecting – likening it to having an affair – seemed to emphasise his sheer good grace.

Val was aware that his act was an acquired taste, and knew full well that many of his viewers were grounded teenagers. As such he was happy to send himself up, turning up on *The Generation Game* to attempt to steal a rocking chair used in a game, or singing 'hello to all the rock fans /

who watch from time to time when mum's around'. Val's talents were also such that he co-wrote all his own scripts, alongside comedy heavyweights such as John Junkin.

In truth the series adhered to the tried-and-tested BBC Saturday night format of musical numbers interspersed by the odd rather silly bit of comedy and lots of musical guests to jolly things along. Of the many acts that appeared, the Nolans were notable for having what appeared to be a monopoly on guest bookings for the BBC's Saturday night shows in the late Seventies. As well as appearing on Val's show, the girls found time to grace *It's Cliff Richard*, *The Basil Brush Show*, *The Morecambe and Wise Show*, *Seaside Special*, *The Two Ronnies*, *Jim'll Fix It*, *Mike Yarwood – in Persons* and *Shirley Bassey* – and all of this in the space of just five years.

As well as his Saturday night series Val also became famous for his Christmas Eve specials, which for many people were the ideal accompaniment to wrapping presents and hanging up stockings. BBC boss Bill Cotton admitted that he'd more or less pinched the concept wholesale from the Bing Crosby and Perry Como specials on American TV, but it worked because Val possessed the lightness of touch to carry it off.

Val's Saturday night series continued until the mid-Eighties, with one of the last episodes finding itself opposite *Live Aid* (although there were four more Christmas specials between 1985 and 1988). Always scrupulously polite, Val admitted he had no problem with his disappearance from our screens, observing that it was right that he made way for something new. What a nice man.

The Wheeltappers and Shunters Social Club

Granada Television for ITV

13 April 1974 to 30 June 1976 (39 episodes)

Although its supporters might not countenance such a thing, in many ways *The Wheeltappers and Shunters Social Club* is the **Saturday Live** of its day. Both series took the traditional variety show and revived it through the injection of new-to-television (although not always fresh-faced) talent. In fact, it could be argued that *Wheeltappers* was the more influential of the two, providing a crucial leg-up to acts of the calibre of Cannon and Ball, Mike Harding and Paul Daniels. So it's doubly ironic, then, that it remains one of the great 'forgotten' shows of Saturday night television.

The series (which intentionally omitted apostrophes from its title in an attempt at clubland authenticity) came out of a themed section from the stage show of the popular series *The Comedians*, during which the entertainers pretended they were performing at a traditional working-man's club. Although Frank Carson had pretended to be club chairman for the live performances, comedian Colin Crompton was the man picked for television. He played the part to perfection, gently mocking the sometimes supercilious manner of those who assumed such a role in real life. A particular treat was his delivery of the latest club news, which usually included the heavily accentuated phrase 'we've had a meeting of the commit-eeee and we've passed a resol-oo-tion' to much riotous laughter from the audience.

While Colin took care of business, it was left to Bernard Manning to assume the role of Master of Ceremonies. Contrary to many people's expectations the rotund comic with a reputation for sexist, racist and homophobic material was charm personified, often introducing acts with very warm words indeed. Not that his trademark acerbic humour didn't make the odd appearance, but when he introduced an act with the words 'Here's someone who can really sell a song. It's a shame he can't sing them', or 'this man can make a cat laugh – pity he can't do the same for people', you knew that it was meant in good heart.

Some very big names appeared at the *Wheeltappers* including Bill Haley, Howard Keel, Gene Pitney, Roy Orbison and Matt Munro. Perhaps less surprising was the presence of traditional northern comics of the ilk of George Roper, Jim Bowen and Charlie Williams (all of whom had worked on *The Comedians*). But *Wheeltappers* also gave exposure to novelty acts such as sword balancer Steve Sabre, exotic dancer Barbara Sharon and the fantastically named Ukrainian Cossack Brotherhood.

Undoubtedly though, the show's lasting contribution was the exposure it gave to new acts. Aside from the aforementioned Cannon, Ball, Harding and Daniels; The Krankies, Little and Large, Dustin Gee and Stu Francis all received early (if not their first) significant television work on *Wheeltappers*.

Over three years *Wheeltappers* injected good old-fashioned

entertainment into the television schedules, and even found time to host a traditional beauty competition (*Miss TV Times of Granadaland from the Wheeltappers* was transmitted on 17 May 1974), as well as a spin-off series (*...At the Wheeltappers*), which provided a different entertainer with thirty-minutes of uninterrupted airtime each week. Sadly, though *...At the Wheeltappers* would prove to be the programme's last gasp, and with very little fanfare *The Wheeltappers and Shunters Social Club* left our screens but, just perhaps, not the affections of those who saw it.

Who Wants to be a Millionaire?

Celador for ITV

4 September 1998 to ongoing
(482 episodes as of 12 May 2007)

Post-*Tiswas*, Chris Tarrant seemed unable to find a decent TV show, as his CV bulged with awful game shows and untransmitted series – **Man O Man** proving to be one of his more successful career moves. There was no real reason to suggest that this latest venture would be anything other than just another footnote in his career. Sure, there was a huge amount of cash up for grabs, but other series, such as the boring *Raise the Roof* which gave away a real house, had proved that quizzes needed more than just big prizes to become hits.

Yet there was something special about *Who Wants to be a Millionaire?* The show started life as a quiz on Tarrant's Capital Radio breakfast show, where phone-in contestants could win big cash prizes, with Tarrant hamming it up something chronic to hook listeners in. The transfer to telly began with a ten-day stint in September 1998 and immediately viewers were gripped.

So what made *Millionaire* special – apart, of course, from its prize? There was nothing to the show: you would answer fifteen questions, each for an increasing amount of cash, until you got one wrong, gave up, or won a million pounds. The show looked minimalist too – Tarrant and the contestant under spotlights, allowing the viewer to get up close and watch the agony as it unfolded.

We were seeing members of the public going through the mill on television. The game took second place to the emotion. Better still, with contestants picked at random from a phone line, it emphasised that these were real people playing for life-changing amounts. Far from getting irritating, the slow pace meant that we were drawn into the contestants' lives, while the stripped scheduling brought viewers back night after night.

When it returned for a second run in 1999, viewing figures were phenomenal, reaching nearly 20 million people on some evenings. ITV made sure it came back whenever the schedules needed perking up, every few months or so, as it was always guaranteed to thrash the opposition. This success all came about despite the fact nobody came close to winning the mythical million for two years.

Inevitably, ITV could not continue to ration its appearances, and from September 2000 it became a permanent fixture in the schedules, normally in a regular Saturday night slot for months on end. It was still big news when Judith Keppel was the first millionaire in November 2000, although obviously it meant some of the excitement wore off.

While still a successful series, it was never the talking point it was in the early days – despite the exploits of Charles Ingram who in April 2003 was convicted of attempting to cheat his way to the top prize. Indeed, Ingram's coughing capers proved to be something of a blessing for ITV, who enjoyed massive audiences for a documentary about it, and were even said to be considering turning it into a film.

Of course, *Millionaire* also proved to be successful throughout the world. The American version on ABC was possibly an even bigger hit than the original, though this too fell foul of overexposure. Meanwhile, series such as *The Weakest Link* attempted to repeat the success, though none matched *Millionaire*'s simplicity.

Come 2007, *Millionaire* was still part of the ITV schedules, but it wasn't the draw it once was. Indeed, now confined to Saturday nights alone, it filled the same role as something like *Play Your Cards Right* or **Bob's Full House**; a reliable quiz show that occupied an awkward gap in the schedule. Ratings were a fraction of what they were in the early days, at around 4 million viewers, and where once it was a special event, it would often be taken off to allow something else to take centre stage.

Nevertheless, if it's now become part of the furniture, it shouldn't be forgotten that for a time it helped the quiz re-establish itself at the top of the charts.

Wonder Woman

Douglas S Cramer/Bruce Lansbury Productions
[shown on BBC1]

1 July 1978 to 17 June 1980 (43 episodes)

Wonder Woman began its television life in the USA in November 1975 as a one-off Friday night television movie entitled *The New Original Wonder Woman* (perhaps to differentiate it from the 1974 *Wonder Woman* movie starring Cathy Lee Crosby). Two further specials followed in 1976 as did a full-blooded series set at the height of the Second World War. Each week Wonder Woman (Lynda Carter) would trounce various Nazis aided only by her trusty lasso (which when wrapped around someone compelled them to speak the truth) and even trustier Major Steve Trevor (Lyle Waggoner).

A hallmark of the series was its fidelity to the spirit of the original DC comics source material. Carter was an almost perfect physical manifestation of the Wonder Woman character, and on-screen comic-book-style captions punctuated scenes on a regular basis. In addition both the beginning and end title sequences featured comic-book illustrations and an astonishing theme tune that sounded like it had been composed by letting a mouse scuttle up and down a piano keyboard.

After the first series the show was revamped to more closely resemble the popular action show *The Bionic Woman*. The primary change this enforced was that adventures now had to take place in the present day. 'The Return of Wonder Woman' laboriously set up the premise that was to underpin the show's final two years. It began with a shot of a modern-day aeroplane, but just to ensure the change in time period was abundantly clear a caption popped up on screen which read: 'Somewhere over the Caribbean today – 1977'.

Now allied with Colonel Steve Trevor Jr (the son of the original Trevor, still played by Lyle Waggoner), the 2526-year old Amazonian's adventures grew ever more bizarre. Not only would she have to contend with sword-fighting robots and evil doppelgangers, but in one episode ('Mind Stealers from Outer Space') the adversaries were extraterrestrial in origin. Yet with all that going on each episode seemed to find itself stuck in a mire of exposition, and viewers tuning in for a look at Wonder Woman coshing a baddie or two always had to wait a long time before any excitement rolled up on screen.

In the US, *Wonder Woman* never really transcended the success of Lynda Carter, and by 1979 the series was axed due to indifferent ratings. In the UK the story was different, with *Wonder Woman* forming a popular part of the BBC's early evening Saturday night schedule with over 16 million of us tuning in. Perhaps we'd all been ensnared by her mesmerising lasso of truth.

The X Factor

Syco Productions for ITV1

4 September 2004 to ongoing
(61 episodes as of 16 December 2006)

When it was announced in 2004, *The X Factor* felt immediately familiar; almost a reality show 'greatest hits' package. At the centre of proceedings was **Pop Idol**'s Simon Cowell and joining him as a fellow judge was Louis Walsh (as previously seen on **Popstars: The Rivals**). Even the host, Kate Thornton, was familiar to viewers of the ITV2 spin-offs from *Pop Idol*. There was one new face in front of the camera though – loose cannon Sharon Osbourne, most famous for being the wife of Ozzy but also a veteran music manager of many years.

According to Simon Cowell, *The X Factor*'s 'x factor' was that it would allow people of all ages to audition for the singing talent competition, meaning (supposedly) that we would become embroiled as never before in the personal stories of each contestant battling it out for that lucrative recording contract. That wasn't the only change though. After the by now traditional open audition rounds in which the nation's exhibitionists and eccentrics lined up alongside the few contenders with genuine talent, we learnt that the judges would each be assigned a different cross-section (16–24-year-olds, over 25s and groups) to manage, meaning that Louis, Sharon and Simon were to be competing against each other to see whose act could win the series.

Unsurprisingly, *The X Factor* developed a tendency for creating a bit of aggro. In the first year Kate Thornton struggled a fair bit, and even went so far as to issue one distraught contestant (Rowetta) with a final warning for not standing on the correct spot on the stage. But this was nothing compared to the sniping between the judges. When Sharon Osbourne snapped and told overall series one winner Steve Brookstein (who had previously been a finalist on Jonathan Ross's *The Big Big Talent Show*,) that he was 'fake', the atmosphere became more poisonous than exciting and the gentle bantering of *Pop Idol*'s Ant and Dec seemed a lifetime ago. This rancour carried on after the series was complete, and less than a week after Brookstein's victory the papers were gleefully reporting that he was booed off during a shambolic appearance on *Top of the Pops*.

Brookstein became a major test of the show's credibility. First of all there was a post-victory performance of 'Against All Odds' that consisted of very little singing and a lot of laughing (which was very off-putting, even for those who had voted for

him). Then tensions surfaced between Brookstein and the new management he had won as part of being crowned champion, with the singer claiming that a promise to allow him to perform on the second series of *The X Factor* was broken.

Things calmed down for a bit as year two got under way, and Kate Thornton at least proved to be a more consummate host. The sniping of the judges returned and hit new heights as Louis Walsh walked out only to come back before the next show, citing Simon Cowell's bullying and Sharon Osbourne throwing a drink over him as his reasons for quitting. In turn, the press deduced that the whole thing had probably just been a publicity stunt.

But worse was to follow as Irish group The Conway Sisters incurred Sharon's wrath when they were saved from rejection by Louis's supposedly partisan casting vote for his fellow countrymen. To see a hard-bitten music manager turn on the girls (accompanied by spontaneous booing from the studio audience) was about as unpleasant a sight as you are likely to catch on a Saturday evening light entertainment show.

With an equally ill-tempered celebrity special in 2006, *The X Factor: Battle of the Stars* (during which ageing magician Paul Daniels vociferously disagreed with how his performances had been edited together as part of an end-of-series montage and Sharon Osbourne snapped away at contestant Rebecca Loos), the programme became better known for its bitching rather than for unearthing any new talent (although series three winner Leona Lewis possessed a set of pipes far superior to pretty much anyone else who's ever entered one of these television competitions).

From its laughable no-hopers to its waves of controversies, there is no denying *The X Factor* remains gripping television; just don't let anyone try and tell you that it's all about the music.

You Bet!

LWT for ITV

20 February 1988 to 12 April 1997 (92 episodes)

Since the demise of **Just Amazing!** Saturday nights had been crying out for a platform for bizarre, anally retentive or just plain bonkers members of the public to parade their special (read – often utterly pointless) skills on television. The similarly exclamatorily entitled *You Bet!* was just such an outlet. Each edition saw people with a special skill attempt to complete a seemingly impossible task, while a panel of celebrities and the studio audience placed bets on the outcome, with points transferring into pounds for charity. Each of the panellists, and the host (originally Bruce Forsyth), would champion one of the participants, and if that participant failed then the celeb (or Bruce) would have to do a forfeit. The series had big aspirations and in fact was the first Saturday night show to be recorded at the absolutely massive Shepperton Studios.

You Bet! served as a platform for all sorts of enthusiasts to show off their skill, yet despite the cavernous studio some of the most memorable challenges were the more low-key ones, such as future comedy stars Armstrong and Miller attempting to perform comedy sketches at high speed or, brilliantly, the two demented Swedish Roxette fans who claimed they could tell which song was playing based entirely on the flickering of a candle in front of a speaker. There were always a few big stunts in each show, though, including a couple pre-filmed on location, with the production team swearing on their lives not to let on the result.

Brucie added a few of his trademark touches to proceedings, most obviously in the form of the wonderful *You Bet!* rap ('So don't fret, get set, are you ready?' 'You bet!') which has stuck in the mind of a million thirtysomethings. Yet Bruce soon got tired of the format, as it ended up giving him a straighter role than normal, simply introducing the contestants and challenges and then taking a back seat.

Therefore, after a few series, he defected to the BBC and the relaunched *Generation Game*. The format was still sturdy enough, however, and so it continued with new host Matthew Kelly. With his experience on *Game for a Laugh* he was used to dealing with eccentrics, and the boundless enthusiasm he would later bring to *Stars in Their Eyes* was in evidence here. Kelly left in 1995, with Darren Day taking over the reins.

Throughout its decade on screen, *You Bet!* was a reliable series yet it never really established itself in the affections of the general public. Maybe it was the sheer scale of the show that meant it was all a bit too brash and slick to really appeal. Nevertheless, when it finally came to a close in 1997 it was replaced by the virtually identical *Don't Try This at Home*.

INDEX